THE TWO CARLYLES

BOOKS BY OSBERT BURDETT

THE TWO CARLYLES

THE BROWNINGS

W. E. GLADSTONE

WILLIAM BLAKE

THE BEARDSLEY PERIOD

THE IDEA OF COVENTRY PATMORE

CRITICAL ESSAYS

THE VERY END, AND OTHER STORIES

THOMAS CARLYLE

THE TWO CARLYLES

BY

OSBERT BURDETT

With Illustrations

Boston and New York
HOUGHTON MIFFLIN COMPANY
𝕿𝖍𝖊 𝕽𝖎𝖛𝖊𝖗𝖘𝖎𝖉𝖊 𝕻𝖗𝖊𝖘𝖘 𝕮𝖆𝖒𝖇𝖗𝖎𝖉𝖌𝖊
1931

920
B89t

19005
April 1942

The Riverside Press
CAMBRIDGE · MASSACHUSETTS
PRINTED IN THE U.S.A.

In the holy tongue, the word which signifieth life is of the dual number.

Sermons, II. 217: LANCELOT ANDREWES

PREFACE

LONG before I knew anything in detail about the Carlyles, a pair of portraits had begun to form in my imagination: incomplete, of necessity, but not confused. Some high lights were there, some shadows rich and tantalizing, but the background, of course, was dim. Yet I seemed to see them, almost as if they were friends, in a house I knew, in a situation familiar to me, in a relation of which fragments appeared to be discernible in the lives of other authors and married people. It was no theory, but a picture that had formed: a picture deriving from some letters. It must be ages since the volumes containing their love-letters occupied a young man's summer holiday, when several of Miss Welsh's witticisms, as keen as the razor's edge, lodged by the laughter that they had provoked in his memory. Some years before that, the day is clear when *Sartor* had first introduced Carlyle's writings to a boy of seventeen; and years were to pass, after both these dates, before the day, memorable to him in another connexion, when he visited No. 5 Cheyne Row to see the setting of the pair, always connected, in his imagination of them, with London.

Those letters, his shorter books, were the only material for these imaginary portraits, but the group deriving from these writings, and shaped by such powers of divination and imagination as he had, contented him. Of their actual lives, even of the legends which have overlaid their lives, unaccountable as this may sound, I knew nothing. It was not until the first of Mr. David Alec Wilson's volumes of mosaic had appeared that I had read a word on their biography. Then, it seemed, all the other biographers fell un-

fortunately into two classes. There were those whom
Froude had led astray, and those who had spared no
pains to convict Froude of prejudice, misplaced confidence, and error.

When, therefore, the present book was undertaken, I
was not a partisan but an innocent, standing suddenly
alarmed at the treacherous path before me, and with
no desire beyond the wish to define and correct the
pair of portraits in my mind by facts and inferences
admitted to be trustworthy. The comedy of this position produced even a passing fancy to write a book
called the Carlyles without Controversy, but that
might have seemed arrogant, and, in certain atmos-
pheres, balm can be as provocative as a bomb-shell.
In truth, neither controversy, nor some pet theory, nor
the bestowal of praise or blame, has entered, then or
now, into my conception of their characters. A pair
of long-suffering sitters were waiting, sitters of whom
I had fondly formed an idea. The time had come to
put the preliminary sketch aside, and to draw them
regardless of preconception.

This I have endeavoured to do, and if, by the light
of agreed facts, a former fancy has not been wholly
contradicted by maturer study, the explanation may
be neither vainglorious nor obscure. A theory, I
repeat, was not in possession; but perhaps a sense of
fellowship for any pair of human beings whose path
is not too straight nor their days unchequered is a
favourable beginning for approaching them. An innocent interest may be less treacherous than one begotten
of dispute, and an eye for the obstructions no less than
the attractions of love, some slight safeguard; while the
practice of letters, and a sensitiveness to the relation
of marriage, as it is to be studied in the living world
around, will aid any one to appreciate the peculiarity
presented, alas, by the marriage of many artists and
authors. Marriage is the hard life. Were it otherwise,

marriage would not be the noble fulfilment, the tragic
disaster, or the precarious mixture that men know
it to be. The admission begets tenderness, for, as
Dr. Johnson noticed,[1] marriage has never been natural to men. Yet no completely satisfactory substitute has been found for it. Its private sanctions and its
legal sanctions often conflict and rarely coincide, and
not only have the two principals to be considered, even
when there are no children, but the two minds of each
principal regarding it. Often and often, each party
is self-divided, whatever the issue may be, and they
are not often of the same mood either for long or simul-
taneously. Where desires are confused decision is difficult, and so, to escape the tangle, men cling to some
arbitrary regulation and impose indissolubility, or
divorce for the asking, as the only solution for the insoluble. In regard to the Carlyles, an author can
imagine what an author-husband means, and assuredly he can respond to the type of woman that an
author might be most tempted to love.

On such premises, at all events, this book was undertaken. To guard against the intrusion of error and
controversy, Froude was reserved to the last. Not until
every charge against him had been heard in the counter-
blasts of his critics was a single page of his turned; and
when he, too, had been read, it still seemed foreign to
these portraits to enlarge on the issues between them.
The Carlyles were my sitters, not Froude's critics nor
Froude. With this hint, the book may be considered,
I trust, without distractions.

Since portraiture, not biography, was intended, a
strict narration has been spared, and much detail hap-

---

[1] 'It is so far from being natural for a man and a woman to live in a
state of marriage, that we find all the motives which they have for remaining in that connexion, and the restraints which civilized society im-
poses to prevent separation, are hardly sufficient to keep them together.'
— Boswell's *Life of Johnson*, vol. I, p. 497 (Macmillan, 1900).
    Dr. Johnson himself did not re-marry after becoming a widower.

pily omitted, for there is far too much! Her letters and his writings are only elements in the design. Even quotations are strictly limited. Nothing, therefore, would please me more than that this study should be called, in either sense of that ambiguous phrase, a work of imagination. In spite of writings based upon the contrary assumption, the story of Jane Welsh and of Thomas Carlyle seems to me, in essentials, to be the story of many marriages. In so far as it is of universal interest, this is because their experience was not extraordinary.

O. B.

ACKNOWLEDGMENTS

TO the following authorities and publishers sincere thanks are given for their permission to quote from copyright works:

Mr. Alexander Carlyle has kindly allowed the citations from the *Love Letters* and *Letters and Memorials*, published by The Bodley Head; Messrs. Longmans, Green and Company those from Froude; Mr. D. A. Wilson permission to draw upon the, at present issued five, volumes of his *Life of Carlyle*, published by Messrs. Kegan Paul. Full particulars of these volumes and their publishers will be found in the Short Bibliography on pages 297–298, together with others.

In so large, and often visited, a quarry quotations, often met in many places, can be confused. Should any attribution have miscarried, I trust that this note, the references in the text, and the particulars in the Bibliography will be accepted as sufficient acknowledgment.

CONTENTS

ILLUSTRATIONS

THE TWO CARLYLES

• •

PART ONE
THE UNLIKELY LOVERS

Define to thyself, judicious Reader, the real significance of these phenomena, named Gossip, Egoism, Personal Narrative (miraculous or not), Scandal, Raillery, Slander, and such-like; the sum-total of which (with some fractional addition of a better ingredient, generally too small to be noticeable) constitutes that other grand phenomenon still called 'Conversation.' Do they not mean wholly: *Biography* or *Autobiography*?

Not only in the common Speech of men; but in all Art too, which is or should be the concentrated and conserved essence of what men can speak and show, Biography is almost the one thing needful.

THOMAS CARLYLE: *Essay on Biography.*

THE TWO CARLYLES

. .

CHAPTER ONE

AN ONLY CHILD

I

THE little human animal who has been wise enough not to leave the world of the unborn until it shall have chosen parents able to endow it with the mixed virtues that maintain a stock in health and quality has started life well. There remains for it, however, a further requirement, for which it can scarcely itself provide. That requirement is: a little brother or sister. An only child begins life, and reaches adolescence (if it survive) at a peculiar disadvantage. To begin with, it misses the human being who can teach it most, perhaps the only human being who can teach it, once it has been weaned, naturally: that is to say, another child of nearly the same age. An only child, again, is too much at the mercy of its parents. The parents are apt to become over-concentrated on one child, and affection, like discipline, should be tempered. If they neglect it, the child may not find an outside companion for itself; if they crush it, it cannot hide behind another victim; if they are doting parents, they may almost suffocate it with love. An only child is, really, an anomaly. It grows in an intensive soil, and there is no telling what queer bias may not be given to its temperament, what accent to its, otherwise desirable, peculiarities, what twist to its nature, at the most receptive stage of human growth. A child is entitled to complain of its parents, should its solitude be deliberate on their part. While it remains an only child, it is one against two, which is not a natural handicap; and the parents, equally, suffer, since it requires more than one infant to educate a pair of adults properly, and no one denies that parents are more or less helpless at first.

In any event, therefore, the hardest work is thrown upon their firstborn, and thus even the first child of a large family is fated to the position of an only child, for at least the first eighteen months of its life. While we still know too little of biometrics (an ugly word, partly because it remains ill-defined) to dogmatize, some such writers as Havelock Ellis or Galton have averred that the best chance in the family falls to the youngest, if only because the youngest is not born until the parents have had time to learn a thing or two. The Benjamin of a family runs, indeed, some risk of being spoilt, but any weakness of the parents in this direction is corrected by the jealousy of their elder children, who are apt to squash the youngest because he is least able to defend himself. So long as the youngest is not an afterthought of middle age, has not been born at too long an interval after his brothers and sisters, he has probably the best chance of any, just as the eldest, however well he may ripen, had the worst. From the point of view of the children, the smallest family should consist of three. In the first place, the two parents are better when outnumbered, and, in the second, as the late Dr. W. C. Rivers, a good observer, remarked, two surviving children only replace their parents, while a third child is a convenient precaution against accidents.[1]

Wider problems than those of the individual child, the parents, the family unit, though not to be neglected, need not here detain us. The character which is to be watched as it unfolded was that of a little girl, who began her life as an eldest child, and was fated to remain alone.

[1] *Through a Consulting Room Window*, by W. C. Rivers (Methuen, 1926).

If we bear this handicap in mind, her own development, which was precocious, the affection and the problems, which she and her parents discovered in one another, fall more or less into shape, and the anecdotes which abound of her early years become intelligible.

We approach her warily, because Jane Baillie Welsh had many gifts, so many that there would have been no temerity in calling her a writer of genius if only the kind and the quantity equalled the quality of her work. This was mainly that of writing letters. Among her gifts, moreover, was a faculty for rendering ridiculous any person or thing which she despised, and, though we know her to have been one of the quality because she never spared even herself when she felt irritated, yet her pen was so pointed and her tongue could be so sharp that she makes us curious of her ancestry, her parents, her nursery, on the chance that one or all of these may have somehow sharpened her a shade beyond her nature.

There seems nothing to suggest that Jane was handicapped, before her birth, either in the breed or the circumstances of her ascendants. The only fact that excites attention is that her parents were namesakes. Jane was, curiously enough, a Miss Welsh on both sides. These parental Welshes, however, were not cousins, not even connexions by blood, however remote. They were namesakes only, and the quintessence of whatever was most Welsh in each of them was to appear distilled in Jane, the most rarefied Welsh produced by either family.

Another of Jane's advantages was that the land, and consequently the human character which is the land's best gift to men who till it, was at the root of both the Welsh families, though, by the time when Jane was

born, brains and nurture had fined the stock, so that it
was now producing flowers as well as bread: a little
above the land, but not yet exiled from it.

The Welshes, too, may virtually be considered families of the Border, thriving (as they did) about midway
between the English and the Scottish Lakes, in the
districts of Dumfries and Annandale. The fact must
not be pressed, but, other things being equal, there is
something to be said for living near a frontier, which is
none the less a frontier of temperament, tradition,
religion, and, therefore, to some extent of race, whatever arrangements the politicians ruling at Westmin-
ster may have made. On the whole, a Border family is
more likely to have had varied experiences, to have
run risks, to have been encouraged in enterprise, to
have been acquainted with more than a local point
of view, than a family settled elsewhere, even at the
centre. If a judge or a critic be a person who is capable,
by definition, of allowing for more than one fact at a
time before coming to any decision, then a Border
family should be able to throw up critics more readily
than others, for it will have been compelled to survive
through the practice of discrimination. In the 'countries of the mind,' at any rate, Jane Welsh was to prove
an alert and wary traveller, and she could certainly
discriminate with skill between the human characters
which she encountered. She could hit herself off to a
turn, and her mockery, never sparing herself or others,
is as appetizing as the hiss from a frying-pan, which,
indeed, it sometimes resembles. The point is that her
raciness of intelligence suggests, to a later century
more sophisticated than her own, a tang of the town,
with Molière or Congreve somewhere at the back of it.
In reality, hers was a more homely salt, a mother-wit,
in rustic idiom, nearer to Mrs. Poyser than to Milla-
mant, and the better for being nearer. Precisely because the soil in her soul was still 'in good heart,' as

they say in the country, the 'share of a high culture could not hurt it. Her mind was tough enough to survive her classics; and she is not primarily to be deemed, as some would have her, a witty young lady languishing in a country town, but a glorified country girl whose family was almost new to the professions.

III

For many generations a succession of John Welshes had been lairds of Craigenputtock, a moorland farm, set in wilds of heather, within a day's walk of Dumfries.

At the early age of seventeen her grandfather, the freeholder, had married the daughter of a farmer, called Hunter, with whom he was lodging while attending Tynron school. It was at Craigenputtock that the youthful pair settled down to the stiff task of bringing up a family of fourteen children.

Their eldest son, John Welsh the second, Jane's father, was born in 1776 and educated at Edinburgh University. Having qualified in medicine in 1798, he became a doctor at Haddington. The general admission of his personal charm and ability seems to distinguish him from his line of namesakes and, as it were, to shift the Welsh centre from the land to the professions. His practice flourished. This enabled him to purchase Craigenputtock from his father, who had been forced first to scant, and then to sell, the property in order to start his large family in the world. Learning had saved the land, but it had been the land which had made learning possible.

In 1800, at the age of twenty-four, Dr. Welsh married an unrelated namesake of his own, Miss Grace Welsh, a local beauty. Her mother, a Baillie, according to tradition was a descendant of William Wallace. Her father, Mr. Walter Welsh, was a stock-farmer of Capelgill. There were both beauty and brains in the family. If Grace was widely admired, she had a brother equally remarkable. He had entered on a business career at Liverpool, and was doing well when the defalcations of a partner made him a bankrupt. Eight years later, however, he invited his creditors to a dinner where each of them found a cheque in full settlement under his plate. Nothing equally decisive is known of Grace Welsh, the mother of Jane, but she seems to have been a beauty in both senses; good-looking, rather moody, impulsive, as women with many admirers often are, and inclined to take a more conventional view of life than her husband. The doctor was handsome, cultivated and urbane. When he recognized ability in young or old, he responded to it by a natural instinct. Such a doctor and such a wife are an acquisition to any neighbourhood, and it is clear that any family of theirs would begin life with a fair start.

A year after their marriage, on July 14, 1801, Jane Baillie Welsh was born. She, too, could boast an interesting pedigree. If her mother did derive from William Wallace, her father traced his family back to David Welsh of Colliston, whose younger brother, John, a well-known minister of Ayr, had married the youngest daughter of John Knox.[1] The home at Haddington must have been a happy one or, in later life, Jane would not have lingered fondly on her childish memories. A precocious little girl, she was specially devoted to her father, and the concessions that she demanded were won more willingly from him. There is no excuse for a blurred conception of her character. She became a great letter-writer, and the series starts when she was only eighteen, while her temperament was sufficiently marked in girlhood to have left abundant illustrations of it.

[1] *Life of John Welsh*, by Rev. James Young (Edinburgh, 1866).

IV

The latest connexion of John Knox was an engaging mixture of affection and vivacity. She had her father's black hair, and her large eyes could be roguish and mocking except in moments of repose, when they were pensive, if not sad. She had a way of impressing herself on those about her, could be daring, mischievous and self-possessed, but she had the art of retaining affection, whatever the age of her associates, or her own escapades, might be. Her maternal grandfather, Walter Welsh, was a great favourite of hers, and her later skill at ticking off the peculiarities of those about her displayed itself very early in her mimicry of his broad dialect. The transition between folk and culture, apparent in her father, received a new impetus in herself, and the question of her girlhood was whether she would be able to develop her possibilities or be checked. Meanwhile, she made no enemies by tricks like mimicry, and when she came into conflict with others she made them respect her, whether by stratagem or resistance.

Her spirit was shown in two early escapades. While still very young she was sent to Haddington school, the school where John Knox himself had been educated. It was a school for boys also, but the girls had their separate schoolrooms except in the mathematical class, where all the children studied arithmetic and algebra together. In this way, it was easy for Jane to make friends among the boys, and she appears, from the first, to have subjugated several. At the same time, she would brook no liberties, and, when one youngster became impertinent, she made his nose bleed with her fist. This placed the boys in an awkward dilemma. The penalty for fighting was a flogging, and, when the noise of the scuffle had brought the headmaster on the scene, he at once asked the culprit to stand forward. Not a boy moved. The word was repeated, but they made no answer. Innocent, this time, themselves, and probably holding sneaking in abhorrence, they could hardly lay the blame on a girl. The master, with automatic ferocity, thereupon threatened to flog the whole school. It was now Jane's turn to show her colours. She owned up, and the master, calling her 'a little deevil,' dismissed her laughing to the girls' quarters.

On a more sensitive point than fisticuffs she was made conscious of feminine disability. Doing well at her arithmetic, she was eager to learn Latin. The boys did; and she asked, explicitly, to be taught Latin 'like a boy.' It was her first attempt at independence, the first reach of her mind after its own food. Her father, who saw her promise, was ready to agree, but her mother, who held conventional ideas of education, dissented. Their only child was bringing into prominence a difference of opinion, and, in the deadlock, Jane thought out a solution of her own. She coaxed one of her boy-friends in the school to teach her a Latin noun of the first declension. The word, prophetic of the future letter-writer, was *penna* — a pen. When she had mastered its cases, she hid herself, after bedtime, under the table in the drawing-room where her parents were sitting. Taking advantage of a pause in their talk, she exclaimed from nowhere: '*Penna — pennae*.' In the astonishment that followed she crawled from her hiding-place, ran to her father, and cried: 'I want to learn Latin. Please let me be a boy!'

The battle was won, though how far her mother was converted remains uncertain. It was a creditable victory for a little girl of eight. We see similar qualities of spirit and resource in a more difficult situation. The school was having a ball, for which dancing was carefully practised, since the parents of the children were to attend. Jane had been chosen for a kind of star turn, one supposes, since it was a *pas seul*, a solo performance. Her mother, accustomed to make the most of her own appearance, always dressed Jane with care and taste, and on this occasion took such trouble that, the street being muddy, Jane was carried across in a clothes' basket. She was about six at the time. When her turn came and the music started, Jane, carefully coached for her special dance, stood still. They were playing the wrong tune! Her trouble was evident; the musicians stopped, whispered together, and started another. It was wrong again. One could not dance the proper step to it. With great presence of mind, Jane, left in the lurch through no fault of her own, threw her skirt over her head to hide her tears, made a curtsy, and retired amid applause.

If this was moral courage, which is probably the rarest, she invited other tests. On her way to school she had to pass a turkey-cock, who stalked behind a gate which was sometimes open. He would gabble at her fiercely, terrifying and hideous to behold. One day, when the gate was open and a bunch of labourers was tittering to see her hesitate to cross his path, Jane's heart swelled. The turkey ran at her gabbling and swelling, whereupon she dashed upon him, caught him by the neck, and flung him to one side, though he was probably as tall as herself.

News of this feat may have reached the school, where the boys had their favourite test of 'daring.' The school-building stood near Nungate Bridge, which rises high over the water, with its arch crowned by a narrow parapet on either side of the roadway. The boys would dare one another to cross the river by this parapet. They do not seem to have dared Jane, but she had wanted to be a boy and decided to qualify herself accordingly. Early one morning she slipped out of the house, and face-downward crawled along the parapet from end to end.

At nine she was reading Virgil, and good enough at

Latin to require a tutor of her own. He proved to be no less a person than Edward Irving, then a young man of eighteen, who, after having taken his degree at Edinburgh, had been appointed in 1810 to the master-ship of Haddington school. Irving was to play an important part in the life of his pupil, and some acquaintance with him is essential to an understanding of their future. The budding orator, remembered by all who saw and heard him, was 'a tall, athletic man, with dark, sallow complexion and commanding features; long, glossy black hair, and an obvious squint.' His appearance was so striking that the squint never injured his reputation for good looks, and the eloquence for which he was to be famed must have made him a good talker. He came from a stock similar to that of the Welshes. His father was a tanner, sprung from a long line of Irvings in Annan, with a drop of inherited French blood, and his mother was a Lowther, whose people were farmers in Annandale. Edward Irving's first school was kept by Peggy Paine, a connexion of the author of the *Age of Reason*. From her Irving had passed to the Annan Academy, conducted by Mr. Adam Hope, before going, at the age of thirteen, to Edinburgh University. Four years later, in 1809, he graduated Master of Arts, and the following year, by the influence of Sir John Leslie, he was appointed master at Haddington.

The young tutor of under eighteen was an acquisition, not only to the school, but to Haddington society. Of this Dr. John Welsh's house was, perhaps, the chief resort. Both the doctor and the schoolmaster were men of remarkable intelligence, and they quickly became friends. Irving was young and brilliant: the doctor a man of recognized attainments and standing in the place. Irving, who was welcomed as an elder son, seemed to be the tutor for whom Dr. Welsh was looking. It is likewise certain that in Jane Welsh he had hit on the most promising of his pupils. During the eighteen months of his tutorship the pair became inseparable. Though the youth was actually twice her age on his arrival, time would soon alter that ratio, and meanwhile he was hardly, after all, more than an elder brother, a being sure to be idealized by a girl who was an only child.

It was one of Irving's attractions that he did not take a pedantic view of lessons. His mind was alive, and imparted life to all that roused it, while it had not begun to yield to the enthusiasm which, one day, was to liken his pulpit to a boat capsizing in a storm. Irving soon interested Jane in other matters beside Latin. He would take her for walks on fine evenings, and tell her all he knew about the stars. A brilliant man, with a gift for enlisting the curiosity of an intelligent child, could hardly have been situated more happily. The quick schoolgirl, too, must have felt that her dream was becoming fulfilled. At an age when other misses had a governess, she had a young man to herself, a man, as we know, with an extraordinary power of communicating his intensity to others. There can be little doubt that her horizon rapidly expanded, and that the vista of a man's education began to open before her eyes. They were still a child's eyes, however, and they were being opened very widely very soon.

A man had arrived able and willing to educate his daughter like a boy, and Dr. Welsh embraced the opportunity. To Mrs. Welsh, on the other hand, Fate must have seemed determined to abet the unwonted fancies of her nursling, for, though the mother was no fool, she saw no reason why little girls should be taught Latin or astronomy, or enlarge upon the accomplishments which she had followed contentedly herself. With tradition on her side, she must have felt that a mother should have some say in the education of her daughter; but against the three fiery spirits of the doctor, the young tutor, and the girl, Mrs. Welsh could not prevail. Before she had reached her teens, Jane was slipping beyond her mother's mental grasp. Luckily, they were fond of each other.

Dr. Welsh left nothing to chance. A boy's education must be taken seriously, even when the 'boy' wore skirts. Irving, therefore, was expected to make a daily report upon Jane's lessons, and, like all lively pupils, she had her moments in which preparation and study were a bore. On one occasion, when she had been idle and he was considering his report, he stooped to her inquiring face and said reluctantly: 'Jane! my heart is broken, but it must be *pessima*.' Where discipleship is the soul of the discipline, a rebuke of that quality tells.

She could not often have been idle or we should not hear of her losing her sleep, and injuring her health by starting work at five o'clock in the mornings. She would awake herself artificially at that hour by tying a weight to her ankle when she went to bed. Indeed, she burnt the candle at both ends, for in her love of mathematics she would sit up late over a problem that she could not quickly puzzle out. There are definite signs of overwork, and nervous concentration. One night she was sitting up late, over some proposition of Euclid. It proved so puzzling that she had to give it up in despair. The degree of rest that she found in bed can be imagined when we hear that, on waking the following morning, she discovered the solution on her paper, already worked out. She had done it in her sleep, and gone to bed again. Her mother does not seem to have known, or at least emphasized, these symptoms, nor her father to have given them professional notice. Yet they were, undoubtedly, warnings of the strain to which Jane was being exposed. That Irving was partly to blame is suggested by an incident, not directly connected with him, that she left on record herself.

It wasn't my religion alone that my Latin studies influenced; my whole manner of being was imbued with them. Would I prevent myself from doing a selfish or cowardly thing... I said to myself simply and grandly, 'A Roman wouldn't have done it,' and that sufficed under ordinary temptations. Again, when I had done something heroic — when for instance I had caught a gander which hissed at me by the neck and flung him to the right about it was not a 'good child' that I thought myself, for whom the half-crown bestowed on me was fit reward; in my own mind I had 'deserved well of the Republic' and aspired to a 'civic crown'!

But the classical world in which I lived and moved was best indicated in the tragedy of my doll.

It had been intimated to me by one whose wishes were law that a young lady in Virgil should for consistency's sake drop her doll. So the doll, being judged, must be made an end of; and I... quickly decided how. She should end as Dido ended, that doll — as the doll of a young lady in Virgil should end. With her dresses, which were many and sumptuous, her four-post bed, a faggot or two of cedar allumettes, a few sticks of cinnamon and a nutmeg, I *non ignara futuri* constructed her funeral pyre — *sub auras* of course; and this new Dido, being placed in the bed with my help, spoke through my lips the last sad words of Dido the first, which I had then all by heart....

The doll having thus spoken, *pallida morte futura*, kindled the pile and stabbed herself with a penknife by way of Tyrian sword. Then, however, in the moment of seeing my poor doll blaze up — for, being stuffed with bran, she took fire and was all over in no time — in that supreme moment my affection for her blazed up also, and I shrieked and would have saved her and could not, and went on shrieking till everybody within hearing flew to me and bore me off in a plunge of tears — an epitome of most of one's 'heroic sacrifices,' it strikes me, magnanimously resolved on, ostentatiously gone about, repented of at the last moment, and bewailed with an outcry.

Thus was my inner world at that period three-fourths old Roman and one-fourth old fairy.

This is a vivid miniature, in which we gain a glimpse of the pair, for the obtuse person who frowned upon

the doll, whose word was law, must, surely, have been
Irving. The old note-book which preserves the story
was written at a much later date, so the teller, too, is
there, for there is no mistaking the savour of her penul-
timate comment. The remark upon 'heroic sacrifices'
is that drop of lemon-juice which gives, as our sauce-
mongers say, the zest imparted by her letters. The
lemon is a fruit which combines opposite virtues. It
is refreshing and tart. It stings and it cleanses, and,
in the shape of verbena, has given its name to an ador-
able scent. In the garden of Eden the serpent would
have tempted Jane, first of all, with a lemon.

The letters contain, for most women, perhaps more
juice than perfume, and we must bend over them if we
would savour the attar of her heart. It was a warm
heart, and susceptible. But it claimed its indulgences
from an early age. The curious mixture of tomboy and
student (which would have made her the very pupil
for Chiron, the centaur), revealed in these anecdotes,
had another element. This, the sense of comedy, never
self-sparing in those who possess it, did not shrink from
setting down her own flaws. Her note-book is just as
candid about herself as her letters are upon those around
her. The thumbnail sketch was her peculiar gift, and
all its studies are character-studies.

With a frankness that is very engaging, she touches
on her schoolroom love-affairs, and confesses that, in
love no less than in work or daring, she could never
acquiesce in the convention that the boy must be the
leader in courtship. Really of course, in love as in
other matters, initiative lies with the person who can
take it, and, even conventionally, the modesty of
women consists in luring men to be explicit in an invitation which the woman (by tacit signals) has stimulated and sanctioned in advance. Few men will risk
a plunge that, uninvited, would probably make them
look ridiculous, for the signs that invite the risk are as

unmistakable as they are subtle. An eye may be a dozen delightful things without being a glad eye, and the distinction has produced a slang phrase that fits the look precisely. Jane, however, had enough of the boy in her to resent, at an early age, the apparently passive tactics of womanhood, which indeed require less awkwardness than is common, both to boys and girls, at school. In her day, too, she went to school early, and it was, she tells us, at the age of nine that she first made herself foolish in love.

One of her schoolfellows was a little boy, the son of an artillery officer, who, with the blind eye of childhood to all but its immediate concerns, awoke a romantic attachment in her. In one form or another, she was bound to be the victim of this unfailing experience at school. Even the astute Disraeli suffered acutely from such romance. Had she been sent to a girls' school, her idol might have been a girl-friend or one of the mistresses, or both. At Haddington, the tomboy in her naturally fixed upon a schoolboy. Their opportunities for meeting were probably slender until the day came when they were both to appear at a dance. If she had been the boy, there is no doubt to whom she would have first walked with her programme, and she felt the injustice of having to dawdle. It is a wonder that she could contain herself when, whether by accident or design, the boy danced off with 'a fair, fat, sheep-looking thing,' and spoilt her party. The affections of childhood are not easily baulked, and, without a brother or sister to receive the overflow of her affections, if she could not have this boy's regard, she resolved to possess his portrait. We know, then, that she had at least been to his house, for she recollected a picture of him in baby-clothes. To gain this prize she conceived a plan worthy of a child's romantic imagination. Since children do not ask gifts of people outside their own homes, but swop the things they want with

one another, she determined to call on the mother and
to propose a bargain. Jane's most valuable possession
was her gold filigree needle-case, but, if she could
persuade the lady to accept this, in return for the
picture, the agreement was not to stop there. To make
refusal impossible, Jane decided to promise that, when
she had grown to be a rich woman, she would return
the portrait, set with diamonds! This heroic plan was
put into execution. It brought her boldly to the bar-
racks. She was admitted to the presence of the lady,
who was astonished to receive from Jane a present of
gold. No explanation was offered, for, her courage
failing, Jane came away empty: on the object of her
visit not having spoken a word. Looking back on the
incident, she said: 'On the whole, my first love wasn't
the smart piece of work to have been predicted of such
a smart little girl, a girl so renowned for her eyelashes,
her Latin and her wit.'

v

Her early teens have left fewer stories than her childhood, but a girl with her eyelashes, her Latin, and her
vivacity cannot suddenly have left exciting experiences
behind. She was growing fast, and, perhaps at her
mother's suggestion, was sent when about sixteen to a
finishing school at Edinburgh, where, it is said, she met
Irving again. The result can be guessed, on both of
them.

At Edinburgh, no doubt, she would not be encouraged to add Greek to Latin, but rather have her boyish
corners eased away, with the aid of a piano, a little
singing, needlework, and other more feminine accomplishments. Mrs. Welsh, herself a beauty, must have
been at least as aware as her husband of the attractive-
ness of Jane, and the time was approaching when the
qualities likely to be agreeable to a husband of 1820
must not be left out of sight. On the tastes of young

bachelors, at any rate, Mrs. Welsh must be admitted an authority. Whatever her daughter's tastes and capacities might be, there was only one future for her: marriage. There was nothing else, then, for a woman to understudy, and Jane, clearly, was exceptionally eligible. If she was, alack, beyond her generation among women, the eyelashes could be set against the Latin, and somehow, as her mother noted with relief, even Latin could not make her daughter either plain or dull. If only Jane had known it, her real danger was different. She was not only beyond the women, but beyond most of the men, and her father and Irving had made her exacting to prospective lovers. Byron was an idol at this time! She wanted some one with brains, with imagination, and also, if possible, with elegance. The meditations of Mrs. Welsh are not hard to fathom. In her more sympathetic moments we seem to overhear her saying: What would be the use of her daughter outstripping society in Haddington, if there was no one else in Haddington with equal feathers to his wings? Jane delighted in Edinburgh, though (except for Irving) she probably had few chances of seeing society of the right kind. The city gave to her, however, a close friend in Eliza Stodart, the first recipient of her early letters.

All this time Jane's affection for her father was deepening, and now she was beginning to enjoy his company on equal terms. His practice covered a wide area, and to make his rounds he had to take long drives. It was one of her keenest pleasures to accompany him, and their hours together gave an opportunity for intimate talks. He had arrived at the most exquisite period of a father's life, at the period when the daughter is growing into a friend, the fatal period which, sometimes, discovers the pair to be strangers to each other. He must have reflected that such companionship could not last unchallenged for very long. He had noticed that the young men were beginning to come round her, that her own vivacity, for companionship as for criticism, touched every society into which she entered with its spell. What would become of her? How could he protect her promise? Where, if anywhere yet, was a fit man for her to be discerned? Unless he could warn her without forfeiting her confidence, he might endanger the very companionship which he loved. But, if this last barrier could be brushed aside, their intimacy would be closer than ever. On her side, though he could not know it, the desire for complete understanding was eager and full. She was still ready to receive all that he would give, and anxious to leave the restraints of childhood behind her that she might stand beside her father in full companionship. To achieve this, the subject of herself must be, as it were finally, disposed of between them; for, so long as father and child reserve some subject, in consequence of their relation, from discussion, the equality of friendship is not theirs.

If she was confiding enough to listen, would he have the temerity to speak? The right moment only comes by waiting, and a forced note, an unsuspected rub, an accident that withers discussion or disturbs attention, let alone some mishap, may miss it altogether.

A few weeks after her eighteenth birthday, Dr. Welsh asked her to accompany him on a long drive. Some chance remark probably decided him, and, as they drove, he began to talk to her tenderly about herself. He told her that she was a good girl, a girl of unusual promise, but that, for this very reason, she was in greater danger than others of making a mistake. She had seen enough of life to stimulate her, but not nearly enough to throw caution to the winds: if a Byron had appeared, even we to-day might tremble for her. So far, her father pointed the argument, he did not think that she had seen any man worthy to be her partner in life. He had expected much of her, and she had not disappointed him. Would she satisfy one expectation more? — would she be wise, as well as good-looking and good? A single glance at the portrait known as the 'earliest likeness' enables us to evoke the figure at his side. The eyes are dark and intelligent, the mouth well-shapen and firm, and the provoking nose is tilted to a saucy and vivacious angle. This face is like a mirror, only waiting the appearance of some object to flash back its very image in reply! Though the curls tumble almost to the eyebrows, the head can be felt behind, for the eyes are plainly brighter from the mental cruse behind them. It is an unforgettable youthful face: the face that is called enchanting because, in it, grace is matched with intelligence, frankness and tenderness are vivified by the features' sharply etched lines.

Whether by silence or quick understanding, Jane's response was full. It was a great day in her life, a day to be fixed in her memory by the climax of this drive. Her father had been visiting a patient with typhus, and that very evening Dr. Welsh himself fell ill. In three days the same fever killed him. Her girlhood, just crowned with its finest intimacy, was over, and her happy life at Haddington was virtually at an end.

VI

Dr. Welsh, who was only forty-three, could not leave his practice behind him, and, not foreseeing this calamity, while leaving a small annuity to his wife, had bequeathed Craigenputtock to Jane.

Deprived of her father's companionship, not only her home became empty, but her life. Mrs. Welsh's interests were divided between tea-parties, making ends meet, and considering possible husbands for her daughter. To relieve her tedium, Jane began to devote herself to Italian and French, and even found three pupils, whom she instructed in geography, French and drawing. In the first shock of her loss, she never allowed herself to be unoccupied, read the books that her father had wished her to read, pursued the studies planned by him, and, in her part as teacher, seemed to assume her father's place. It was a valiant, if imperfect, effort, for Haddington, without her father, was dullness unredeemed. She gives a vivid record of her feelings in her correspondence with Miss Stodart; and, in one of her early letters, the refrain 'Mother bids me say' runs as a motive: to introduce directions about making marmalade, about hens that need medicine, about jam-jars, directions which rise to a climax in the cry: 'Not one word more will I write for her, by God!' Judging by the comments that this explosion has received, Miss Welsh must have been the first lady in her century to swear by post. The doubtful duckling had become suddenly a swan, a swan too big for the duck-pond of Haddington, where the tradesmen stood gaping at their doors, and the visitors, including the young men, were ninnies. The voice that was to startle English drawing-rooms in the seventies when Mrs. Besant won her independence from home, of which George Eliot was a pioneer, in act, for many silent women, which was heard across Europe in the person of Ibsen's Nora in the eighties, found one of its earliest instruments in Jane Welsh; for, when she now described herself as 'hemmed in all round, straining my eye-balls and my neck to no purpose,' and concluded: 'here is no sojourn for me. I must dwell in the open world, live amid life,' she meant what she said. It was no passing aspiration, no transient mood. She had that faith which is the will in action. Her fate was to be born too soon, but the pioneer who utters a demand before his fellows none the less opens a door, whether or no personally able to find his or her own exit through it. Her letters are as authentic a record of this spirit as the writings and deeds of later comers, who afterward made in their own lifetimes more noise in the world. Jane is not one of those women whom an eventually famous husband has dragged into the limelight.

Meantime, it was a husband that she sought, for only a husband could secure her escape from Haddington, and she was not one of those women, who, from the first, are dedicated spinsters. Thus, when she cast her eyes about her, and ticked off the possible young men, she could count at least six whose advances had been considered, but none of whom, unless it were George Rennie, the nephew of the engineer who built Waterloo Bridge, filled the part suggested by the example of her father or of Irving. Rennie, indeed, proved a disappointment. In the very room 'where — but no matter' — an eloquent phrase! — he came to say good-bye, Rennie took his leave, before starting for a foreign appointment, without a sign of sentimental regret. It was annoying to find that anxiety for his safety at sea was stronger than her indignation with him, stronger, even, than her humiliation at herself.

She took refuge in books, and found one precisely to her mind in *La Nouvelle Héloïse*. This confirmed her own high standard for her cavaliers, whom, she now saw, must combine the virtues of St. Preux and Wolmar in Rousseau's novel. By that measure, the six names that she totted on her fingers were no use. Cured of what, in self-reproach, she termed 'flirting' by the faithless Rennie, she discovered that sincerity was her favourite virtue. Her future husband must be pre-eminent in sincerity. He was nearer than she fancied, for, within two years of her father's death, Irving paid a visit to Haddington. He brought with him another teacher, Thomas Carlyle, and we read with interest how this studious peasant, as duly constipated with genius as an egg-bound hen with eggs, compared with St. Preux and Wolmar. Carlyle's 'talents, independence, high-souled principles of honour' impressed her, but he would kick over the fire-irons and 'make puddings in his tea-cup.' Beyond a doubt, 'want of elegance' was the defect that she found in her latest acquaintance, and she was no less conscious of the want than of his gifts.

CHAPTER TWO
THE MASON'S SON

I

THE Carlyles, whatever their lineage, had become a family of peasants, sometimes feckless and reduced to hunting for hares to fill the larder, and sometimes settling to steadier work, which varied from the trades of joinery or building to farming. In the two generations which preceded Carlyle's, the grandfather's life was the most chequered. This Thomas Carlyle, after whom the author was to be called, was born about 1727, and his grandson described him 'an honest, vehement, adventurous, but not industrious man.' It was his habit to amass sufficient money to pay his half-year's rent, and then to leave his wife and her seven children to shift very much for themselves. He liked to go hunting, sometimes in attendance on his kinsman the laird of Bridekirk, while his family, except for what he could bring to them, were occasionally in straits even for meal. Potatoes were such a luxury in those days that a sieve-ful would be stored to make a feast at All Hallows. The children were oddly clad, Carlyle's father sometimes going in leather. The grandfather, at any rate, had some fun out of life. He became a joiner, and not only travelled as far as Lancashire to get work, but one winter skated home across the Lakes, and saw the Highlanders in 1745 take his friend the laird of Bridekirk a prisoner, after whom he was sent with a message by the laird's wife. A restless being, he gave up joinery for farming, and settled at Brownknowe, where, in the end, he was supported by the future sage's father, James. If hardly a family man, old Thomas had a warm heart, for, before his death in 1806, he said to James: 'Thou hast been a good son to me.' The best of his qualities, fire, 'the toughness and springiness of steel,' he transmitted to his second son and fourth child, James, the future author's father.

In earlier days the family had been farmers at Burrens, Middlebie, and, according to tradition, had had their farm filched from them by the then Duke of Queensbury, early in the eighteenth century, about the time when Carlyle's grandfather was born. For our purposes, the man to note is Carlyle's father, who was, if his famous son is to be believed, and such evidence as we have is not negligible, the sterling product of the family. 'I have a sacred pride in my peasant father,' Carlyle wrote: 'perhaps among Scottish Peasants what Samuel Johnson was among English authors.' The contrast between his natural capacity and his limited opportunities dwelt with Carlyle to the last. A man of granite, with a strong tinge of religion, James Carlyle filled his children, and even his wife, with a certain awe. His courage, his industry, his pride in his work, his thrift, and his generosity impressed them; but they dreaded his wrath — even the gentry quailed when he rose to oppose some injustice in the Tax Courts — and the children did not dare to show much love for him, for he was a man of few words and rarely inclined to unbosom himself. He can be compared to a rich field which has never been fully cultivated or developed, and those who saw the richness sighed, as men sigh to-day when they note the land of England unploughed, unmanned, and turned into pasture, or houses. Some scraps of natural beauty are reserved, like town-parks, as the countryside degenerates into one vast suburb.

The turning-point in the life of James Carlyle occurred at the age of sixteen or thereabouts when a certain William Brown, a mason from Peebles, came to do

some job in Annandale. Perhaps he boarded with old
Thomas; anyway, he taught the Carlyle boys to be
masons, so that 'instead of miscellaneous hunters and
labourers' they became 'regular tradesmen.' The
ability of the young James is seen in the fact that,
though not the eldest, he was regarded as the head of
the family; and, when work was wanting in Annandale, he slung his tools over his shoulder and accompanied William Brown, as his apprentice, to Auldgirth
in the Nithsdale Hills. At that place a bridge was then
in building, and, except Craigenputtock in his old age,
this was the furthest distance that he ever strayed from
home. His job was that of a hewer with 'some few
pence a day' for his wage. The work on the bridge was
being superintended by a mason from Edinburgh, who
saw ability in James and wanted the boy to return
with him; but James stuck to his friend and master,
Brown, and became in time the best mason in his
neighbourhood. When Carlyle thought of the houses
that his father had built, he said: 'They stand firm and
sound to the heart all over his little district'; and again:
'Let me write my books as he built his houses.' James
Carlyle must be numbered with those sturdy, but
mostly anonymous, builders whose work, where posterity has not destroyed it, like the epics of anonymous
bards of old, seems to defy time; whose barns seem
designed to outlast our civilization, and who could not
bridge even a culvert without the mark of magnificence
upon the stone. His chief building, his son fancied,
was Cressfield House, which brought to him the largest
sum that he ever earned in one year, £100.

About 1791 James Carlyle married a distant namesake, one Janet Carlyle, by whom he had a son, John,
eventually an emigrant who died farming in Canada;
but, within a year or so, James was left a widower, and
in March 1795 he married again, one Margaret Aitken,
then in domestic service to her aunt because her father,

a farmer, had fallen into bankruptcy and was sacrificing everything to pay off his creditors, which in the end
he did. By this time, James and his brothers were
master-masons in Ecclefechan, and the steadfast and
formidable man was upright on his own feet. He and
his wife presented one of the engaging contrasts that
are conspicuous in many marriages. He was honest as
the day, full of natural capacity, a man with whom
nobody would idly meddle, and with a laugh, when it
chanced to come, that rang loud. His wife, Peggy, was
gentle, with a low harmonious voice, not a woman, at
first sight, to fall in love with a fighting mason, for so,
though not through quarrelsomeness, James's set were
called. The truth was that the Border, at that date,
was infested by Irish vagrants, gipsies and other vaga-
bonds, so that farmers did not ride unarmed, and
masons, often at work in lonely places, took care not to
be attacked with impunity. The something dangerous
in James was confined to self-defence; insubordination
was as alien to him as an ill-laid course in a wall. His
son recalled how James would stand bare-headed before a certain landlord who, he said, ruled his estate
well, and it was from his landlord, a baronet of the
name of Maxwell, that James Carlyle formed his idea
of what a gentleman should be. His own type was the
man of action, always attentive to any fact or idea
worth hearing, and, though he never had more than
three months' schooling, he would read what came his
way, except poetry or such romances as the *Arabian
Nights*, which he held to be idle fictions. It is expressly
recorded that he never glanced at the poetry of Robert
Burns. His talk was pithy; he could sketch an object
to the life, and his 'I don't believe thee!' his sceptical
'Hah!' or his grave 'It's no idle tale' would reduce a
company to silence. His expressions were racy, and the
slack reaper remembered his reprimand: 'Thou maun
alter thy figure or slant thy bog. Thou hast every

feature of a bad shearer.' He had that natural poetry of speech that elementary education kills, for, by a well-observed fact, the moment an ordinary man knows what a metaphor is he loses the habit of coining metaphors. His talk was a local reservoir for conversational anecdotes, and he had the sign-manual of the poet, a power of exaggeration for the sake of the humour to be extracted from it. A good proof of his natural intelligence was that he did not fear the effect of education on his children, even when warned that they would despise him if they became better educated than he. James Carlyle himself would have passed unscathed through many schoolmasters. He had the character which could survive book-learning, and an intelligence critical enough to test, rather than to swallow, print. He had that fear of death which seems peculiar to healthy, wholesome people, and his stoic strength was infused by a faith in God which made him careless of public opinion, and prepared him for what he called 'that last, that awful change.'

It was 'exclusively he,' Carlyle tells us, who insisted on educating his son, and, what is more remarkable, who did not interfere even when education seemed to have unfitted this son for earning his living. He taught little Thomas division, and, when his mother said that the child would soon forget it, her husband replied: 'Not so much as they that have never learned.' He it was who took Thomas, in 1806, when he was eleven years old, to Annan Academy; he wrote regularly when Thomas was at college, and when Thomas denied the hope of his father's heart by refusing to enter the ministry, and thus seemed to have been educated in vain, the old man quietly let him have his way. There were severer tests. Education which does not lead to the pulpit is expected to lead to schoolmastering, and, when Thomas revolted even from teaching, the old man, though convinced of his imprudence, refrained from reproaches, even though the young man loitered, for several summers, under the paternal roof with no proper occupation, no prospects, and suffering, as his father might have thought deservedly, from sickness both in body and mind. One cannot imagine a greater strain on a father's forbearance, especially as so much as a chance word of impatience 'in those sour days of wounded vanity' might have driven the youth from home.

When Carlyle was twenty, his father left the trade of mason for a farm at Mainhill. He was shrewd enough to see that times were changing, that population and industrialism were putting a premium on jerrybuilding, and that, as he put it, 'honest trade was done.' At the new farm he soon had trouble with his landlord, and, when a proposal that he deemed to be unjust was made, his answer was: 'I will not do it; I will rather go to Jerusalem, seeking farms, and die without finding one. We can live without Sharpe (the landlord) and the whole Sharpe creation.' The last meeting of this rugged pair was memorable. Carlyle said something that the old man admired, whereupon James Carlyle, with a sparkle in his eye, remarked: 'Man, it's surely a pity that thou should sit yonder with nothing but the Eye of Omniscience to see thee; and thou with such a gift to speak.'

Carlyle did well to think of his father as the sunken pillar on which his own life was built, but his own gift of speech was none so free as it should be in a healthy author. Burns had this freedom. Why not Carlyle? Though Carlyle spoke of a wall about his father's heart, and that 'he had not the free means to unbosom himself,' yet it is not certain that, had James had the opportunities of the son, he would not have proved a less trammelled worker. To wrench and strain, to agonize, to choke with stifled thoughts, in Carlyle's way, is to suffer from some inhibiting disease. A great man will, indeed, wring beauty out of the hurly-burly, but this last can occur only in a mind somehow distorted and deformed. When father and son are set side by side, the father is the healthier, and his stones, wherever men have left them alone, will last as long as Thomas's books. It would not be quite fair, but there are moments when the father's comparison of a confused preacher to 'a fly wading among treacle' recurs to the reader of Thomas Carlyle's works. Burns, on the other hand, was a genius who could suck the Muses' honey without getting stuck. The psychological impediment that made Carlyle roar must not be confused with the inarticulateness of the peasant. He suffered from genius as gentlemen suffer from gout.

II

When his mother had recovered from his birth, which occurred on December 4, 1795, and contemplated her first baby, she called it a 'lang, sprawling, ill-put-together thing.' For some time she doubted whether she would ever rear him. Before he was two, he had a fright in the kitchen where a can that he had set on the fire boiled over and sent him shrieking from the room. Since he never forgot the incident, it must have left a mark upon his mind. His emotions were easily excited, and he could be roused, very quickly, either to a blow or to tears. He was an active and inquisitive child needing to occupy both his fingers and his mind. He listened greedily, and amused people by his childish mimicry. He had the run of the village, and, though taught to read very early by his mother, preferred to watch the swallows and the crows, to keep the pig away from the potatoes, to stand by the door of the smithy, where work and altercations would go on, to peep round the door of a neighbouring bakehouse, to watch the weavers and other villagers at their crafts in what proved to be the last days before industrialism.

He was no little bookworm. Like a certain Miss Welsh, who was soon to make her appearance in this world, Thomas was fond of his grandfather, and would sometimes be encouraged to show his affection in the same way, by repeating the old fellow's locutions. This knowing boy, a tough youngster the local clog-maker would call him, was sometimes led on to his own confusion, and he never forgot how a pair of old women, whose mysterious box was a fascinating problem to him, induced him to take a large pinch of snuff, and how he thought his head would be blown off by the cruel explosions that followed.

At the age of five he was solemnly breeched, and he was awakened to the horrors of existence by seeing the joiner measuring his little sister for her coffin, and by the accidental sight of his uncle, ghastly in death. For months his mother was inconsolable, and his memory of her daily tears, and of the nightly dreams of the dead child which she recounted, was vivid throughout his life. At the turn of the century, times were hard and food was scarce, so scarce that when a beggar arrived at the house, from which his elders were absent, and little Thomas could find no food, he took down the money-bottle in which he kept his pennies, broke it and handed the money to the man, through the great pity that, even then, he felt. He had looked on death, been frightened badly, and had proved his susceptibility to violent emotion, before the age of six. It is significant that it was the touch of Pity which first opened the door of Heaven to him.

The first school worth mention to which the boy was sent was a mile off, at Hoddam, and his feeling for poetry is seen in the ballads that he would shout to the weavers, raising his voice above the hum of the looms; for, while they worked, they liked to have some one reciting. He impressed a visiting examiner, who told his father that he must start Latin or be wasting his time. In three months, we are told, he could construe Horace and Virgil, and the tongue of Cicero became a living reality to the boy when some Roman stones were shown to him and he found that he could translate the inscriptions. He was happy at his first school, and his mind was growing; fed by the natural and human sights that met him in the little town and on the hills about it, and by the sermons at the Meeting-house which, like other children, he was encouraged to repeat from memory. Hectic homilies were then popular, and these sermons sank in, so that Carlyle was to remain to the end a Calvinist with a difference, or, if this be thought too strict a definition, an evangelical with doubts. If some of these preachers were like volcanoes belching the pleasant lava of damnation on their hearers, the boy had in his father one who did not hesitate to leave the kirk when the preacher out-Heroded Herod. In more senses than one, James Carlyle was the sunken pillar on which his boy's beliefs could feel firm ground. It was, indeed, the father's sense of reality that became the son's touchstone of fact. The difference was that schooling and book-learning opened to the son a world of cant, and the dread he had of cant was so peculiar that it became almost an obsession, an obsession from which the father seems to have been wholly free. For cant Carlyle had a most uneasy fear. Physically Thomas was not so sound a man as his father, and the ill-put-together bundle of humanity that Mrs. Carlyle observed in the cradle was perhaps the outward sign of some instability within. He shot up early and became a six-foot man. Perhaps he overgrew his strength.

There is no alloy in this sketch of James Carlyle which Mr. David Alec Wilson has recorded: 'A very conspicuous Christian, marshalling his family into the front pew of the gallery every Sunday; and he's honest and pays well and doesn't quarrel and all that; but what if he thought he should hit you?' We are also told that James Carlyle never knew what doubt was; and the offspring of this splendid son of the soil, turning from action to literature, in his awkwardness resembles nothing so much as a bookish man nobly trying to do manual work. However hard the pensive fellow tries, the movements of such a man betray that he was not bred to manual labour. Moreover, a fine physique is not always inherited, and, if the physique be exceptionally fine, it is apt to prove a drain on the stock and to throw weedy children. Like his parents, Thomas Carlyle was to live to a very ripe old age, but, unlike them, he was chronically unstable.

III

Certainly, it was not want that made him so, and the first problem in his biography is to find the cause of his spiritual inhibitions and of his physical dyspepsia. They were probably connected, but which came first it seems impossible to say. His father was now a thriving man, and, in his deep way, a devoted parent. His mother the boy adored, and the home was happy. Religion, work, affection, combined to make it so. What, then, was it that deprived the lad of equilibrium? The only early clue we have is slight. Up to the age of ten Carlyle was regularly in the company of his father, and we have seen how his inquisitiveness, aptness to listen and readiness to reproduce what he had heard, made him welcome to his neighbours. Yet, when he speaks of his father with ungrudging admiration and love, he is forced to add that it seemed 'as if an atmosphere of Fear repelled us from him. My heart and tongue played freely only with my mother.' Somehow, and unconsciously no doubt, the father choked the little boy, and here, for want of a better explanation, seems to lurk part of the cause of the trouble. Compassion was so characteristic of Carlyle in his manhood that it suggests he had felt the need for it himself, and, since his home was a true home, with the best that the land can breed of men, we can only assume his nature to have suffered unawares by some experience beneath the surface.

Yet father and son had much in common, even in unexpected ways. James Carlyle, for instance, had read *The Wealth of Nations*, but what he thought of the dismal science that that great work had introduced, we do not hear. If the *Arabian Nights* were lies to him, and the poetry of Burns no concern at all, he did not snub the boy of ten when, inflamed by the hammer-on-anvil verses of Campbell, Thomas would recite the 'Battle of the Baltic.' Burns and Campbell seem to have been the first poets to have fired Thomas Carlyle's imagination, and Reynard the Fox the first prose. He had a hero-worship for Robert Burns, and, recalling how, at the age of eleven, he had identified the tomb of the poet in Dumfries churchyard, he declared it to have been an unforgettable experience.

His outer troubles began in the rough and tumble school at Annan, where his first two years were miserable. The boys were unlicked cubs, whose chief pleasure was fighting, and Thomas was not only under a vow to his mother not to fight, but added to this the crimes of working, of being so a favourite with the ushers, and of letting his tongue wag rudely when tormented. The one oasis in this desert of barbarity occurred at each week-end, when he would return home. As with many another sensitive child, it may have been his schoolfellows who destroyed his inward peace and his digestion. At last, they taught him the necessity of self-defence, and, once he had taken his own part vigorously, he was let alone; but two years, especially at school, are long enough to damage a boy's humour. Something or some one upset his disposition, and the tall tree was full of knots against the grain.

IV

The Annan Academy was an odd arena in which to find general literature, but the man in whose house some of the boys boarded had a library, which was open to borrowers, and here the novels of Smollett, and even a history by Robertson, were eagerly devoured. To be nearly drowned in the bathing-pool at Annan was another experience which, as the present writer can testify, is never forgotten. For workers it must have been a solid school, since algebra, geometry and French, were soon added to the boy's acquirements. Beyond letters, however, none of the arts came his way, and he seems to have been introduced to Shakespeare by the accidental sight of a bust of the poet on a show-man's booth, with some lines from 'The Tempest' inscribed below it. It was a lucky quotation, the one that compares human life to the stuff of dreams, for it confirmed the religion that made mortal existence a transient thing, and so prepared Carlyle for the music which makes the lines memorable. Who can doubt that Carlyle's growth would have been smoother had he had pictures to see, statues to show him the grace that is the perfection of strength, and music to infuse him with rhythm? He acquired, partly by study, and there was then a tradition, a beautiful and sensitive handwriting, and it is said that he would have liked to learn to draw, an art, we are told by those who know, the elements of which any child can get if taught sufficiently early. The visual arts were wanting, and Carlyle never learned to see that strength should wear grace as the bloom on its sincerity. Beauty and strength need never be opposed.

V

On the eve of his fourteenth birthday, Thomas started on foot for the University of Edinburgh, exciting rumours from which had reached him through

Edward Irving, a brilliant old-boy, who once paid a visit to the school. The journey took three days. Here Greek also was studied, and the mind was opened to intellectual fashions in the students' debating societies, to which Erasmus Darwin's writings had long brought the idea of evolution. Dr. Darwin's books, as we can see from Butler's summary in *Evolution Old and New*, provided such exciting topics as the origin of man, some of the young debaters holding that he had sprung from a cabbage, but others from an oyster. At Edinburgh growing pains were felt. The young student began to halt between diffidence and contempt for others. He had reached the awkward age.

Among Carlyle's opinions on the many authors, classical and modern, whom he read at this time, it is interesting to learn that he disliked Horace for being 'light in the touch.' It is odd that the only grace which evangelicals understand should be grace of soul, and even into this they import their own limitations; and that men of their hands, who delight to see expert lightness in the handling of tools and rough materials, should be blind to the same light touch in the arts. Perhaps we all recoil from the beauty which rebukes our want of it.

Carlyle did well enough in his studies to be able to take pupils in his vacations, and was meeting people, worthy of admiration, whose opinions took small heed of some facts that he had been taught axiomatically at home. In William Allingham's *Diary* is one significant remark: 'Mother,' Carlyle is reported to have asked, 'did God Almighty come down and make wheelbarrows in a shop?' a question which made the poor woman lie awake all night, in prayer and tears. This did not silence him, but he kept his peace when he next shocked her by asking how it was known that the *Song of Songs* symbolized the relation of Christ to His Church? After the pang of this inquiry he kept his own counsel, for his next problem was how to maintain his inquiries without causing his mother needless and cruel pain. Mr. Wilson compares the mind of his hero, at this stage, to 'a raw wound'; and the best argument in favour of the interpretation of Christianity that he had begun to question, was the brainless materialism that he encountered in Edinburgh. So he still studied Christian evidences in the gradually extinguishing hope of being convinced. He was too much of his age to surmount all its superficialities.

Thus far he did see: that the piety which he was leaving had tougher virtues than the crude rationalism of the town, and it was the impact of Edinburgh that led Carlyle to show his exaggerated impatience with insincerity. He did not see that denunciation flatters vice, the best rebuke of which is the example of virtue. His growth is a fascinating study. He chose good friends, and he had one horrible experience, the sight of a man being hanged, whose twitchings haunted his dreams until, divining the teaching of a later psychology, he freed himself by drawing the horror upon paper. Less inhuman activities were provided by the Law Courts, where he heard the sprightly Francis Jeffrey plead. He also listened to preachers, and became observant of elocution. The scientific studies in which he was mainly engaged were more than satisfactorily concluded, and the time had come for Carlyle to realize his father's wish, the end of all this education, and to prepare for the ministry. There were two ways of doing this, and Carlyle chose the longer: no doubt to gain time.

This time was often spent in the forbidding University Library, the use of which was sternly discouraged by the nominal librarian, and by the sturdy henchman whom he employed. Yet it was in this cemetery of books that the man of letters struck his roots, and from there that he dug out Shakespeare, at whom good taste was still inclined to jeer. In the other books that he read there, on subjects ranging from chemistry to history, he searched instinctively for the man behind the writing, and formed his opinion of the fellow by applying, to the ideas expressed, his own foot-rule of good sense. This is not a fantastic occupation. Many must have been the unscientific minds, lured by the words 'The Calculus Made Easy,' which, though unable to acquit Professor Sylvanus Thompson of exaggerating, have no doubt whatever, from the quality of his preface alone, that superior wits have done their best there. Franklin on Electricity and certain Scottish writers were among Carlyle's finds in the University Library. There was much virtue then in Scotsmen. Scott was publishing *Waverley* in the year before Waterloo; Burns was a living memory; and letters were opening a new field of fame with the enormous prestige attaching to Byron, as, with the rise of Scott and the general welcome beginning to attach to novels and their writers, the grubs were emerging from Grub Street, almost as if poets and authors could claim to be mistaken for respectable men.

In some few letters that survive from this early time, the latent force in Carlyle issues with surprising ease, but, occupied with coaching, he does not seem to have made any attempt on the Reviews, then in their pride, though there is allusion to some later contributions (1816) to the *Dumfries Courier*. In books annotated by him there is a prayer to Fortune,[1] 'that with a heart of independence, unseduced by the world's smiles, and unbending to its frowns, I may attain to literary fame.'

This desire may be the last infirmity of a noble mind, but it is one of the first to make its appearance. Carlyle outshot this vanity, in theory, but it taught him to rail at it in others, and there never was an author more apt

[1] D.A.W., I, p. 93.

to judge from his own belly the condition of the world.

Edinburgh was the capital; and rank, fashion, celebrity paraded Prince's Street with such pomp and regularity that the unfashionable scarcely dared to thread the gay throng. Everybody who was anybody could be seen there, and even a poet would not pass without glances of recognition. It is not so long since these processions have disappeared from our towns, and with them a welcome element of colour. In London, there are still riders in the Row, but the tub-thumpers survive in better strength than the traditional Sunday promenaders after church from the Marble Arch to the Achilles statue. Only twenty odd years ago, young people returning from the theatre, if they could escape the parental eye, would linger toward midnight in Piccadilly Circus for a nightly spectacle. On the stroke of twelve, when the hansoms were thinning, and other pleasure-seekers had started for home, the doors of the Continental, a notorious hotel of naughty reputation then standing in Waterloo Place, would open, and a troop of men and painted women would appear, keeping their loose ranks up the hill till the pairs dispersed, in company, at Gilbert's fountain. Depressed and respectable young men, not bold enough to enter the Continental, would talk of this procession as one of the minor sights of the town, and it certainly gave unity to the solitary young people who glanced, then as now, at one another between the two poles of their wanderings, Waterloo Place, and 'the home of ballet' in Leicester Square. It was in Prince's Street that Carlyle had his first glimpses of gigmanity, and men of pleasure.

At the age of nineteen, we are told, a friend expressly advised Carlyle to fall in love: 'you will be the better for it.' Instead, he applied successfully for a vacant mathematical mastership at Annan Academy. The annual salary was £70.

VI

One of the good writers whom Carlyle scorned was Lord Chesterfield, for the young man had enough in common with Johnson to shy at the earl's seemingly slight, but really profound, advice to study manners. Carlyle, however likeable, was scarcely couth. He was apt from the first, also, to misjudge a good when its abuse was more conspicuous than its goodness; so, when he found Annan to be a place where social pretensions were rising, and where astuteness and smooth behaviour could get a man further than he deserved, he raged at the false airs and graces of the prosperity-hunting crew, already inclined to patronize a young schoolmaster whose father 'is a mason, I believe.'

He was not indifferent to young women, but he refused to cultivate the parents, and would make the girls smile in their sleeves by quoting good jokes — from books. Late hours at work, and loneliness in a cold room — writing, at the best of times, is freezing to the legs — were fraying his nerves and ruffling his temper. He began to suffer from sleeplessness, and to be exasperated by noise. Mr. Wilson thinks that his liver was affected by these excesses. Carlyle was not an ordinary teacher. He did not flog his pupils; but he would stand nonsense from nobody. After an elder colleague's abortive attempt to humiliate him in class, Carlyle was let alone. The pity is that he should have provoked hostility, for he needed to be thawed, and was probably harmed by his isolated superiority. He had quite enough pride already; and this was his danger, for your proper peasant has good reason to be proud; nor is Blake's advice, to be 'humble to God but haughty to men,' sound, though it is a great temptation to the underestimated and the inexperienced to think so. If we are only to be good to those who deserve it, there will be precious little opportunity to be good at all. One does not like to accuse Carlyle of reading superficially, but his standard was apt to be his immediate like or dislike, and the consequence was that he was punished all his life for deliberately shutting his eyes to the truth of Chesterfield's maxim: before all else, remember the graces. This is, in substance, St. Paul's opinion of Charity, compressed into four words. The finest motto in the world is that chosen by William of Wykeham for his two foundations; and there is no better proof that Manners makyth Man than the rewards which their affectation alone constantly brings to people who have not even sincerity, much less virtue, to recommend them.

It is more surprising to learn that he was not drawn to Hume, but the ingenuity and reasonableness of some of the Essays soon led Carlyle, who was preparing a trial sermon and a discourse on divinity with the ministry in view, to alter his opinion. Such adjustment in his attitude to orthodoxy as was necessary was not very severe. Hume was no longer impossible in all evangelical circles, and the popular preachers of the moment were those who indulged in 'plain sermons,' stuck closely to moral admonishment, and left dogma, which is the foundation and life of religion, alone. Good works were the vogue, and muddle-headed muscular Christianity was dawning. At the moment, indeed, there was more hesitancy among Carlyle's young friends about entering the ministry than in himself. After all, to what could education lead except to the pulpit or the schoolroom? And Carlyle was not blind to the sacrifices made by his father.

Meantime, he delivered, with approval, a Latin discourse on Natural Religion in the Divinity Hall at Edinburgh, and, while there, was introduced to Edward Irving with whom his friendship began with a passage of arms. He maintained his interest in mathematical science, which at least seemed sure as far as it went, and even found spiritual refreshment in Newton's *Principia*. Carlyle is one of the few imaginative writers who have been capable of mathematics. At that time, when beliefs were crumbling in protestant countries, anything which could be proved to be true possessed a religious value, for all the world as if nothing that could not go into a test-tube could be tested, though all the while young men and women were falling in love without even wanting to prove a superiority in their sweethearts incomprehensible to outsiders. We can imagine the strain of all these growing-pains on a lanky young man who worked too hard, was thinking too much, and sleeping too little. It needed only a sudden strain to affect his constitution, and this occurred when, after sitting up with a sick uncle for a night or two, Carlyle saw the old man die, not too peacefully, under his eyes.

For a month he was ill with sore throat, sad heart, and mental depression. Undiagnosed indigestion is said to have been a trouble; too little exercise out of doors a cause; and that condition of thwarted virility which caused even the healthy Browning to become a martyr to headache before his marriage set him free.

Recommended for a mastership at Kircaldy Burgh School by two professors whose advice had been sought, Carlyle received the appointment, and it is pleasant to recall that, though the new master was intended to bring the Council's school on to a level with the private school conducted there with great success by Irving, Irving gave to Carlyle the warmest of welcomes, and remained a very good friend.

VII

Exactly a calendar month before Christmas 1816, Carlyle started for the second time as schoolmaster. His salary was to be £80 for the year. Irving lived over the way. He also was veering between the min-

istry and teaching, and had become engaged to Miss
Martin when Carlyle arrived. In off hours he went
for enormous walks with Irving, and there is nothing
like a long walk beside a friend for loosening the tongue
and getting to the bottom of an argument. In school
he kept order mainly by scowling. Mr. Wilson speaks
of some one who cherished fearful memories of
Carlyle's scowls. Perhaps these scowls were something to show for the inflamed throat that again
attacked him in 1817, the year too in which, without
parade on his part and without a show of impatience
on his father's, Carlyle definitely turned his back on
divinity and Holy Orders. Carlyle absented himself
from family prayers, but this, too, provoked no question from his father. In the gospel of silence James
Carlyle was a more perfect practitioner than his son.
Only once, apparently, did the old man's metal melt,
and that was at this time, when Mrs. Carlyle fell ill and
suffered so cruelly from sleeplessness that, for a moment, the old man feared that she was losing her
reason. His distress was overwhelming, and he col-
lapsed moaning on the ground. Only less hard to bear
were the well-meant condolences of neighbours who
attributed part of the old man's anguish to the apos-
tasy of his son, which was bruited abroad. James told
these meddlers roundly that his son had better work
to do than to preach at them. It was nobly said, and
fine proof of his magnanimity. Poor Mrs. Carlyle had
not yet realized that she would never sit below her son
in the kirk.

To decide to refrain from a course of action is one
thing. The moment when the heart and brain ap-
prove as decisively as the instinct may not occur simul-
taneously with such decision. It is queer to learn
that the man who destroyed Carlyle's belief in Christianity was Edward Gibbon, which tells us better than
any disquisition what the kind of Christianity was in

which Carlyle *had* believed. There is also a point of
some literary interest in Gibbon's influence. It seems
that Carlyle felt the thrusts of Gibbon's irony, and
so, for once, Carlyle acknowledged the quality of a
weapon that he could not himself use. He was generally afraid of wit, as a bull may be afraid of a gadfly,
and, when he met a young lady who was an adept at
mocking illustration, he confessedly quailed, telling
her that he much preferred her tender moments. Perhaps he would have thrown aside even Gibbon in contemptuous irascibility, if the intention of Gibbon's
irony had not been congenial to his own doubts. We
have had another century for learning that religion is
not to be measured by the size of a whale's throat, and
that the literal lies of poetry are no more empty of
truth than the heavens are of stars when the sun is
shining. If certainty is to be measured by the mul-
tiplication-table, neither love nor beauty are certainties. Having, like his contemporaries, become deeply
confused, it is no wonder that Carlyle was to spend the
rest of his life scrambling out of such a muddle. Bad
theology is a good riddance, but the faith that moves
mountains abides, as Carlyle found. He had taken his
road, however, and, with Doubt gone, it was hard that
fate should now send Dyspepsia to gnaw at him.

VIII

We are inclined to forget how much Carlyle saw of
Irving at this time, and to what extent, except in
sacred enthusiasm, he was under Irving's influence.
Their long walks on holidays, and the tours that they
took on foot, explain much; but Irving had the active
self-confidence of which Carlyle had the desperate
side only. Irving, a careerist to the marrow, was feeling the call of the arena; he knew that his voice was
destined for other hearers than his townsmen, and
Carlyle's shyness in society and equivocal social stand-

ing, in his neighbours' eyes, threw him back on Irving's society.

When Irving decided to leave his school, his independence was infectious; and, among the people who were thrilled by the news was, it seems likely, Irving's attractive young friend, Margaret Gordon, to whom Carlyle, inwardly hungry for a woman to please, had been introduced. Girls of quality in the place were taught by their elders to think schoolmasters poor creatures, and certainly the wages of teaching were no recommendation to the parents of eligible young women. Since Margaret was the first woman to attract Carlyle, it is interesting to know that she was 'witty and merry, yet...as kind as she was bonny'; for a sensible young man, who can keep his susceptibilities in check, is apt to preserve a preference; and the order of Mr. Wilson's adjectives suggests that it was indeed a counterpart for which Carlyle was open. He was sensible rather than witty, atrabilious rather than merry, though, in looks and feelings, certainly bonny and kind. Margaret added to her other attractions a fondness for reading, and we may note that her admirers were not few. A good deal of their converse, as it happened, was carried through the post.

With this stimulus to think less and to thrive more, Carlyle's temperament began to expand, but a vocation was still beyond his decision. Engineering was vaguely, the law more seriously, mentioned; private teaching offered a stand-by, and, though he seemed to welcome introductions to editors, the idea of becoming a man of letters was not born. He was at the awkward moment, not uncommon in the lives of artists, when he was no less positive of his disinclinations than vague of his destiny. Even so, he was to enter letters by the drudge's door of translation, which for some reason remains a sweated industry to this day. The proof arrived of his first rendering, and, as other proofs began to follow, the habit was forming, for printer's ink is one of the deadliest of human gratifications. Even a writer who has abandoned authorship for years, once the smallest paragraph has been coaxed from him, may be made again prolific by the receipt of a proof.

Meantime, Irving had been reviving acquaintance with Jane Baillie Welsh, then acquiring accomplishments at Edinburgh, and also finding that, in proportion as he was drawn to his former pupil, the Martins were holding him to his word. The crisis in Miss Welsh's life at this time, 1819, was, as we have seen, the death of her father in September. The part of Irving in the life of Carlyle is full of surprises. He not only warmed him by his talk, encouraged him to leave schoolmastering, introduced him to Margaret Gordon, destined by her aunt for a good marriage, took him to the Welshes, but entreated him to write, and showed his worldly wisdom by pointing out that translations and work for reference-books led nowhere, while a future was open to men, if they would only learn to be persuasive, who wrote for the Reviews.

In vacations he lingered with his people at Mainhill, delighting his father by his talk, and taking care not to wound his mother. It is pleasant to think of him healthily inactive, being, for a while, content to grow and not worrying about the future. No doubt, with Italian and German to bite on, he was doing quite enough, but the fluting note of leisure is as welcome in his story as a butterfly is on a stone wall. If work, as distinguished from forced drudgery, could ever be hateful, it is made hateful by Carlyle's admonishing growls. His hunger for work was almost a disease, and we soon hear of him reading 'quartos of shorthand notes' on law! An Irish peasant of the past century, scraping stones from a mountain in the famines, is hardly more disgusting. The peasant under compulsion we can pity: the voluntary student of these quartos

raises the gorge. His own was to be raised by them
shortly, and, at the same moment, on the orders of her
Aunt, Margaret Gordon had bidden him farewell.
Indigestion recurred, and the winter of 1820 was
passed in odd jobs of writing and translation. It also
brought the last letter from Margaret, in which we
may note one piece of advice: cultivate, she told him,
'kind and gentle manners.' As there has survived a
letter which describes his hideous dyspeptic sufferings
at this time, we must allow that Nature made it harder
for him than for most rough diamonds to 'remember
the graces.'

It was an enormous blessing that his close friend
Irving was sunny, sanguine, generous, encouraging,
and at hand. With his head full of *Faust*, some attempts
beyond hackwork at writing, the gradual conviction
that he must work with his pen, the disappearance of
Margaret Gordon was being left behind him. His
efforts were failures; his biliousness returned, when the
good angel Irving carried him off from Edinburgh,
walked him to Haddington (where he was to preach)
and left him, suddenly content, at Dr. Welsh's. If Miss
Gordon's style of talk was at all like the formal letters
with which she discreetly closed her correspondence
with Carlyle, then a better foil to the vivacious wit of
Miss Welsh could not be imagined.

CHAPTER THREE

A COMEDY OF COURTSHIP

I

IT was toward the end of May 1821 that Jane Welsh and Thomas Carlyle first met, and we have seen the sort of persons that Thomas and Jane had grown, thus far, to be. This month of May, in which they became friends, is important, more important probably than the better-remembered month of June 1822.[1]

In this eventful year 1821–22, also famous for the composition of Shelley's ode in memory of Keats, two crises occurred in the life of Carlyle. In May 1821 the inflammable young man was introduced to Jane Welsh. In June, the year following, occurred the crisis of his 'conversion,' that sudden wrestling with the Dark Angel who had long tortured his body with dyspepsia, and had choked his spirit. The genius was struggling with its clay, and, though the stiff integument had cracked, it still clung and weighed down his spirit.

A peasant visited by imagination, above the soil but tethered to it, who had lost his traditional religion and, as yet, had little in exchange; a seer, above his comrades in ability, behind them in professional scope, knowing much better his unfitness for common pursuits than the work appropriate to his own talents; in these, even, more aware of natural impediments than of the way to master them; a man, suffering from the effects of overwork and prolonged celibacy, with a disordered digestion and undiscerning doctors; a body, pinning its faith to violent exercise and calomel, as if what he needed was cathartics with their legacy of physical

[1] June was traditional until Mr. D. A. Wilson gave reasons for preferring July. *Carlyle Before Marriage*, pp. 250–51.

weakness, instead of satisfaction, harmony and repose; a youth, for he was younger than his years and cursed with an earnest temper, who, already rejected by one girl because of his straitened circumstances, had now fallen head over heels in love with a very vivacious and intelligent lady, again in present circumstances beyond his immediate reach, and very far from having decided to prefer him to her numerous suitors; a lover, kept for a year on tenterhooks by the indecision of a young woman who would neither close with him nor let him go; a being, in sum, with the heavens dumb above him, the earth below unstable, the future hazardous, health precarious, heart without rest: such a man was ripe for some explosion.

The nature of the crisis is more easy to divine than to describe. Carlyle's own account is symbolical. There was no witness; and the chapter in *Sartor*, called 'The Everlasting No,' gives the poetry of his situation only. His general condition may be guessed from his despairing, if momentary, glance at opium, from which he was delivered, very characteristically, by reading a book. De Quincey's description of the pains of opium was decisive. With the pathetic belief of the man of letters in the value of exercise in the open, Carlyle had taken to bathing. In Leith Walk, on his way to the beach, with a towel under his arm and his brain teeming, he suddenly experienced the nether side of egoism: the side in which the ego, from having been the sum of reality, shrinks to a nothing; while the universe, into which its infinite pettiness has emerged, stretches like the desert of eternity on every side. At that moment, the ego differs from an electron only by its ghastly pretentiousness.

The nature of this desert, however, will depend upon association of ideas: Bunyan on the village green; Richard Jefferies lying on his back in a field in summer; Whitman, on the sea-shore and in a crowded tram, have all known it; the form in which it comes to nun and novice is familiar enough. The Abbey gave it to Blake; a Welsh cataract to Wordsworth; a child to Francis Thompson; the shadow of an invisible beauty to the boy Shelley; and, within living memory, the sightless stars and a recollection of Dürer's *Melancholia* to James Thomson; while a field of ripe corn, and the children playing in the road, presented, to a happier imagination, the joyous sense of the same reality to Traherne, in Bunyan's day. The experience is one, but its note, and its effect, depend upon the background of the person. To the puritan it will say No: to the poet Yes; since we receive what we bring, even here. The moment in which the contemplative may taste the beatific vision brings to the puritan a sense of unforgivable sin; to Psyche the embrace of Eros; to Jack the endowment of his Jill; to the nature-mystic an ecstasy in which he seems to be dissolved into animal and vegetable existence; but Carlyle, an off-shoot of Calvinism, had been reading Hume, and to him it was a shattering sense of physical mechanism which his poetic recoil from materialism converted into a cosmic but mechanical corpse.

It is worth notice that anyone alive enough to be a poet will experience just the same exhilaration whatever interpretation, glorious or ghastly, he may draw. How like the clangorous beauty of a trumpet-call is the rhythm of these verses,[1] though the thought which they set to song is intended to be as depressing as lead:

> How the moon triumphs through the endless nights!
>   How the stars throb and glitter as they wheel
> Their thick processions of supernal lights
>   Around the blue vault obdurate as steel!
> And men regard with passionate awe and yearning
> The mighty marching and the golden burning,
>   And think the heavens respond to what they feel.

. . . .

[1] *The City of Dreadful Night*, section XVII.

With such a living light these dead eyes shine,
  These eyes of sightless heaven, that as we gaze
We read a pity, tremulous, divine,
  Or cold majestic scorn in their pure rays:
Fond man! they are not haughty, are not tender;
There is no heart or mind in all their splendour,
  They thread mere puppets all their marvellous maze.

Not the thought of the poet, nor the subject of the draughtsman, nor the statement of the mystic, matters much; the life is in the line about either which his intellectual imagination draws. Thus the rhythm chosen by James Thomson is the splendid denial of his negation, and that negation his upbringing and his circumstances explain. So, too, with Carlyle at this moment. Calvinist by inheritance, peasant by blood, inarticulate by some inhibition, Carlyle was a man for whom the life within had become damped down to the point at which it must collapse and surrender, or else, in such a character, defy: a naked, puling proton of vitality more abject than Caliban in fear. The force before which he quailed was nameless, impalpable, appalling, until, in his recoil, his intelligence bluntly asked him how, of anything actually so nameless and so impalpable, could anyone but a coward be afeared. Where was the danger? What was the enemy? Granted that it existed and was terrible, what was the worst that it could do? Was Death the only answer? and could the mere cessation of breathing, a sleep from which there was no awakening, produce such nightmare-terrors? In men not lost to courage, simple questions remove mountains of illusion, and Carlyle was not the last to find all the fires of Loki vanish at an honest word. In an instant the terror departed, and his soul was flooded with life. This moment made a man of him, he tells us, and pusillanimity fell from him like an outgrown illusion. Thus, the outcast on the beach became a proper fellow, with defiance for his watchword, since, even at such a moment, the dour creed from which he came could no more sweeten than a converted blackamoor can alter the colour of his skin.

In his own retrospect Carlyle does not mention love among the factors in his situation, but it would be agreeable to experience that the meeting in May, and its year of distracted correspondence, should have provoked or hastened the spiritual crisis at its end. The dawn of love is 'wonderful for light.' In a rich nature, when it rouses a whole being, it produces a climax beyond personal ecstasy. If Carlyle, already blessed with a divine cruse, had cried 'Lead, kindly light!' his prayer might well have been answered by the vision of a young woman; and undeniably Jane Welsh possessed precisely that vitality, light touch, perspicacity of mind, and clear-eyed criticism of which Carlyle, the heavy-laden, just then stood much in need. To this extent, he was a moth to her candle, as, in her turn, she felt herself to be a candle to his rising star.

II

Between their meeting in May 1821 and their marriage in October 1826, there lay five troubled years, during which the process that eventually united them is more significant than its climax. For this reason, some patience is requisite to follow the tortuous windings, rich in human comedy though these are, that distracted the two ardent correspondents. The tale contained in their love-letters when sketched objectively from without, has been compared, by one sympathetic biographer, to the preliminaries in a complicated lawsuit, and no one can deny the forensic skill or the wealth of argument possessed by either party. The facts can be presented as a comedy. The letters occasioned by the facts take us behind the scene.

Indeed, we scarcely know whether to admire more the perspicacity of the twain or their extraordinary power of disconcerting one another. Let there be no mistake. The dossier of this disturbing correspondence is not bulky by reason of pettiness on either side, by reason of variable temper, by changeability of mood, by little explosions of vanity or of caprice. The lovers do not display littleness of soul. They display something more vital, more human, more universal: the inexhaustible power conferred by Nature upon man and woman whereby their force of mutual attraction is secured through their mutual ability to confuse each other. Ordinarily, we observe this in mean degrees: in the triviality and caprice of a woman and in the petty selfishness of a man; but, when the lovers are as large-minded and as intelligent as Jane Welsh and Thomas Carlyle, we have an epic picture of Nature at her work of conjugation, in which she carefully arranges the proportions of obtuseness and intelligence, so that each shall be blind where the other sees clearest, in order that the quality which tantalizes each sex in the other shall never be scanted of its food.

There must be more than physical attraction if the two are to hold together, beyond their courtship, through the long process of gestation and the rearing of a family. Woman, like ivy, naturally clings. If man possessed (as many do) physical desires only, he would be, so far as he could, a pleasure-seeker, sireing the whole sex within his range, and a husband (developing into a father) to none of them. To keep him constant during courtship, constant during gestation and the infancy of his progeny, his imagination and his intelligence must also be engaged, and, for this, the satisfaction of his passion would be entirely insufficient. The beauty that tantalizes him to embrace it, and to make it his own, must, therefore, be accompanied by other mysteries: the mystery of a mind which fills him alternately with wonder at its acuteness and with amazement and fury at its stupidity; the mystery of a character marvellous for its loyalty and affection, but no less marvellous for its indifference (if not contempt) to aims and ideals as consubstantial with himself as the fruit of her womb is with a woman. The woman, too, must wonder that a lover so passionate and devoted shall become, without a moment's warning, suddenly oblivious of the face that he has kissed, apparently centred far outside the limit of those beauties which he has, again and again, declared to be the breath of life to him. The nerves of the pair must be wrung, and wrung again; an intense feeling of repugnance must balance their ardours, for so only shall they remain mysteries to each other, and, unless they severally remain a mystery, there will be nothing to keep them attracted once the moment of embrace shall have passed. It is, therefore, to misunderstand the nature of love, with its proverbially chequered history, to read a love-story or a marriage-story in terms of praise or blame. It must be read in terms of human nature, with one eye always upon Nature, the impersonal mother of mankind, who intends, for her own purposes, that many misunderstandings shall occur.

In all love-stories worthy of the name, it is Nature that we should be watching rather than her victims. Lovers are her destined prey. They are chosen to be sacrificed remorselessly to ends of which, were they conscious and not purposely by her bewitched, they would cry to be relieved, so little have these to do with their immediate hopes and purposes. Nature almost seems to grudge the brief delights with which she first ensnares them. They are fated to suffer, for suffering is one of the bonds that love can least afford to lose. This is no less true after marriage than before it. If there were no quarrels in the morning, there would be no makings-up at night, and the consequence would be, no children. This, and this alone, Nature refuses to tolerate. We have not out-manœuvred her yet. From her point of view, an empty cradle is far worse than any quarrel, and quarrels are provoked by her, to the complete bewilderment of both parties, for the sake of the reconciliations that they stimulate. The quarrels can be as terrible as the corresponding transports are divine, since, to justify the irreconcilable irritations of two temperaments of opposite gender, there is no more reason than in love itself: homicide is as much the logical end of one as the nuptial embrace is of the other. Thus the misery of marriage is not a fact for which either man or woman is primarily responsible. They should no more blame each other for this misery than preen their individual selves for the sweets that somehow make love bearable, in spite of everything. The shadows that will darken the pair after their wedding begin to cloud them in their courtship's days, an exquisite prophecy of the light and shade awaiting them. Once remember that this is true of all lovers — only a proportion of those who kiss or marry — and we shall read with sympathy and interest the experiences of the future Carlyles. These are further worth attention because there was genius in both, and genius, being an elemental energy, brings us as near to Nature herself as human beings can come when studying themselves. In this pair of Scots Nature was nearer the surface than usual, and their remarkable powers of expression enable us to watch Nature at close quarters, and to overhear. The correspondence has been misunderstood by those who have seen in it only the idiosyncrasies of an eccentric couple. Here, as elsewhere, we receive according to our capacity; and the foolish have so stupendous a majority that genius, intended for our illumination, produces fog. The smaller natures and the meaner intelligences never can understand such a story as this. Yet the truth must be stated: we can measure it justly by the average experience only when we remember that the average experience fails to provide a similar record of Natural revelation.

III

To make the courtship and the correspondence intelligible, and so as not to lose ourselves in the mazes that
beset the pair, it is convenient, at the beginning, to emphasize four phases in its development.

The first occupied two years: from the date of their
original meeting, in 1821, to the moment when Jane,
admitting that she loved him, yet declared: 'Your
friend I will be... but your wife never.'

The second period runs from this act of 1823 to Jane's
decision in 1824 to marry Carlyle if and when he should
be able to support her in the circumstances to which she
was accustomed.

This conditional agreement involved the pair in
many discussions, which only concluded in 1825, when
Mrs. Basil Montagu precipitated matters by an act of
indiscretion, an act leading Carlyle to beg Jane not to
marry him upon impulse, an act inducing Jane herself
to visit his father, with whom Carlyle happened to be
staying at Mainhill, where the sight of the stonemason's
family decided her to marry Carlyle as soon as matters
could be arranged.

The final year before their marriage in 1826 was
spent in an agonizing debate: should the new husband
and wife make a home for themselves, or should they
live with his family, or should Mrs. Welsh, for whom
Jane was naturally much concerned, take up her abode
with her daughter and her prospective son-in-law.

If we bear these points of rest in mind, a progress,
otherwise elusive, can be discerned in the tangle, and
the correspondence becomes, not merely the record of
conflicting hesitations, but the working out of a complex problem partly of temperament, but partly of circumstances.

Jane, it will be remembered, was still, in 1821, considering eligible husbands from among the young men
who, as her father had observed on the eve of his own

death, were beginning to be bitten by her. It is plain, despite certain protestations in her letters to Eliza Stodart, that she had contemplated matrimony from her childhood. Men would have agreed that she was too attractive to remain single, and, as for spinsterhood, she had never seen herself in the part. When she exclaimed that she would never marry if she found herself single by the age of twenty, she was complaining that no thoroughly eligible husband had appeared, and her essential condition was that her husband should be a genius! This momentary display of petulance was natural in a brilliant young woman who knew intuitively that she was being wasted in the Haddington circle, a circle from which a husband was the only means of escape. The petulance meant that she would never marry any of the local creatures, not that she would not marry at all. The dreadful problem was how the circle could be enlarged by any man who was not too brilliant to belong to it. Carlyle, beyond it in imagination and force of character, was below it in the graces of behaviour. When it came to the sticking point, which quality did she value more? This question gives the key to her attitude after their first meeting.

The delicious clarity of her mind prevented her from self-deception. Like the artist in words that she was, she took an artistic pleasure in defining precisely what she meant by his 'want of elegance.' This was no less clear to her, and we can scarcely put it more strongly, than his genius. Since the obstacles to his self-development were equally plain to her candid eyes, it is remarkable that her faith in his possibilities remained unshaken throughout. She also perceived that any wife whom he might choose would have to share his sufferings. She was intelligent enough to realize that genius can hardly be called a personal advantage. It is far more often a crushing weight, a tragic destiny. All married people have to bear, to some extent, a double

burden, but this becomes more than double when one
of the pair has a double fardel of his own. In the hardly
to be exaggerated importance of minor graces of behaviour, any lady who married Carlyle would have
something to bear. In the major matter of life with
him, a lady, a woman even, would have still more. He
was not only a dyspeptic but an author. Therefore, if
he married a woman with no streak of genius in herself,
that woman would be cut off from her principal source
of compensation. If, on the other hand, Carlyle found
a woman capable of intellectual sympathy, and such is
rare, what of the complications that such a woman
would add from the very quality that might enable her
to bear with him? When two artists or two authors
marry, their choice lies between a great failure or a
great success. It is an interesting question whether he
ever realized that such a woman would demand from
him more, and not less, of the little responses that he
was least capable of giving. Whatever insight has been
claimed for Carlyle, insight into womanhood has never
been one, certainly not into a woman with a streak of
genius. Among the heroes that he has held up for our
example, there is no heroine: no Saint Catherine, no
Saint Joan, no Aspasia, and no Phryne. If we may
judge by his utterances, the kind of woman whom Carlyle visualized, the kind of wife whom he anticipated,
was not a Mary but a Martha: an affectionate and industrious woman, for whom to obey would be better
than sacrifice, and to hearken than the fat of rams.

If it was a stroke of irony that Carlyle should have
been cast for the part of Saint Preux in the destiny of
Jane Welsh, fate was no less impish when the Martha
whom she offered to him should have had several points
of resemblance to Madame de Sévigné.

To a girl of fine intelligence, however, genius is a
mighty argument. The deepest need of Jane's own
nature responded to the noble quality in his. Her re-

sponse, it must never be forgotten, was, moreover, twofold. Jane was not only a lover in her bloom, but also a
mother in the making. We shall see her, more than
once, spending her mind and her heart upon poor children and exiled idealists in whom she believed that a dash
of genius was to be discerned. Passionate as her own
nature was, it was rich also, and there is little doubt
that, if she ever wondered whether her passion would
find satisfaction in Carlyle, she foresaw, from the first,
that her mother-instinct would be fully taxed if she
married him. If the marriage could provide her with
children, she would have much less to fear, for a woman
with the mother-instinct knows immediately that, of the
two loves felt by man, love for the mother and love for
the mistress, the former is more enduring. The mistress
who becomes the mother to him is the mistress of whom
the lover and the husband does not tire. The converse,
unfortunately, is not equally true, for Nature looks beyond a pair of single lifetimes: all husbands are children to their wives, but no husband can fill the place of
children. The great saying of Isaiah, that a little child
shall lead them, is profoundly true of married life.

For the moment, however, the childishness that Jane
discerned in Carlyle, a quality that genius preserves,
was sufficient. With his twofold appeal to her imagination and to her maternal instincts, Carlyle was well
worth considering. When the alternatives among her
suitors intruded themselves, his claims seemed vast, and
his 'want of elegance' sank to dust in the balance. If he
could supply the great thing, could not she herself supply the small? As a fountain of graces, there could
surely be an overflow to provide the light touch, the
finer shades, in which he was deficient. Love did not
blind her to defects in her idol, but it may have made
her momentarily vain; vain in the belief that love can
compass miraculous changes. If the average woman,
when attracted by a man too fond of his liquor, finds no

difficulty in believing that she will be able to reform his habits once he shall have become her husband, a subtler woman is hardly less open to the same delicious creed. For Jane, too, there were peculiar advantages in aiding him. She knew that he must find great difficulties arising, chiefly, from his own nature. His health was odd; his spirit was clogged with a kind of peasant clay, and his struggles to set it free would be immense. To confirm his faith in himself, to sympathize in advance with the right issue of the struggle, to make him fitter to meet the circle in which his gifts would eventually be appreciated, was a natural aspiration in a believer who was already equipped with what he needed. Intelligence of her degree does not need to be feminine in order to nurse the signs of genius half-maternally. Where no personal rivalry is involved, and in fine characters not even then, does ability fail in respect and in charity toward its likeness. Genius, indeed, if character be part of it, and the word be not pared to one special faculty, is in charity with all men. Its glance is embracing, its sympathy boundless, its smile as indifferent as sunlight. Suffuse this with personal liking, make one of the pair woman and the other man, and the opposition is transformed into an embrace. All this love was accomplishing for Jane, but Jane was also a practical young lady.

Her faith in Carlyle made his future appear more certain than his present. Already detached from the soil, Carlyle was not destined to remain a schoolmaster. Even in the arts, society applauds success, and what an advantage for him to be prepared, in advance, for its reception! From her reading, Jane knew what aristocratic salons could be, was at home and happy in their records, felt equal to defending herself against the wit that might be lurking where Carlyle at first might prove unarmed. If anyone could polish him, it would be she, and, under the rays of her vivacity, to which he was indulgent, even when their victim, the clay in him would

melt, the granite mellow. How could she doubt that
her gifts would prove less infectious than his own? how
question that he would absorb with no more resistance
than she offered to his domination? To the spirit in her,
the power of comedy may well have seemed the stronger
power of the two, and Carlyle, great in his simplicity,
offered to her keen eyes many opportunities for comedy.

But to this inspired peasant she could bring not only
the sympathy of criticism. In her small way she was an
heiress, and the expectations of a wife are an advantage
to a sage who has left, without so far transcending, the
soil. To brains, in the battle between dullness and
intelligence, intelligence, if it will be patient, seems
bound to win. All the cards lay in her hand, if, guided
by love and intelligence, she played them adroitly. The
mental need of her nature was promised satisfaction
in Carlyle, and, compared with this, what did some
smaller and more superficial requirements matter? The
final test, that of living with him, she could apply no
more than any other girl before her marriage, but few
young women have imagined their future lot more
clearly than Jane Welsh. Various matters of immediate
importance — a home, her mother's future, his people,
a house in town or a farmhouse, a combined or separate
household — confronted her. In the manœuvres ne-
cessitated by these questions a situation arose unusually
rich in comedy.

IV

Carlyle had arrived about the date of George Rennie's departure, and Jane, still clinging to study, gave
up teaching to become a pupil again, a pupil to Carlyle, with whom she began to read German. During
the lesson he scratched the fender with his boots, and
made violent gestures with his hands. Only his tongue,
she declared, should be left unpadded or unhand-
cuffed. Luckily he found her apt, and she discovered

German, when taught by Carlyle, to be a noble language. She suffered a slight reaction, none the less. Possessed by the impossible figure who should combine the virtues of St. Preux and Wolmar, she confided to Miss Stodart that this vision was happier for her than the sight of any solid husband, eating beef.

An offer now came to her to assist a projected magazine of local origin. Her account of her interview with the founder, who called to invite her support, is not unlike a page from a Restoration comedy. Mr. George Cunningham had been in the mathematical class with Jane at Haddington School, but that was long ago, and at the time of his visit, she had ceased to be even 'on bowing terms' with him. Thus she fancied that he must be wanting subscribers for some mathematical work of his own, unless, indeed, as it amuses her to fancy, he might have fallen in love with her upon hearsay! That Mr. Cunningham should seek her support for his project shows that her talents were not unknown to her neighbours, but they can scarcely have seen many of her writings except, perhaps, some sentences quoted from her letters.

At the age of fifteen she had written the little poem upon Byron, already noted, and a year earlier still she had composed a tragedy: 'very wild and bloody' according to the recollection of one friend whom she invited to pass a written criticism upon it, and according to herself 'just an explosion' in which no one was left alive to speak the epilogue. The stage was peopled by corpses before the fall of the curtain. No doubt Jane's conversation was passed from ear to ear, and served to justify belief in her literary talents. These had begotten many projects, but had accomplished little. At the time of Mr. Cunningham's visit, she was planning a novel. The heroine was to be 'a very monster of perfection,' who, though 'an empress of a thousand male hearts,' was to 'live a maid, and die in an elegant little garret.'

The novel was to be her whimsical atonement for having laughed at old maids, a company that Jane was proposing to join now that no man corresponding to her fancy-picture was available.

It might have seemed that, with her head full of such subjects, Jane would have welcomed Mr. Cunningham's request for her co-operation, but she declined until she should be assured, from the first number, that 'it would not go to the Devil.' We can overhear her inward question: can any good magazine come out of Nazareth? For once, her 'too lively sense of the ridiculous' led her into error. The *East Lothian Magazine*, published monthly by no less a person than Tait, ran from 1822 to 1828 and attained a considerable circulation. Mr. Cunningham tried his hardest, but in vain: 'the literary man looked into the fire, and I looked at the literary man; and a queer, little, odd-shaped man it was.' Hearing of the affair, Mrs. Welsh said to her daughter, you really are 'a very great character,' and even the defeated Mr. Cunningham himself was much amused by Jane's sallies.

There was a trace of contempt in her refusal. Possibly the editor's blue pencil would have removed, had she consented, the characteristic outbursts in which she excelled. Had the request come from some established magazine that she liked, it might have proved more welcome, and we cannot but think such writing would have been more healthy for her than the pungent letters in which her literary instinct was to vent itself. Letters, indeed, can relieve the soul, but the relief is mainly subjective because it escapes the healthy discipline of criticism. Even in authorship and in art, a profession is partly impersonal, whereas the private correspondence of a natural writer remains, by itself, too introspective to be wholesome. One lingers on the offer, however, because an opportunity seems to have been missed. Through presenting itself in a questionable guise, the chance passed, and that it never came again is a pity. Jane, capable as she proved, was not exclusively domestic, and both before and after her marriage, she needed an activity apart from her household. There are many examples of abortive, but genuine, authors. Perhaps she suffered more than she was to realize for having been too disdainful of Mr. Cunningham's successful magazine.

Meantime she was enjoying herself, and there is little doubt that German lessons from Carlyle were more agreeable to her than writing for any magazine. Her appetite for such companionship was keen. She had to snatch at the present crumb, or go without. Irving watched the rise of Carlyle's influence with mixed feelings. Knowing how susceptible to influence of this quality Jane was, Irving felt that his old favourite was slipping beyond his grasp; for Irving's religious ideas were beginning to run away with him, and in Carlyle and in German authors there was not much countenance for Irving's sublimities. The two men remained friends, however, and, when Irving had been translated to a ministry in London, his influence with the Bullers, whom he had bewitched from his pulpit, persuaded them to appoint Carlyle, now stranded in Edinburgh, since his retirement from Kirkcaldy in 1818, and a victim to translations and dyspepsia, tutor to their two boys.

This gave a chance for Jane's friendly correspondence with Carlyle to develop, and literary projects were discussed between them. Their collaboration in a novel was one of these. She was now in the pleasant state when she could rebuke him for advances without endangering her friendship. At this moment, too, Irving informed her that the parents of Miss Martin had refused to allow him to break the engagement into which he had entered soon after his departure from Haddington. If Irving had not returned and seen Jane again, he might never have discovered that she was still his real choice. Their re-meeting had unsettled him sadly. It proved Miss Martin, good as she was, to have been a passing impulse, but he had promised to marry her and he was not allowed to falter. Jane supported the parents' attitude, and was herself now better able to appreciate what Irving's future would be. We can scarcely imagine her dutifully seated beneath the spray from his pulpit, and, though she esteemed him, she remarked later, that, with herself beside him, 'there would have been no gift of tongues!' When Miss Martin shortly became Mrs. Irving, Edward obtained a peaceful and affectionate wife. It was not Mrs. Irving's fault that Jane remained a poignant memory to Mrs. Irving's husband.

The suitors of Haddington were now dispersed when, in October 1822, Carlyle returned home to visit his mother at Mainhill. Old Mrs. Carlyle was the dearer to him because she was pathetically unable to fathom his spiritual condition. She feared that he was falling away from the pure milk of the word which sustained the rest of her family. The farmhouse offered a sharp contrast to the 'elegant whim-whams' (as he called them) of Jane's home, into which his letters blew like a moorland breeze through a drawing-room window. There were visitors there, kinsmen, whom even Mrs. Welsh found it fatiguing to entertain, while Jane sat impatient, talking or silent, with her eye upon the German or Italian authors whom the company forced her to neglect.

By way of relief during this winter, Jane sketched the feminine character which she herself admired. It was as vital as that of the Magdalen, and equally fitted to explain why our Lord chose His friends, and found His favourite company, among great sinners. The fine text, 'other sheep I have which are not of this fold,' applied, we may believe, to this disreputable company.

Telling Elizabeth Stodart to read *La Nouvelle Héloïse*, Jane wrote: 'Ask your heart, or rather your judgment, if Julia be vicious. I do not wish to countenance such irregularities among my female acquaintances; but I must confess, were any individual of them to meet with such a man, to struggle as she struggled, to endure as she endured, to *yield* as she yielded, and to repent as she repented, I would love that woman better than the chastest, coldest prude between John o' Groat's House and Land's End.... This book, this fatal book, has given me an idea of love so pure (yes, you may laugh! but I repeat it), so pure, so constant, so disinterested, so exalted, that no love will ever fill up the picture my imagination has drawn with the help of Rousseau.' When she wrote this confession Jane was half-way through her twenty-first year, having previously sworn to die a virgin if she should reach the age of twenty 'in vain.' In moments of delight or of disappointment, the imagination flies to extremes, as a bird to its nest, and throughout her life Jane's expressions are easily misunderstood by those who cannot conceive so vividly as she.

Meantime her correspondence with Carlyle continued, and he was constantly tantalized by a variety which made it impossible for him to tell what caress or what rebuke his own letters might provoke from her. That she could be critical as well as tender made her tenderness twice welcome. He found her reactions unpredictable. He never knew whether he would catch a fish or catch a crab when he angled for her pleasure. She was beginning to teach him that his special talent was far from being a standard of honest ability, and that to parade his dread of cant was sometimes the surest way of becoming a target for her ridicule. The picture of the young pupil, making her sage instructor feel bewildered, is delightful, and it gradually dawned upon Carlyle that she was mistress of some secrets

hitherto beyond his experience. To his surprise, he
found that he could stand almost anything from her: almost, for at bottom still he expected to be lonesome,
and maintained his rugged independence. It was just
here that she, in her turn, suffered from surprises. With
the other men whom she had known, her mockery had
produced further protestations. She had not yet found
a man, as nearly in love with her as Carlyle, who would
withdraw if he were rebuked too sharply. She was not
quite so independent as she liked to appear, and was
very far from wanting to suffer a second time the humiliation that George Rennie had thrust upon her. If it
came to a tussle between Carlyle and Jane, we can already divine which would grip the other tighter. He
had his dreams, whatever fortune love might hold in
store for him. Her dreams involved a second person.
She was not, primarily, in love with herself.

v

In a letter of 1823, dated from 'Hell,' because she
was bored in the house where it was written, she made
an avowal which the simple man interpreted to mean
that she was consenting to marry him. Oh dear no, she
replied in effect: 'I love you...though I find the expression a rash one. But were you my brother, I should
love you just the same.... Your friend I will be...but
your wife never.' By taking this to be final, Carlyle's
simplicity served him well. Nothing was more likely to
make her think twice than his answer: 'In junctures of
this kind' he replied unconcernedly, 'my heart is made
of sterner stuff than to break,' and he explained that he
had no intention of dying in the style of a heart-broken
shepherd in Arcady. There seems, indeed, little doubt
that Carlyle could have done without Jane, and that
Jane, if her circle had been wider, might have turned
to some one else.

Love at first sight is not the only kind of love. There

is more than a conventional lie in the assertion that marriage can, sometimes, produce it. The ties which bind human hearts are manifold, and a common life, common troubles, and common responsibilities are more apt to make love enduring than the prejudice of youth for personal beauty of body or mind. It would be a mistake to suppose, because their mutual approaches were chequered, that the Carlyles were fated to remain unsuited to each other to the end. The element of recoil, not being final, was indeed an excellent foundation on which to build. Whether their marriage was the best possible combination for either is a different question. The man or woman by whom only one other person can be contemplated exists, but is very rare. We are tempted to ask the pair which makes this boast, what would have happened to you if you had not met each other? That both would have remained single is possible, but not likely. In nine cases out of ten, the constant factor is the capacity of loving, not its chosen object; and if Jill does not meet Jack, she will marry John. Once John has safely appeared, even Jack may seem out of the question. The only one, to the warmhearted, is the one who has been accepted first. The might-have-been may make a delightful dream, but love is substantial enough to be content with present reality. Those who range most freely are those incapable of feeling love at all.

At this moment, Jane's intelligence suggested to her that she was more interested in Carlyle's future than in the degree of his feeling for herself. The problem for her was how to keep him within range without committing herself too far for the privilege. It seemed odd to his bluntness that a woman could be so much concerned about a man whom she did not intend to marry. On his side, the needs of his own nature, so often thwarted, had to come first. Charm as she would, Carlyle was not going to sacrifice his peace of mind to love of her or of anyone. He wanted to know definitely where he stood with her. If she would marry him, so much the better. If not, let the matter be settled. Carlyle did not say so, but his idea of comfort predicated a wife. Was he to look elsewhere in the hope of finding one? To become involved with a dedicated spinster would be a waste of his energy and time. In these cross-purposes there was much matter for correspondence, and he could not understand why Jane would not make the matter clear. Her own aim, at the moment, was to avoid defining the situation too narrowly. To keep him at arm's length without losing him was her wish, not because she was a flirt, but because the thing that she most needed was his head rather than his hand. In nothing was he her ideal except in his 'genius,' and to help that to expand gave her solicitude and excitement enough.

His letters kept her alive in the midst of work mainly undertaken to dispel dullness, but her instinct to mother budding talent appears in the care that she took of a beggar boy and of a child of eight, who turned out rather disappointingly. Other admirers, old and new, she weighed in her critical mind. There was an old fogy of a doctor who now tried to 'dazzle her wits' with white hat and yellow leggings, and any fresh young man who passed across her vision was weighed in her bright balances for the fun of setting down how far he, too, fell short of a husband's sterling. At this time life in Haddington was often dull, and in the spring of the year 1823, in which she had said to Carlyle 'your friend I will be... but your wife never,' Jane had complained to Miss Stodart: 'Often at the end of the week my spirits and my industry begin to flag; but then comes one of Mr. Carlyle's brilliant letters, that inspires me with new resolution, and brightens all my hopes and prospects with the golden hues of his own imagination.' Two years had passed since their meeting, and the upshot, so far as avowals went, was her definite refusal to marry him.

VI

At present, Jane was more interested in the future of Carlyle's genius than in the possibility of becoming his wife. To Carlyle, of course, interest in the genius was the becoming prelude to interest in the man. The pair was so much concerned with each other that the situation, provoking and puzzling to him, though appropriately vague to her, was always threatening to pass beyond their control. Had they been less sincere in their intellectual sympathies, the matter would have been concluded more quickly. In ordinary cases, one of the two would have brought the other to book by showing an alarming interest in some third person. There would have been a hint, a challenge, an awkward explanation, and then a complete reconciliation or a break. Jane's horizon was too limited to allow of such a climax, and Carlyle, wanting a home of his own, was the last person to seek one so long as his tantalizing friendship with Jane endured.

The degree of her attraction to Carlyle and of her extraordinary attachment to genius is apparent from an experience of hers during the summer of 1824. Her cousin, Mr. James Baillie, came to Haddington upon a visit of a fortnight. During the whole of his stay, Jane wrote to Eliza, 'I never wearied once.' Apparently the cousins spent the entire time in one another's company. Jane was whole days, it would seem, alone with him on the brink of dangerous avowals. In the mornings they paid visits together. In the afternoons they went for long walks in the woods and across the fields, or sat on a green bank and 'talked sentiment' with one another. The evenings were filled with games of chess or cards. It was a delightful time, one of those fortnights on which life looks back with the keenest pleasure. The young people were indulging their youth, without committing themselves beyond indulgence. They were on the verge of a love-affair without quite falling in; as much involved, but no more, as a pair of swallows in flight, or as two partners joined in the dance with no tie beyond their pleasure and the music.

Mr. Baillie was an apt partner at this game, for he was master of some of the surprises which Jane was less accustomed to suffer than to spring. It would seem that Mr. Baillie (though she did not rumble him) began to play with her the very game of contrasts that Jane delighted to play with others. At one moment, she wrote to her friend, he is 'as sentimental as the Prince of Denmark, but ... often in our conversations, when his imagination had risen to the highest pitch, when his fine eyes full of tears, and the melancholy, impassioned tones of his voice showed me he was ready to be overpowered by his feelings, he would start away to some theme of ridicule or folly, and efface the impression he had just made with the laugh of a Mephistopheles.' Turning upon her her favourite weapon, which few people had the brains to use, Mr. Baillie caught her off her guard, and had her at his mercy. The surprise is not so common but that instances are worth noting. One other example the reader may appreciate.[1] When the late Samuel Butler was investigating the authorship of Shakespeare's sonnets, he chanced to meet Lady Ritchie, who asked what he was about now that he had settled that little matter of the authoress of the Odyssey. Butler mentioned the sonnets, whereupon she said that she had her own theory about *them*. Butler, incautiously, asked her what it was. 'My theory is' replied the lady 'that the sonnets were written by Ann Hathaway.' Butler thought this fatuous because he took her seriously — a fact incredible, were it not that

[1] One of several good things in *A Nineteenth-Century Childhood*, by Mary MacCarthy (Heinemann, 1924).

the inventor of any particular form of humour may easily become its victim should an apparently innocuous member of the opposite sex apply it unsuspiciously to himself. Mr. Baillie reduced Jane to a condition of bewilderment by the same move. Either he found that her romantic appetite was beyond his power to sustain for very long, or, a student of Byronism himself, anticlimax was one of his enjoyments. It was certainly one of hers, but a shock which she was more used to giving than receiving.

She did not resent his dazzling manoeuvres, for the core of her letter is this: Mr. Baillie 'is my very *beau-idéal* in all respects but one. His nature is the most affectionate I ever knew, his spirit the most magnificent; he has a clear, quick intellect, a lively fancy: with beauty, brilliance, sensibility, native gracefulness, and courtly polish, he wants but *genius* to be — the destiny of my life.' Byron, her inevitable hero, was lately dead, and Disraeli was only twenty at the date of this letter. She was probably lucky not to have met Byron, to whom she might have proved a Cleopatra, possibly even a Medea; and one cannot be certain whether she would have accepted Disraeli for a *genius* or not. She was, however, intended for the world in which they moved, and, with or without Carlyle, the one genius within her orbit, she was too fine a soul to have escaped the skirts of tragedy. It was Mr. Baillie who taught her that people might be charming without possessing any genius, but she was right to make the tragic choice, and to reject the more reasonable, because this last would lead her, as she put it with whimsical accuracy, to descend to earth, 'marry — and, oh Plato! — make a pudding. I do not say puddings; for sure I am, the first would be the death of me.' Domesticity was not, she felt, the purpose for which she had come into the world. Meanwhile, she was accompanying her mother on a round of visits; but though the people were pleasant, she was irked by idleness. She needed employment for her brain. This Carlyle could give, and without it not all the graces with which Mr. Baillie was endowed were capable of satisfying her.

Moreover, before the year 1824 was out, Carlyle was further to appeal to her cherished sympathies. A few days before Christmas, the postman brought to her at Haddington two letters. One was a 'letter of fifteen pages' from Mr. Baillie. He was on the verge of matrimony, and about to suffer one of those revulsions of feeling which was often the fate that Jane extended to her former favourites. The other was from Carlyle, containing a fragment of a letter from Byron and another from Goethe to Carlyle himself. Carlyle asked Jane to keep the latter as 'the most precious of your literary relics,' and her comment upon it was: the letter 'is highly complimentary; and coming from the man whom he honours, almost to idolatry, must have gratified him beyond measure. I question if a charter of nobility could have gratified him as much.' That is sympathetic but detached. It was the fragment of Byron's handwriting that threw her into a transport: 'I kissed the seal with a fervour which would have graced the most passionate lover.' When she had heard of Byron's death in the previous April, she had writen: 'I was told the news in a room full of people. If they had said that the sun or the moon was gone out of the heavens, it could not have struck me with the idea of a more awful blank in the creation,' and Carlyle had answered that it fell upon his own heart like 'a mass of lead.'

In the spring of 1825 Carlyle paid a visit to Haddington, where he had the pleasure, we may suppose, of seeing Jane discomfort another Mr. Baillie who had unexpectedly arrived 'to recruit his strength' in her neighbourhood. The unlucky man, she wrote, 'looked — just as I did when he passed me on the Waterloo Bridge, and I felt that I was revenged.' Instead of paying attention to him, she insisted on talking to Carlyle about the Peak of Teneriffe, until, after having been left in the cold for two hours, the gentleman departed. For her he had become 'but one more bubble melted into thin air.' Indeed, one is tempted to think that Jane enjoyed pricking her bubbles as much as blowing them, and sometimes revenged upon her suitors the romantic tendencies that she detected in herself.

In June Carlyle returned to London in order to resume his duties of tutor, but he soon wearied of dancing attendance, and was glad to take advantage of Irving's hospitality. Among the people whom he met in London was Mrs. Montagu, of whom we shall hear more, and various literary people. He crossed to Paris, became critical of friends and acquaintances, and was plainly irritable from ill-health of mind and body, to say nothing of the nervous strain he always felt when finishing one of his books. The *Life of Schiller* was his present task, and his letters contain remorseful tributes to his friends, as if he was aware that grumbling was as natural to him as his broad dialect. The correspondence with Jane continued, and he had made enough money to save something, despite the help that he was giving to his brothers. A place like London could not yet become natural to him, and his thoughts followed his letters, for he dreamed of country quiet with some one beside him to relieve him of all domestic cares. All the qualities, except perhaps one, that he needed could be provided by a capable and attentive housekeeper, and we are only chilled by his very human selfishness because he wished a wife and not a housekeeper to fill the part. A bachelor is allowed to be exacting. No one blames him for studying his own comfort with care. Carlyle, at this time, was a man of typically bachelor tastes and habits, yet we observe him brooding on a wife as if his housekeeper must necessarily be married to him. It was not Jane, altogether, that lent this bias to his thoughts. There was nothing surprising that he should find her very attractive. Most men agreed with him about that. The surprising thing, whatever his physical needs, is that he should suppose home meant marriage, and his marriage to some one to be inevitable.

Meantime his prospects were less blank than they had been, and his native restlessness led him to confide in Jane's sympathetic ear. He supposed himself to want very little: as little as the parent who only wants perfect obedience and perfect truthfulness from his child! If he wanted quiet, repose, and the devotion of some woman to his comforts, it seemed to him that no woman, who professed to be devoted to him, could want more! If nothing more entered into his thoughts, it was because his thoughts were self-centred. Most egoists are unaware of their condition, because egoism is, precisely, this unawareness of other people. They can therefore be blamed no more than the colour-blind, since revelation means the cure of the disease.

He therefore proposed to rent and stock a farm in Annandale, to entrust the management of the farm to his brother Alexander, and to live himself in an adjoining house. By this means he hoped to find the quiet for writing, and to gain enough money from the farm and from his work to provide a wife with a home. The news came with rather a shock to Jane, partly because, like Irving, she had thought that London would open its arms to her friend's talents, and partly because she supposed that pensions and sinecures were readily, by deserving talents, to be found. Here what she was to call their 'inequality of birth' produced an amusing misunderstanding. At her suggested solution the pride of independent poverty was up in arms: 'A sinecure! (he exclaimed in answer). God bless thee, my darling! I could not touch a sinecure.... For affection, or the faintest imitation of it, a man should feel obliged to his very dog; but for the gross assistance of patronage or

purse, let him pause before accepting them from anyone.'

It is becoming conventional to pay lip-service to this
attitude, though why a man should be too proud to accept patronage when he is not expected to be too proud
to accept a legacy is not obvious. There is a pride proper
to all men, but one suspects that the poor are sometimes so much prouder than other people because they
may have so little but their pride to be proud of. At all
events, each class in society has its own code in these
matters, and Jane's innocent expectation that Carlyle
would find an endowment in London seemed as proper
to her as it seemed improper to him. All people capable of fine work feel it to be a waste of time merely to
be earning their living; and Carlyle's recoil from her
prospect for him may have been partly due to the feeling that such a person as himself ought to be spared any
obligation, for he repudiated the idea of hackwork as
vehemently as the idea of patronage.

In all men of slow development a despairing period
has to be bridged. They may not be able to work at
anything but their vocation at the very time when they
can scarcely work even at that. Carlyle, a victim to
agonizing inhibitions, was somewhat in this plight all
his life. We cease to be greatly irritated at his perpetual
croaking when we remember that the world could not
but be mirrored for him in his own spleen. The painful
condition of his own stomach seemed to him, sometimes unfairly, to be the normal condition of the world.

Though the confession was not made till later in the
same year (1825), Jane told Miss Stodart that she had
suffered from the bile for 'several years, and have never
been able to work out more than a few weeks of truce.'
In this very August, Jane added: 'My life is passing in
the usual alternating manner. One day I am ill, and in
bed; the next in full puff at an entertainment.' She
complained that, between headaches and visiting, her

education was completely at a standstill. She found an excuse for her idleness that is amusing in its insight: 'It is in vain to think of toiling up the steep of knowledge with a burden of sickness on one's shoulders, and hardly less difficult for a young person with my attractions to lead the life of a recluse, however much I wish it.' How much did she really wish it? She pined, I think, for that particular society in which no such fission occurs: for the salon which is an exercise in manners as well as an exercise of wits. She was intended to be a great lady with a gentleman of genius at her side. Ill-health and ill-luck played a part in her life, and she too was later tempted to take, at moments, a rather bilious view of the world. In this respect, between her and Carlyle no comparison is possible, for his psychological disorder remained chronic, though, on the vital point, he had better luck with books than she with babies.

When she dismissed his plan for conveying her to a farm, he was naturally disappointed. Since he could not see the scheme of such a life through any other eyes, it seemed to him to be a rejection of himself. Anxious to know exactly how he stood with her, he offered to set her free, for the facts of their relation were closer than its formula. When he discovered that she did not want to be set free, her criticism of his plans appeared to him unaccountable. A woman who was willing to marry a man must surely want what he wanted. Carlyle had no other conception of marriage. So he returned to the charge with an alteration so slender that she unmasked all her critical guns in her reply. He had heard that her farm of Craigenputtock was to let, and jumped at this solution of his difficulties. Life in the country, if not a country life in the farmer's sense, was his native and appropriate background. Its quiet, its seclusion, its simplicity were also dear to him, as they will always be dear to many authors; but, beside this background, he needed to be relieved of all domestic cares by some one who would fulfil her own destiny in ministering to his peculiarities.

Jane seemed to him exceptionally fitted for such a task. Without being in love with him, she loved him, and had willingly admitted this. She also admired him, and was in full sympathy with his aspirations and his ideas. Beside this, she was not happy in her single life, and it seemed to him that she had only to take the plunge to find full scope for all her qualities. Carlyle failed to realize the retrenchment that his plan would entail upon her. She was a town-bred young lady, and was asked to exchange the comfort and the circumstances to which she was accustomed for a rustic existence which, while it would provide him with everything that he desired, would deprive her, on his present income, of some comforts which she 'lacked the fortitude to despise.' The solid gain that she would find would be the companionship of a 'genius.' This was undoubtedly her chief demand, but our chief desires are pursued on the assumption that our humble necessities will be taken for granted. We may expect to sacrifice something, but not the elementary habits of our life. There are, indeed, vocations for which no sacrifice is held to be too great. Marriage, however, is scarcely one of these, and a woman about to marry expects her husband to provide her with a home substantially similar to that which she is leaving, if only because this necessity is assumed as a matter of course. On the plan that he was proposing, Carlyle would be sacrificing nothing. [He would be receiving more than he bestowed. It became necessary for Jane to explain to him that she, also, had to be considered.

When therefore Carlyle told her, in January 1825, that literature could not be the sole nourishment of life; that she was unhappy because she had not yet found a serious work to do; that to be mistress of a house was her proper destiny; that she had it in her to be a model wife,

which was 'the highest distinction of the noblest women'; that thousands managed life 'in comfort' on resources more slender than his own; that he must recover health and refuse to become a hack writer; that
it was for her to decide whether he should become 'a
right man' or only a bitter Stoic; and that the great
question for her was whether she dared to trust her fate
to him, he was scarcely looking at the matter with a
woman's eyes.

In her reply, Jane analyzed her feelings as carefully as
his proposal. First of all, the love she had for him was
not a passion which overclouded her judgment or absorbed her to the exclusion of everything else. On
the contrary, it was 'a simple, honest, serene affection,
made up of admiration and sympathy.' While she
thought these 'temperate sentiments' to be, perhaps,
the best foundation for 'domestic enjoyment'; while her
present consent would secure to her 'the only fellowship and support' she had found in the world, and
might also 'shed some sunshine of joy' on his existence
which had 'hitherto been sullen and cheerless,' there
was an obstacle. As things were, she explained, her
consent would involve both 'in numberless cares and
difficulties,' and, in her own words, would 'expose me
to petty tribulations which I want fortitude to despise
and which, not despised, would embitter the peace of
us both.' With fine precision she added: 'I do not wish
for fortune more than is sufficient for my wants — my
natural wants, and the artificial ones which habit has
rendered nearly as importunate as the others. But I
will not consent to live on less; because, in that case,
every inconvenience I was subjected to would remind
me of what I had quitted, and the idea of a sacrifice
should have no place in a voluntary union.... I conceive it a duty which every one owes to society not to
throw up that station in it which Providence has as-
signed him; and, having this conviction, I could not

marry into a station inferior to my own with the approval of my judgment, which alone could enable me to brave the censures of my acquaintance.'

This impeccably clear argument, so just in respect of herself and so free from offence to him, was clinched by a question. Had he any certain livelihood to maintain her in the position to which she was accustomed, or any fixed rank in the society in which she was bred? 'No! You have projects for attaining both, capabilities for attaining both, and much more. But you have not attained them.... Devise, then, how you may gain yourself a moderate but settled income. Think of some more promising plan than farming the most barren spot in the county of Dumfrieshire.... I would as soon think of building myself a nest on the Bass Rock.... Depend upon it, you could not exist there a twelvemonth. For my part, I could not spend a month at it with an angel. Think of something else, then. Apply your industry to carry it into effect; your talents to gild over the inequality of our births — and then we will talk of marrying.' If Mrs. Welsh could have been looking over her daughter's shoulder while Jane was writing these lines, she might well have said that no mother in the world could have stated the case more fairly. But, when we consider what Carlyle's feelings may have been when he reached this logical conclusion, when he found that Jane was as firm in her stipulations as he in his own, we can share his relief to find that logic was not to have the last word, after all. The feelings, especially her feelings, were engaged and they allowed him, and therefore herself, a concession. 'I will marry no one else,' she wrote. 'This is all the promise I can or will make'; but even outsiders know that such a promise is half the battle. The argument was further softened by a final sentence: 'If there is any change to be made in the terms on which we have so long lived with one another, it must be made by you, not by me.'

In sum, she had rejected his plan, but not his proposal, and had admitted that only his circumstances now stood between him and their marriage.

VII

In his answer, Carlyle wrote: 'Believe me, I am not hurt or angry. I merely wished to know. It was only in brief moments of enthusiasm that I ever looked for a different result.' This sober conclusion, however, was prefaced by two remarks in which he tried to do justice to both their feelings for each other. 'I find (he told her) my affection for you intertwined with every part, connected with whatever is holiest in my feelings or most imperative in my duties.' She seemed to him, he explained, as much out of place in her circumstances as he in his own, and it was perhaps natural for him to fancy that he could supply all that she needed since, to an imaginative man, the bare machinery of existence slips readily out of sight. Moreover, in no practical sense, would he, on his side, be any worse off after their marriage.

Was it her hesitation to share his circumstances which made him declare, 'your happiness is not by any means irretrievably connected with mine?' for, in reality, she was the more dependent of the two. His main desire was, in his own words, 'to rebuild his own destiny,' a desire certainly not dependent upon any woman's help. She, being less self-centred, was more at the mercy of fate, and she could not fail, therefore, to be moved by his following plea: 'I would ask a generous spirit, one whose happiness depended on seeing me happy, and whose temper and purposes were kindred to my own — I would ask such a noble being to let us unite our resources; not her wealth and rank merely — for these were a small and unessential fraction of the prayer — but her judgment, her patience, prudence, her true affection, to mine, and let us try if, by neglecting what

was not important, and striving with faithful and inseparable hearts after what was, we could not rise above
the miserable obstructions that beset us both...' in
other words, to overlook what was important to her,
but was trivial to him. It was natural that his argument should thus come full circle, for they were measuring the question by two different standards, and, in the
long run, such a difference is bound to come out. Since
she had left him no room for self-deception about her
wishes, he concluded by saying: 'You are such a generous spirit. But your purposes and feelings are not such.
... If we must part, let us part in tenderness, and go
forth upon our several paths, lost to the future, but in
possession of the past.'

Without going back on what she had said, Jane in her
reply advanced another inch toward him: 'I have
shown you, in declaring that I would marry no one else,
not only that I esteem you above all the men I have
ever seen, but also that I am persuaded that I should
esteem you above all the men I may ever see.' Then
she gave a picture of herself that we may believe to be
profoundly true — true not of her only but of her feelings for Carlyle:

I am prudent, I fear, only because I am not tempted to be
otherwise. My heart is capable (I feel it is) of a love to which
no deprivation would be a sacrifice — a love which would
overleap that reverence for opinion with which education and
weakness have begirt my sex, would bear down all the restraints which duty and expediency might throw in the way,
and carry every thought of my being impetuously along with
it.

But the all-perfect mortal who could inspire me with a love
so extravagant is nowhere to be found — exists nowhere but
in the romance of my own imagination.... In the meantime I
should be mad to act as if from the influence of such a passion
while my feelings are in a state of perfect tranquillity.

Self-knowledge of this quality is very rare, and might

have chilled or terrified Carlyle if his own dependence
had been equal. There are good reasons to believe that
his attraction to her was less strong than hers, despite
his drawbacks, and it is possible that one of the things
which Jane missed in life was the passion in another
which she herself was capable of experiencing. No lack
is comparable to this. We have only to glance round at
the richer souls about us to see the emptiness that occurs when a heart, capable of overflowing with affection, finds no answering energy qualified to reciprocate,
or even to appreciate, its resources. Warmth answered
by coolness, generosity by egoism, meet our eyes wherever we turn. How few are the mothers even who experience in their children a return adequate to their affection once the stage of infancy has been passed. Not
all mothers are warm-hearted, but such a mother is the
type of a generous nature which rarely meets with its
return. Jane, I think, at this stage had primarily a
lover's nature, and to this there must be a full equiva-
lent or none.

In an even more candid letter Jane then confessed
that she had objected to his circumstances partly in the
hope that, while he was improving them, time might
intensify her feelings. 'I thought (she added) that the
most decided objection to your circumstances would
pain you less than the least objection to yourself; while,
in truth, it is in some measure grounded on both. I
must be sincere, I find, at any cost.' The personal objection was out at last, and she was not sure that her
sentiments 'are proper for a husband.' Her doubt will
be shared, and Carlyle had certainly not pressed her,
but, when it came to the point, she would rather marry
his genius than part with him. This admitted, we can
understand why critics, cool to her, have laid on her the
responsibility for many of the crises that followed. 'Not
many months ago (she went on) I would have said it
was impossible that I should ever be your wife. At pre-

sent I consider this the most probable destiny for me. In a year or two I shall perhaps consider it the only one.' The degree of her self-detachment is only equalled by her determination, in the last resort, not to let him go. When she makes this clear she can be insinuatingly tender, saying: 'I know not how your spirit has gained such a mastery over mine, in spite of my pride and stubbornness. But so it is. Though self-willed as a mule with others, I am tractable and submissive towards you.... How comes it, then, that you have this power over me? for it is not the effect of your genius and virtue merely. Sometimes, in my serious moods, I believe it is a charm with which my good angel has fortified my heart against evil.' With such confessions as these before him, what could Carlyle do but wait, feeling that only circumstances, which time and patience could remove, stood between him and his marriage. She had given everything except her immediate consent, and to him most of her circumstantial objections were, as we have seen, unreal.

Matters stood thus in the spring of 1825, when Carlyle betook himself to Hoddam Hill, which his brother, Alexander, was farming. The life there only wanted the companionship of Jane to realize the atmosphere that Carlyle had dreamed of, and it is not surprising that he should have looked back on this time as an idyll in his life. He was on a farm but not farming; he had plenty of literary work, for he was busy on translation from the German, and he had an Irish horse upon whose back to fight his demon of indigestion. Carlyle's remedies were all strenuous. He had the touching faith of the literary man in the value of vigorous exercise, although the glory of riding is to provide movement without fatigue, and rather to oil than to galvanize the muscles. Those who have tried both long walks and long rides will appreciate the distinction. After a twenty-mile walk the feet break, the legs are heavy

with fatigue, the body is a load of weariness, but you
return from hours in the saddle gloriously tired, with a
head cleared, a heart clean, and your organs function-
ing in harmony. If you want the luxury of fatigue without exhaustion, you can find it in the saddle better than
anywhere else. It is not decisively clear how far Carlyle was really in want of a wife at Hoddam Hill.

A further step toward their union was taken when
Jane and Carlyle agreed that she should transfer to
Mrs. Welsh for life her interest in Craigenputtock, which
was worth about £200 a year. By this plan Mrs. Welsh
would not suffer financially if her daughter married,
and if Jane married Carlyle no one could say that he
had married her for her money. Jane was anxious to
protect him from such a charge, and he was anxious to
be protected. It was a mutual wish, and did honour to
the independence of both of them, but in the meantime it made it doubly necessary that Carlyle should
increase his income if he was to provide Jane with a
home like that she would be leaving. The deed which
made the transfer, moreover, secured Craigenputtock
to Carlyle on Mrs. Welsh's and her daughter's death.
Jane had thus done everything in her power to safeguard her mother and her lover.

In the momentary deadlock at which their engagement had arrived the only solution seemed to be that
Carlyle should somehow make some money, and of all
literary work translation has proved to be the least
remunerative in any century. From this point of view
their prospects were pathetic, but fate had a stroke in
store which hastened matters unexpectedly.

The good angel who was to bring them closer together appeared in an odd disguise, and was so little
prepared for the result of her interference that she
seemed only bent on making mischief. Mrs. Montagu,
one of Irving's friends in London, and 'Barry Corn-
wall's' mother-in-law, was one of those women who de-

light to manage the most private details of other people's affairs. She loved to receive confidences, and with
great faith in her own wisdom shrank from keeping these
confidences to herself. When, therefore, the expansive
Irving poured the story of his old attachment to Jane
into Mrs. Montagu's willing ears, she scented a romance
out of which further crises could be created. It was in
these crises that she delighted, for they gave a zest to
her days. Irving, who had not been allowed to withdraw from the engagement to Miss Martin that he had
repented, easily seemed a martyr to Mrs. Montagu's romantic heart. It is simple to blame him for not keeping
his past to himself, especially as his wife was proving a
devoted wife to him; but we all luxuriate in our secret
sorrows and are apt to unburden ourselves into a sympathetic ear. Filled with the news, Mrs. Montagu, who
had made Jane's acquaintance by correspondence, conceived the idea of telling Jane what she had heard. She
pictured Jane languishing with disappointed love, and
enjoyed the thought of telling her that Irving, though
married, had not forgotten. To heighten the emotional
strain was an irresistible temptation to Mrs. Montagu,
to whom romantic situations were as nectar. She never
paused to ask herself if her 'comfort' would be welcome,
or what rebuke her action invited if it were not.

Since no practical good could result either to Irving
or to Jane from this interference, whereas Mrs. Irving
might suffer acutely, we can measure the luxury in
which Mrs. Montagu was indulging herself. In the
guise of trying to allay the feelings that her action, if ef-
fective, must excite, she hinted to Jane that Irving was
scarcely worthy of a life's devotion, and that his new
ideas and ambitions would probably make him a disappointment to any woman who confided her heart to
him. This was surely sufficient presumption, but, with
the excuse of having once made some such avowal herself, Mrs. Montagu's appetite for emotional gossip was

not easily assuaged. Therefore, in complete ignorance of Carlyle's present interest in Miss Welsh, Mrs. Montagu confided the confidence that she had received from Irving to Carlyle also, for she supposed Carlyle to be aware of the feelings once subsisting between Irving and Jane. This was entirely news to Carlyle, to whom it was presented as an existing and painful fact. As Carlyle was writing love-letters to Jane and receiving love-letters from her, he was so little disturbed that he informed Jane of the strange delusion which appeared to possess Mrs. Montagu. She was really living in the clouds, for when Jane, instead of rebuking her for impertinence, soberly replied that she was not languishing for Irving, but was indeed eventually to marry Carlyle, Mrs. Montagu refused to believe her! Jane, on this occasion, was in a merciful mood, for she wrote to Carlyle: 'I had two sheets from Mrs. Montagu the other day, trying to prove to me that I did not know my own heart. Mercy! how romantic she is!' So true was this that Mrs. Montagu wrote again supplicating Jane not to marry Carlyle if she retained any tender feelings for Irving. Since Irving was already married, a disinterested friend might have been relieved to hear that a former lover of his had outgrown her feelings for him. Romantic people, however, rarely find romance in happy solutions; sacrifices, confessions, and humiliations self-inflicted are as manna to them; and to Mrs. Montagu, no doubt, it would be far preferable that Jane avow something painful at the risk of languishing in virginity, than to leave the past alone, for Jane was the last person in the world to imply that she had for her later lover a passion which did not exist.

The effect of Mrs. Montagu's second letter was to make Jane realize that she had not been candid about Irving with Carlyle, and therefore she felt the time had come to admit that she had once been 'passionately' in love with Irving. Since she had also helped to hold him

to his engagement to Miss Martin, Jane had no conventional excuse for reproaching herself, but it was now desirable that Carlyle should hear the whole story, and
that her scruples and her passionate feelings should be
made equally plain. No man attracted by a woman is
much troubled by any previous love-affairs that she
may have had. He is in love with her present, and, except as a subject for conversation, little concerned with
any past. But since Jane, at bottom, was desperately
anxious not to lose Carlyle, it was with trepidation that
she told him the story. 'Woe to me! then,' she concluded, 'if your reason be my judge, and not your love.'
Of course, her anxiety was the strongest appeal to his
generosity, though in a situation of this kind 'generosity' is only a convention of the stage.

Carlyle, as sensible as Mrs. Montagu had been in-
fatuated, after an accidental delay, replied: 'You exaggerate the matter greatly.... You ask me to forgive you!
... Come and see, and determine.... As I am, take or
refuse me; but not as I am *not*, for this will not, and cannot come to good.' This was the crux of the matter.
Jane did not want him, precisely, as he was, and Carlyle had little prospect of improving his circumstances,
and none of altering himself. The discontent was almost
wholly on her side, and, to bring the matter which had
halted so long to a decision, Carlyle boldly asked Jane
to come and visit him at Hoddam Hill. There she
would meet his mother and his brother, and then go to
the farm at Mainhill where his father and his sisters
were living. In this way the circumstances which
charmed him, but frightened her, could be inspected in
their native simplicity, and Jane could gather at first
hand what family life meant to the entire Carlyle
family. As he had no itch for gentility, the invitation
was not difficult for him to give. To accept was more
adventurous for Jane, but then Mrs. Montagu's interference had brought the pair nearer.

After some debate, for the two delighted in forensic discussions on paper, discussions in which Carlyle repeated that she must take him as he was and must realize that he might not be able to make her happy, Jane set out from Templand, where she had been staying with her grandfather, and on September 2, 1825, took the wrong coach. She was in good spirits, and when, late in the evening, Carlyle was not to be seen, she found a lonely lodging for the night at Kelhead Kilns without ill-humour. If anyone doubts that she had charm and good humour, even when she was a victim to mischance, let him consider the note that she wrote in this almost humiliating situation:

> Good morning, sir — I am not at all to blame for your disappointment last night. The fault was partly your own, and still more the landlady's of the commercial inn, as I shall presently demonstrate to you *viva voce*. In the meantime I have billeted myself in a snug little house by the wayside, where I purpose remaining with all imaginable patience till you can make it convenient to come and fetch me, being afraid to proceed directly to Hoddam Hill, in case so sudden an apparition should throw the whole family into hysterics. If the pony has any prior engagement, never mind. Anyway, pray make all possible despatch, in case the owner of these premises should think I intend to make a regular settlement in them.
>   Yours
>   JANE [1]

A poet, perhaps, would have waited all night.

This is a delightful letter. Only a lady could have written it, for a lady is one who makes the least, instead of the most, of any embarrassment. It also shows grace and good-humour, and her consideration for the family and for the pony is a charming touch. No young man attracted to the writer of this letter could fail to feel safe from temper after reading it. To the Carlyles, who were a little nervous, the mishap must have been per-

[1] *New Letters and Memorials*, I, 3–8.

turbing, for they now knew that Thomas and Jane were virtually engaged to be married. But, in Carlyle's words, 'from the first moment there was no embarrassment; even my mother's, tremulous and anxious as she naturally was, fled away without return.'

Jane stayed about a week, and not only enjoyed herself but made the Carlyles enjoy her visit too. Jane had now seen but one half of the family. Accompanied by Mrs. Carlyle, she then went to Mainhill, where Mr. Carlyle, called in from his work, shaved and changed into his Sunday suit before receiving her. This visit also was successful. Jane was too vital a person not to appreciate the substantial good of peasant existence. There was a touch of adventure in her new experience, but whether such an existence would prove natural to her remained to be seen. If she had recoiled from its details as Carlyle had recoiled from the 'whim-whams' of Haddington, it would have been no discredit to her. Because Carlyle sometimes made a pudding in his tea-cup, he was inclined to believe the habit essential to a noble character. The truth is that life on the land, like other noble lives, is a life one must be born to, and that manners, whether simple or gentle, have no absolute value apart from the surroundings which give rise to them. Carlyle naturally preferred those in which he was most at home, and took a lover's advantage when he used Jane's discontent with the Haddington circle as an argument that she only needed his company on a farm to make her happy. From his point of view, Jane's visit to his family had been a complete success, but Mrs. Welsh heard with dismay that her daughter, after this visit, had resolved to marry him.

VIII

All the easy arguments were upon the mother's side. Mrs. Welsh did not like Carlyle in the sense that he was not the son-in-law that she would have chosen. She did not make puddings in her own tea. She was dubious of his temper. Her own dominant ways recognized his autocratic disposition. She was indifferent to his intellectual pretensions. She knew that his income was too small. There were painful talks between her and her daughter, and Carlyle was too much detached, if not too generous, to press his claims. He begged Jane, if she wavered, not to heed himself.

Later in the autumn Jane paid a visit to Edinburgh, and attended several 'fine entertainments.' The comparison was not really fair, but it enabled her to write to Mrs. Carlyle that she had never been so happy as she had been at Hoddam. Mrs. Carlyle must have been glad to hear this, but she may have paused over Jane's dramatic description of the discomforts of her journey from Edinburgh to her home. Could a young lady be healthy who was 'woefully sick' upon an ordinary journey, and who, though swathed in four petticoats, was benumbed with cold?

Meantime, Carlyle continued his work very happily. He was idolized by his family, and wrote: 'There is no grumbling at my habitudes and whims. If I choose to dine on fire-and-brimstone, they will cook it for me with their best skill.' These are the well-known privileges of a bachelor, and bachelors will never learn that they are not compatible with marriage, for marriage is intended to be the satisfaction not of one person but of two. Carlyle was right to call this time an idyll, for it came to an end very soon. His family left Hoddam Hill because of some trouble with the landlord, and as the lease of Mainhill was also up, the two groups joined forces and retired together to Scotsbrig, a commodious farm where his parents spent the rest of their lives.

For some reason, Carlyle's content ended with this removal. Was he less considered than before when the whole of his family was about him, when his father naturally became the proper head of the household? Or was Hoddam, after Jane's visit, a more agreeable place to him than Scotsbrig proved to be? He may have been growing fastidious, and thought one devoted wife preferable to a large devoted family. At all events, he became keenly anxious to be master in his own home, and Mrs. Welsh, accepting the inevitable, offered to restore Craigenputtock to her daughter. Jane would not hear of this, and then a fresh debate began on the question whether, once they were married, she and Carlyle should make their home near Edinburgh or in the country. His idea of a country cottage was now abandoned.

It was Jane's turn to accuse him of waywardness, and she wrote: 'Now I call this a trial of patience and obedience — and say! could I have complied more readily though I had been your wedded wife ten times over?' Their nerves were becoming frayed with these discussions, and it was natural that she should exclaim: 'At times I am so disheartened that I sit down and weep.' To Carlyle, it seemed that all would be well if only they were once married. It was a decision that he craved for: 'if you judge fit' he replied 'I will take you to my heart as my wedded wife this very week. If you judge fit, I will this very week forswear you for ever.' What was she to make of that?

Since the difficulties of which she was conscious did not exist for him, it was logical that the impatient man should throw on her the burden of deciding. He begged her, if she really cared for him, to accept the inevitable: 'take me, and be content with me, and do not vex yourself with struggling to alter what is unalterable — to make a man who is poor and sick suddenly become rich and healthy.... If you are reconciled to be my wife (not the wife of an ideal me, but the simple, actual, prosaic me), there is nothing frightful in the future. I look into it with more and more confidence and composure. Alas, Jane, you do not know me. It is not the poor, rejected, unknown Thomas Carlyle that you know, but the prospective rich, known, and admired.' There was an element of truth in this, and Jane did not wince at its expression. Carlyle had the main essential, but he had not the manners, or the temper, or the habits which should have been included as a matter of course.

Forced into a corner by the argument, realizing at last that nothing was to be gained by prolonging hesitation, Jane made up her mind.

IX

Their theoretical difficulties being over, practical difficulties began. Where should their home be, and should it be a joint or a separate household? When Carlyle, happy in his family and with slender resources, suggested Scotsbrig, he seemed aware of the difficulties of a joint household only when Jane proposed that her mother should join them in a separate home. Jane was naturally concerned for her mother's future, and Mrs. Welsh seems to have agreed to the marriage in the hope that she would not be parted from her daughter. Mrs. Welsh would not have been tempted by Scotsbrig or its neighbourhood, so Jane suggested that, as the home at Haddington was to be given up, her mother should take a new house near Edinburgh for all three.

Before the possibility of a disputed supremacy Carlyle naturally quailed. The 'habitudes and whims' which were indulged without grumbling at Scotsbrig had not escaped Jane's critical eye. To a man's instinctive desire for his own home upon his marriage, Carlyle added the assertiveness of all thwarted and explosive natures, the unwitting selfishness of an egoist, the obstinacy of a peasant, and the absorption of an author. Knowing himself not an easy person to deal with, he naturally demanded considerations in

proportion to his need, for he suffered as much as anyone else from his own temper. To become his own
master was difficult. To complicate the difficulty with
a mother-in-law, naturally more interested in her
daughter than in himself, would have been intolerable. Carlyle firmly refused, and he was right to do
this, though we cannot help smiling when he asked
Jane if she really thought that her mother would consent 'to make me her guardian and director, and be
a second wife to her daughter's husband.' It is this
extreme demand, or rather the use of the word wife to
denote the complaisance required of a mother-in-law
not otherwise welcome, that inclines women to jib at
Carlyle's views of matrimony, which were as follows:

The man should bear rule in the house, and not the woman.
This is an eternal axiom, the law of nature which no mortal
departs from unpunished. I have meditated on this many
years, and every day it grows plainer to me. I must not, and I
cannot, live in a house of which I am not head. I should be
miserable myself, and make all about me miserable. Think
not this comes of an imperious temper, that I shall be a harsh
and tyrannical husband to thee. God forbid!

Since some one must be head, the modern recoil
from this assumption means that the head must not be
the man, who now, in his turn, has all the weight of
prejudice against him. Carlyle still had tradition on
his side, and, in justice, we must not confuse this tradition with the personal egoism that accompanied it. He
was the sort of person who could be selfish or tyrannical without knowing it, and the complete candour
of this letter is fine testimony to his honesty of heart.

The only solution seemed to be that Mrs. Welsh
should join her father at Templand, that the marriage
should no longer be postponed, and that Jane should
make a home with her husband at Scotsbrig, a farm
that would be within visiting distance of her mother.
It was then the turn of the Carlyle family to cry out.

Their consent seems to have been assumed by Carlyle, who had apparently taken it for granted, but they were wider awake to actualities than he, and declared that Jane, whom they had seen and liked, 'even in summer' would find it difficult to live there, 'and in winter impossible.' The conditions of the place were alive to Carlyle himself as soon as he contemplated the thought of *Mrs.* Welsh's future visits. He wrote to Jane:

> You have misconceived the conditions of Scotsbrig, and our only possible means of existence there! You talk of your mother visiting us! By day and night it would astonish her to see this household. Oh! no! Your mother must not visit mine! What good were it?

While he emphasizes the wisdom of keeping Mrs. Welsh and his family apart, the unsuitability of the place to his young wife was apparent to the disinterested eyes of his own people. Since Mrs. Welsh and the Carlyles did not clash when they met, it seems clear that Carlyle was really dreading her intrusion. He was so made that he could not help thinking more of his own comfort than of Jane, but many of their difficulties arose from the fact that their standards of comfort were different. If the habits and standards of the two families had been the same, most of these problems could not have arisen. The mixed marriage is a problem in itself. It cannot help magnifying the selfishness of either party. We need to bear this always in mind and to make it our postulate if comments on the attitude and even the blindnesses of either are to be fair.

Mrs. Welsh wished to leave Haddington for many reasons. She was less well off, and her friends there, admiring the young woman, did not regard Jane's prospective husband with enthusiasm, and their attitude, whether sympathetic or the reverse, was humiliating to her pride. To Carlyle, seeking for an alterna-

tive to the rigours of Scotsbrig, the house at Haddington offered a simple solution, but he forgot that it
would be no less awkward for Jane to return there as
his bride than for Mrs. Welsh to remain there as his
mother-in-law. He could not look at the matter from
another's point of view, nor was his solution more
agreeable that he and Jane should shut the door on all
'intrusions' there. Naturally Jane was sensitive to the
awkwardness, and unconsoled by the solution, but her
refusal puzzled a man who failed to see that a marriage
so difficult to accomplish was in itself a difficulty. 'The
vacant home at Haddington' he wrote to Jane 'occurred to my recollection as a sort of godsend, expressly suited to our purpose. . . . Even yet I cannot with
the whole force of my vast intellect understand how
my project has failed!'

The distracted lovers now considered once more a
country cottage, and Carlyle pointed out that with his
'£200 a year to begin with' there was nothing to fear.
Oblivious to the last of the disparity in their 'habitudes,' he tried to overcome Jane's hesitation by remarking that 'wives are supported . . . on all incomes,
from £14 a year' upward, and that he trusted her 'for
good sense enough to accommodate her wants to the
means of the man she has chosen before all others, and
to live with him contented on whatever it should please
Providence to allot him.' Fortunately, Jane had too
much good sense to do anything of the kind, and she
is remarkable among lovers of either sex in that good
sense did not desert her even when her heart was
deeply engaged.

Therefore, when Mrs. Welsh departed from Haddington, she took and furnished a house at Edinburgh,
where she was to live with Jane until her marriage,
now fixed for October 1826. Comley Bank was the
name of the new home, which was to be occupied exclusively by Jane and her husband once they had been

married and Mrs. Welsh had gone to live at Templand with her father. In the long run, therefore, all compromises were abandoned. The upshot of this protracted discussion was a separate and independent home for the young couple, with no third parties to disturb Carlyle and no unnecessary rigours for Miss Welsh's acceptance. Jane herself appraised it in the following words: 'It is by no means everything that one could wish, but it is by much the most suitable that could be got, particularly in situation, being within a few minutes' walk of the town, and at the same time well out of its smoke and bustle. . . . As for interior accommodation, there are a dining-room, and a drawing-room, three sleeping-rooms, a kitchen, and more closets than I can see the least occasion for, unless you design to be another Blue Beard. So you see we shall have apartments enough on a small scale — indeed, almost laughably small; but, if this is no objection in your eyes, neither is it any in mine.'

It was now the summer of 1826, and Carlyle was naturally content that a decision had been reached at last. As the month for their wedding approached, however, the nerves of both began to show the strain of all this preparation. These highly strung people recoiled from the public ceremony, which, in the Scottish way, was performed at the Templand house, more sensitively than most couples. A bridegroom always feels embarrassed and uncomfortable. A wedding is not his occasion, whatever he may feel. But Miss Welsh too spoke of the 'dreaded ceremony,' the 'horrid circumstances,' the 'odious ceremony.' If he became aware that he was 'a perverse mortal to deal with,' and had tried to confirm himself with the aid of Kant's *Critique of Pure Reason*, she had her own misgivings about him. In a touching letter she wrote:

I am resolved in spirit and even joyful — joyful in the face

of the dreaded ceremony, of *starvation*, and of every horrible
fate. Oh! my dearest friend, be always so good to me, and I
shall make the best and happiest wife. When I read in your
looks and words that you love me, then I care not one straw
for the whole universe besides. But when you fly from me to
smoke tobacco, or speak of me as a mere circumstance of your
lot, then, indeed, my heart is troubled about many things.

Again: 'Do you perceive, my good sir, the fault will
be wholly your own if we do not get on most harmoni-
ously together.' He tried to reassure her, but the note
of assurance in life or in love he could not give. He was
self-troubled even in his affectionate words to her:

You are very kind, and more just than I have reason to expect in imputing my ill-natured speeches (for which Heaven
forgive me!) to their true cause — a disordered nervous
system. Believe me, Jane, it is not I, but the Devil speaking
out of me, which could utter one harsh word to a heart that so
little deserves it. Oh! I were blind and wretched if I could
make thee unhappy!

She was taking a risk in marrying him, and he a risk
in marrying at all. Imagine her feelings when Carlyle
proposed that his brother should accompany them on
their journey after the ceremony: 'I absolutely prohibit
John (she replied) from going with us an inch of the
road; and he must not think there is any unkindness in
this. I hope your mother is praying for me.' They
both approached the altar as if not a blessing, but their
blood, was to be shed; and Carlyle's exclamation 'Oh!
we are two ungrateful wretches, or we should be
happy' was the sign of strained nerves. 'I will always
love thee' was his conclusion to their correspondence.

CHAPTER FOUR

THE ARGUMENTATIVE LETTERS

THE love-letters of the Carlyles differ from most of their kind by the unromantic tone that pervades many of them. While, even in these, we never doubt the sincerity or the genuineness of either writer, we do not often feel while we read that we are invading a privacy. The typical love-letter is much nearer to those penned by Charlotte Brontë to M. Héger than to anything, but one or two, written by Jane Welsh, or to all but a few written by Thomas Carlyle. The emotion that compelled Miss Brontë to address her master in language which she believed was proper to a friend, who could be no more than a friend, and for whom, perhaps, she was unconscious of more than friendship, makes by comparison several of the Carlyle letters seem remote; yet no one doubts that Miss Welsh had a passionate nature or that Carlyle was as deeply moved as it was in his nature to be. But the pages from his pen which show him most deeply moved occur mainly in his books, not in his letters, and there is even more emotion, more personal feeling, in his reflexions as a widower than in the majority of his love-letters. Until late in the series, it cannot be said of him, and can rarely be said of Jane Welsh, that 'the heart has its reasons which reason does not know.' Jane, perhaps because she had a head to lose, never lost it. The intelligence and the imagination which drew these two into each other's orbit controlled their hearts to nearly the end of this correspondence, and the result is that the story unfolded in the letters has been detached without much loss. The story, in the dramatic and literal senses of the word, resembles an argument. In the typical love-letter, the argument is inseparable from the feelings and the words. The unadulterated language of the heart, Charlotte Brontë's for example, could be conveyed by quotation only.

In the Carlyle love-letters a partisan reader is less concerned with the motive, without which, in most such letters, nothing would remain, than with the characters revealed, the observations provoked, the intelligences excited by them. Many seem rather the cream of a general correspondence, than the unique secret of two hearts. If, for convenience, we group the earlier letters with those that famous friendships have given to the world, how charming, how tender, how distinguished is this emotion which will prefer a thousand hints to one avowal; which is everywhere implied, and rarely uncontrolled; which can pack a phrase with meaning, and make a bouquet of the briefest note! Jane was a born letter-writer, and in the single form of composition which she shared with her husband she has no comparisons to fear. She lives for us by her correspondence. Her volumes of letters, to Miss Stodart, to Carlyle and to later friends, are a delightful addition to our shelves. A portrait of her would miss a quality that overlooked her writings. In a sense unforeseen by her early ambition, she became a woman of 'letters.'

It is an interesting detail that Jane was bad at spelling. Even the name of her lover continued to be misspelt, until Carlyle, half exasperated and half diffident, begged her to pay more attention to the word. The same tendency can be observed in other instinctive people. Perhaps it is harder for them than for more sophisticated persons to master the convention of English spelling, a feat of memory so arbitrary that proficiency in it, together with pronunciation, is made a social test, so that no Englishman can spell or pronounce an unfamiliar word without running the risk

of a social solecism. Jane, not easily awed, gaily refused to memorize our phonetic Chinese-puzzles. Her
pen ran as fast as her tongue, and in her letters we can
overhear her talking.

She evidently talked very fast. We can still catch the
gallop of her tongue in the quick rhythm of her letter-
writing, where the sentences ask to be read at high
speed. Indeed, it is impossible to read them aloud
slowly, and they are made to be read aloud. Knowing
them to have been penned by a young woman, we find
them, unless we are elderly and rather sentimental
women ourselves, arch, sprinkled with satire, and
laughing with comedy: letters that a young playwright
of talent might write. The overtone of masculinity in
this girl's intelligence is delicious to intelligent people.
Time was to bring a touch of acidity, which the later
letters and the later portraits confess, but the earlier
correspondence is neither hard nor cold, and with this
we do not need to hope that time will mellow, and
suffering season a little, this heart so high-spirited and
young. To a 'dry' appreciation a tinge of masculinity
adorns a charming young woman, in the same degree
that sensitiveness will crown the genius of a man.

The best of these letters make us dream, and our
dream is of a theatre where the magnet, though a
woman, should be, for once, not an actress but a playwright. It should be a theatre of comedies, written by
Jane Baillie Welsh, a theatre where the woman-
dramatist nursed the ambition to let Congreve set the
pace for her. The passages of dialogue, in which her
letters abound, the vivid thumbnail portraits, the inimitable little situations that frame the dialogues, raise
a provoking question: Why did so much talent stop
half-way?

She had written a tragedy when she was fourteen; it
had five acts, though they were short. She had tried
her hand at verses, which (we can still see) showed a

certain precocity. She, now a young woman, had welcomed Carlyle's suggestion that they should collaborate in a novel, portraying exactly the situation in which, to his eyes, they found themselves. He plied her with suggestions: for tragedies, for essays, for a critical life of her favourite, Madame de Staël. They were to produce a volume of tales, taking it in turns to cap one another's. Nothing, except some early reminiscences, came of all this. The first tale that Carlyle sent to Jane drove her, she told him, to despair. Even the novel on which they started after their marriage was given up. Her literary ambition had possessed her before she met Carlyle, but as soon as he came, and nursed it, her production was limited to her letters. There have been people who could write excellent letters, but have never desired to write anything else. People with her desire and her capacity do not generally outgrow it. What is the explanation?

The situation in which she found herself when her correspondence with Carlyle started, in June 1821, is explained in a letter of November 11, 1822, a letter of great interest. 'When you found me for the first time (she wrote), I was wretched beyond description,' under the shock of her father's death. 'Without plan, hope or aim I had lived two years when my good Angel sent you hither. I had never heard the language of talent and genius but from my father's lips. I had thought that I should never hear it more. You spoke like him; your eloquence awoke in my soul the slumbering admirations and ambitions that his first kindled there.... But in my studies I have neither the same pleasures nor the same motives as formerly: I am alone, and no one loves me better for my industry.... Your friendship restored...the counsels and incitements I have lost.' Thus, Carlyle was the third man to appeal to her instincts of discipleship, and, like her father, and like Irving, he found a pupil for whom discipleship and affection were almost one. Her studies required a human interest. They were not imperious instincts in themselves, and, had they been, the social round in which her mother delighted was a perpetual encroachment on her time. Her aunt Grace was never tired of tilting against learned women, or of warning Jane that gentlemen disliked such girls. Jane herself enjoyed society, but not the society which was at hand. The truth slips out in her confession: 'I shall never hold a respectable place among literary ladies. But I know I can be a first-rate fine lady whenever I please.' The salon, not the library, was her proper field, and correspondence was her appropriate form: in a great lady, the grace of authorship.

This, again, throws a light upon her correspondence with Carlyle. He was the third of her inspiring tutors, and, when occasion arose, she alluded to Irving with friendly frankness. 'Fewer people love me than you might imagine. You do. My mother does. Mr. Irving does.' The language of friendship could hardly be clearer. Indeed, it is not very easy to fix upon the letter in which her feeling first passed beyond friendship. In January 1823 she asks him to come to her, but in March he professes to have no idea of marrying her, though his letters grow steadily warmer throughout the summer, and here, alas, some of her replies have not survived. In July he has decided that, whatever happens to her, they must never part, and a month later that he must love her till the last moment of her existence. There is no mistake where he stood then, except that his affection for her did not associate itself with the possibility of marriage. Her reply, as we have seen, was: 'Your friend I will be... but your wife never,' a remark that still seemed to Carlyle a reasonable recognition of the facts. Nevertheless his letters soon resume their former strain, and she came to accept a language which, even when she caught its

tone herself, was still the language of an ardent friendship. It began, however, to be expedient to read these
letters to her mother, and, in consequence, Carlyle
was asked to confine his endearments to the German
language. The position that he occupied in her mind
is whimsically stated as follows: 'Have you got rid of
that infamous accent of yours? Remember that I can
never enjoy your society to the full until you do. My
poor ears are in a fever every time I hear it. Why
do you speak Annandale? Why are you not as elegant as Colonel Alex? My beau-ideal would then be
found.'

'Would then be found'! That qualification of hers
lasted for some time. She was conscious of a but to the
end, and her final surrender was not free from misgivings. She knew herself better than Carlyle knew
himself, for his attraction and affection for her, intense
as they became, blinded him at moments to inherent
difficulties. When she said that she loved him without
being in love with him, she summed up her position
exactly. His can scarcely be described in so neat a
formula. He was in love with her, but no woman,
however necessary, was the object of his being. With
his gifts and his ambitions, she was a crowning delight,
not a necessity of his existence. Short of being in love
with him, she found him a necessity, and thus, ulti-
mately, the whole nature of neither was involved in
their union. Had they been less remarkable people,
this might not have mattered. Her heart was set on a
genius, but unfortunately Carlyle's included idiosyncrasies so pronounced that he became almost the
genius of caricature. The poor man could not help
himself. His sufferings were acute, and in him we can
study in their exaggerated form the worst drawbacks
ever attributed to the tribe of authors. If his imagination as well as his mind had fully awakened to the
difficulties inherent in his temperament, he might have

hesitated to marry anyone. He knew the facts. He
failed to realize their implications. His letters to Jane
show him, in his need, wavering between a strong
desire for her, a proud confidence in his own superiority to fate, and a prey to recurring, but intermittent,
doubts of what would be best for her happiness. The
love that could put another's interest constantly first
was scarcely possible to a man so driven by interior
conflict as to make his own need of peace a dominating
hunger. Without passing idle criticism, we may yet
think that Carlyle would have done the best for himself if he had met some one more ordinary than Jane or
even had inquired of himself if he were, perhaps, born
to be a bachelor. In so far as he was helpless and
dependent, it was only with the selfishness of a child.
It was, I think, in his affection for his mother that he
found the relation to woman most satisfying to his own
nature and appropriate to hers. He had his work.
Jane, capable of becoming a fine lady to a man of
genius, had found only the genius. Fate was thus able
to drive a hard bargain with her. If Jane renounced
Carlyle, she renounced the best thing within her reach.
If she surrendered to his genius, she surrendered half
her desires. The 'little more' and the 'little less' of
Browning's fine distinction happened to be perversely
embodied for Jane in the same man.

With this situation before us, and Jane (as late as
January 1825) wished, in her own words to him, 'to
see' Carlyle 'earning a *certain* livelihood and following
the profession of a gentleman,' let us turn the letters
over for sidelights, for those glimpses that lurk between
the lines. Hers are the more akin to talk because, perhaps, she was not on the way to become a professional
writer. Even when Carlyle explodes, it is into turbu-
lent prose. His letters contain more promise of his
books than mirrors of his conversation, however crusty.
Since neither was to find a Boswell for their talk, the

later Carlyle characteristically making his memory of Coleridge's conversation a prose-picture or impression but not a record, these letters are our only substitute for Boswell. We seem to enter Templand, where the atmosphere was much that of her Haddington home, when Jane writes: 'I am quite tired out with my present manner of life. I think, for the last six weeks, my mother has not been in the same humour for two hours at a time; and then her jealousy of me is so intolerable that I am actually frightened when anyone shows me kindness.' To see Jane in as many moods as possible, we will simply listen, and scarcely interrupt her with comment, whatever we may overhear. 'Miss Kitty Kirkpatrick — Lord what an ugly name! "Good Kitty!" Oh, pretty, dear, delightful Kitty! I am not a bit jealous of her, not I indeed — Hindoo Princess tho' she be! Only you may as well never let me hear you mention her name again.'

When she gave rein to her imagination, it would bound from such a start very readily:

Well, if I do not go... I shall escape the danger of becoming 'a fashionable wife.' Oh, thou goose! to fancy for an instant that I could end in this!... I will never be anything so heartless! I have pictured for myself a far higher destiny than this. Will it ever be more than a picture? Shall I ever have the wish of my heart fulfilled? A 'sweet home' calmly embosomed in some romantic vale; with wealth enough to realize my ideal of elegant comfort; with books, statues, paintings and all things suitable to a tasteful, intellectual manner of life; with the friendship and society of a few, whose conversation would improve the faculties of my head and heart; and with *One* to be the polarstar of my being — one warm-hearted, high-minded, *dearest* Friend, whose sublime genius would shed an ennobling influence on all around him; whose graceful and splendid qualities would inspire a love that should be the heart and soul of my life! Such happiness is possible; and alas! it is next to impossible to assemble the circumstances which compose it.

Wit and romance were not her only moods. The lover could sometimes be equally candid:

How often do your letters bring me comfort, dearest! I wish there was a glass window in my heart, that you might look into it. You can never know by words how much I love you, and how gratefully I feel your kindness.

With her many moods to choose from, Carlyle, the stiffer, confessed: 'Do not mock and laugh, however gracefully, when you can help it! But for your own sake, I had almost rather see you sad. It is the earnest, affectionate, warm-hearted, enthusiastic Jane that I *love*; the acute, sarcastic, clear-sighted, derisive Jane I can at best *admire*,' a confession in which we come very close to both of them.

Carlyle had *his* picture of his own destiny and needs:

Freedom is the very life of man... and the very search for peace in some degree is peace.... One item lies at the bottom of almost every scheme I form: it is a determination to have some household of my own; some abode which I may be lord of, tho' it were no better than the Cynic's tub; some abiding home, which I may keep myself in peace by the hope of improving, not of changing for another. I have lived too long in tents, a wandering Bedouin; the fruits of my toil wasted, or spent in the day that witnessed them: I feel the sad effects of that arrangement; every hour they are becoming sadder. The point, then, is to alter it, to find the means of altering it.

The rising rhythm of his prose, which has already begun to flood this letter, then overflows into a passage that might almost belong to the unwritten *Sartor* itself:

O thou detested Fiend, Disease! most hideous of the progeny of Tophet! Could I but meet thee in some questionable shape, though it were frightful as the Hyrcanian Tiger, that I might grapple with thee, and kill thee, and scatter thy fragments to the four winds of heaven! but it is vain to imprecate: Ernulphus himself could make no impression here. I am sick and must recover; and if so, in sickness itself provide the helps for getting out of it. Till then my mind lies spell-bound, the best of my talents (bless the mark!) shut up even from my own view, and the thought of writing anything beyond mere drudgery is vain. I see all this: but I will also see the plan of conquering it, if it can be conquered.

The writer, not yet started on his proper task, lurks in Carlyle's letters, as clearly as the play of mind and mood which made Jane popular in company is reflected in hers. She is like a butterfly beginning to clap its wings: his are still wrinkled from the cramped cocoon whence he is crawling painfully into the sunlight. In the midst of his uncertainty, he could only look to time, crying: 'Shall I love you forever, or am I a fool for loving you at all? I *will* love you to the end of time, betide what may!' She too, for him, was becoming not only a hope but a complication.

His need for health, his love of the land, and the tie between his imagination and nature, led him to sketch a home with some, but not many, likenesses to the 'romantic vale' that Jane had desired. 'Had I land of my own (he told her), I should instantly be tempted to become a farmer! Laugh outright! But it is very true. I think how I should mount on horseback in the grey of the morning; and go forth like a destroying angel among my lazy hinds; quickening every sluggish hand; cultivating and clearing, tilling and planting, till the place became a very garden round me! In the intermediate hours, I could work at literature; thus *compelled* to live according to the wants of nature, in one twelvemonth, I should be the healthiest man in three parishes; and *then* — if I said or did nothing notable, it were my own blame, or nature's only.' There were, properly enough, no 'statues, paintings' in his picture, just as there were no 'hinds' or 'tillage' in hers. What a curiously different cross each was between the town and the country! Thus, when he jumped at her mention of Craigenputtock, she laughed, not at his proposal to farm it, but at the suggestion of living with him there.

When they passed from the ideal garden to the pair who should inhabit it, she had desired one 'of sublime genius' whose 'graceful and splendid qualities would inspire a love that should be the heart and soul of my life'; but circumstances, she admitted, stood in the way. Here is his companion picture: 'Were it in my power, I would ask a generous spirit, one whose happiness weightily depended on seeing me happy, and whose temper and purposes were of kindred to my own; I would ask such a noble being to let us unite her resources, not her wealth and rank merely, for these were a small and unessential fraction of the prayer; but her judgment, her patience, prudence, her true affection, to mine; and let us try if by neglecting what was not important, and striving with faithful and inseparable hearts after what was, we could not rise above the miserable obstructions that beset us both, into regions of serene dignity, living as became us in the sight of God and all reasonable men, happier than millions of our brethren, and each acknowledging with fervent and unspeakable gratitude that to the other he owed all, all.' It is hard to decide which was drawing the more romantic picture: she a woman's, he a man's. Carlyle ended: '*You* are such a generous spirit; but your purposes and feelings are not such. Perhaps it is happier for you that they are not.' Where lay the lurking contradiction that made each feel the several pictures to be conflicting? He pleads for his plan with the question: 'After all, why if we love each other, should not everything be well?' Why, if? because parts of this pair were incompatible, while the word love implied a unity still lacking to them.

This letter of his, and her long reply, dated January 29, 1825, are very characteristic, and indeed vital in the lives of both. Though Jane would only admit

Carlyle to be her 'probable destiny,' yet from this time, in truth, she held herself to be engaged. Carlyle's allusion to parting, moreover, produced the answer: 'How could I part from the only living soul who understands me?' This let loose in him a flood of curious feeling, in which he seems to confuse some implied fault in her with the personal gifts and different standards that separated them. Otherwise, how can we reconcile his wish that she 'had been some humble maiden with no possession, no accomplishment but the ethereal spirit, the true fervent heart, which Nature gave,' with the criticism implied by the words: '*Were* you (the italics are his) but the being which your endowments indicate, with what entireness could I give up my whole soul to you...?' What was the shortcoming that he discerned but did not define, the shortcoming which made him say in the same letter, 'it seems as if I *dared* not love you!' There can be no doubt what it was. She was not some humble maiden, as he wished her to be. It seemed to him a flaw. He wished it away. He did not wish that he himself were of her circle. Nothing is prouder than a peasant's pride, and so the marks of breeding peculiar to her were defects, while those peculiar to him were unimpeachable. In the very temperaments of the twain a disguised sense of misalliance makes itself felt.

The unavoidable word is still avoided: family sympathy has led some of his biographers to affirm that the Carlyle family had exalted ancestors! Who needs to linger upon evidence that does not touch the point? The lovers were comparing the present not their lineage, and, as it chanced, at the time when they were corresponding, the Welshes happened to be nearer the professions. It would be false to exaggerate the difference. Carlyle's brother and Jane's father were both doctors, but, in the professional sense, the Carlyles at this period were one generation behind.

The slightest difference is always the most sensitive, and the sensitiveness more than the difference explains the lovers' puzzle.

As this correspondence progressed, Jane came to share his view that she was responsible for their difficulties. 'What hinders? (she exclaimed, in March 1825). Nothing but the miserable perversion of my own sentiments!' She said that she had lived so long among people who did not understand her that she had 'grown as difficult to come at as a snail in a shell.' This had ceased to be true of her feelings which answer Carlyle's as clearly as a bell, and there occur at this time some of the happiest of all their letters.

In this mood they began to plan the visit that Jane was about to make. She was to stop the coach at Kelhead where Carlyle was to meet her with a pony, and take her the two miles to his mother's home and tea. His health was improving; his mind was more at peace, and, amid the exhortations and the fulminations, too characteristic to be wholly banished even from his love-letters, there is a passage which promises *Sartor* at its best: 'The chambers of the East are opened in every land, and the sun comes forth to sow the earth with Orient pearl; Night, the ancient mother, follows him with her diadem of stars; and Arcturus and Orion call *me* into the infinitudes of space as they called the Druid priest or the shepherd of Chaldea.' Even Mrs. Montagu's intrusive letter could not utterly destroy this interlude of calm. Yet Jane's heart, which 'beats faster than usual when I think of walking into the midst of your family,' which could meet his wishes over her property by writing gaily, 'my money matters are all arranged; and now I am as poor as yourself,' was to be wrung beyond all foreseeing by Mrs. Montagu's urgent advice.

Jane's confession was made and posted.

If we are now to see Jane in the throes, there is her

shortest letter, written, through no fault of Carlyle's, after an agonizing week of suspense:

Mr. Carlyle, do you mean to kill me? Is it just of you to keep me so long in doubt? Your displeasure I have merited, perhaps your scorn, but surely not this terrible silence! Write then, for Heaven's sake! and kindly, if you can; for I am wretched beyond all expression. Had I but strength, I would come to you this very day; and when I held you in my arms, and you saw my tears, you would forget everything but the love I bear you... the loss of your affection was the very last thing I feared. And have I indeed lost it? Speak, tell me. It is inhuman to leave me in this suspense....

Before this had reached him, Carlyle, of course, had reassured her, and he too becomes frank in *his* confidences: 'If this accursed burden of disease were cast away, nine-tenths of my faults and capacities would pass away with it.' After such a crisis, her visit to Hoddam Hill could not fail to be a success for both of them, and the finger of fate can almost be claimed for arranging this climax on the eve of her arrival. That, too, was made the more moving from the mischance which caused her to take the wrong coach, so that she did not reach Kelhead till so much later than eight in the evening that Carlyle had given her up in despair. The little note, already quoted (p. 90), that she sent from her improvised lodging is a perfect complement to the appeal wrung from her a month before.

Her seventeen days on the Carlyle farm were decisive, and remained among the happiest memories of her life.

The consequence of this visit was an interlude of sunshine, an interlude, lasting from October to the end of February (1826), which occasioned the happiest letters. It was not even marred by Jane's difficulties with her mother, in whose mind, we are told, a storm had been brewing for weeks. The storm broke over Jane's head on the day after a flying visit of Carlyle's to

ot averse from showing Jane in a
querulous light, calls the complaints 'bitter, hasty, and
not well-founded,' so fatal has it proved to all the
Carlyle biographers to desire to be fair to — only one.
Carlyle went on to lament that 'there is no unity in my
condition,' and wins us by sympathizing with Mrs.
Welsh's views: 'They coincide too nearly with my own.'
In this gust of opposition Jane's love rose into a flame,
and now fame itself seemed to her a poor thing in comparison. Busy with his translations, a weary labour to
one who would one day write out of himself, Carlyle
records his state for us pithily. 'Alas! the matter lies
deep and crude, if it lies at all, within my soul; and

much unwearied study will be called for, before I can shape it into form. Yet out it shall come, by all the powers of Dullness!' The clay was dull, though in this clay the soul, which 'is form,' was painfully working.

Their troubles were opposite: his within, hers without, and the troubles served, since they were now in love, to humanize and gladden both of them. They even catch sometimes each other's quality under its influence, which makes it pleasant to read in Jane's letters a prose, like Carlyle's but clarified of scum: 'Strange as you may think it, young man, I have an affection for thee which it is not in the power of language to express; and I wot not what evil or combination of evils could prevail to make me entirely wretched, while thou art within reach to comfort me with sweet words of hope or love.' Equally do we catch her echo in his sentence: 'There are many miracles in this world; but for a woman to descend from relative superfluity to live with a sick ill-natured man in poverty, and not in wretchedness, would be the greatest miracle of all.'

Toward the end of January (1826), he was able to prophesy, truly as it turned out, 'who knows but by this time twelvemonth we may be married!' The air seemed to clear with the return of good spirits to Mrs. Welsh, who now began to speak of leaving Haddington. In a long and friendly discussion with her daughter, Mrs. Welsh learned that Jane did not propose to part with her even after her prospective marriage. 'At this,' Jane explained, 'she burst into tears, and, throwing her arms about my neck, exclaimed, "why have you never said as much before?"'

Though Mrs. Welsh was sometimes dubious about Carlyle, undoubtedly she also shrank from being separated from her daughter. For his part, Carlyle was considering a little house in Edinburgh, whither he would bring his sisters to keep house for him. It was a

passing notion, but it provoked an interesting comment from Jane. She had begun to be fond of the
Carlyle family, and, thinking of them, she wrote: 'Indeed, my darling, they would make but sorry house-
wives in a situation so new and strange; and you, with
all your kindness and wisdom, would make a still
sorrier mother. Whatever you do, never think of
carrying off little Jane. *She* is my child, and shall go
no such road until I am there to guard her.' Against
a joint household, as we have seen, Carlyle was firm:
'My prospective cottage (he wrote) would be calcu-
lated for different objects than your mother's,' and,
again, 'it is impossible for two households to live as if
they were one.'

This demur, on each side, to the other's project produced a serious tension, in which she accused him of
changing his mind from a country cottage to a town
house, and recalled her previous compliance. Thereby
she provoked a lecture, grave and reproachful, from
him. This misunderstanding is only worth attention
because it shows the different logic of a man's and a
woman's mind. Carlyle had changed his plan because
his circumstances had altered. He was being drawn to
Edinburgh because a project for a new paper, on
which he was to work, was in the wind. In a passing
mood of impatience, she even wrote, 'suppose we take
different roads!' Indulging a dangerous fancy, she
then began to sketch two roads, in company, moreover,
with different partners. It was naughty of her to give
her imagination such a free rein, and her summer
lightning was quickly followed by his thunder. Carlyle
had the better case, but his conduct of it was no less
distressing to her than her naughty suggestion had
proved to be to him.

Carlyle had had a disagreement with his landlord,
and was feeling forced to move. It was natural, but
unlucky, that he should discuss her fancy, about dif-

ferent partners, with equal seriousness. With deliber-
ation, he replied as follows: 'Your half-jesting enumer-
ation of your wooers does anything but make me laugh.
A thousand and a thousand times have I thought the
same thing in deepest earnest. . . . Look round with calm
eyes on the persons you mention or may hereafter so
mention; and if there is any one among them whose
Wife you had rather be — I do not mean whom you
love better than me — but whose Wife, *all* things considered, you had rather be than mine, then *I* call upon
you, I your brother and husband and friend thro'
every fortune, to accept that man and leave me to my
destiny.' Not even his closing words, 'O Jane, Jane,
I could weep too, for I love you in my deepest heart,'
effaced the effect of his having treated her suggestion
'reasonably.' After all, she had ended her own tirade
with the words: 'But what am I talking about? — as
if we were not already married — alas, married past
redemption! God knows, in that case, what is to
become of us. At times I am so disheartened that I
sit down and weep; and then at other times! Oh,
Heavens!' His solemn answer to this, 'we are *not* married already,' so right in cold logic, seemed but treason
to her heart. Though alert in her self-defence, and
now keeping a quiet pair of hands upon the argument,
she could not resist one thrust: 'It is so unlike *you*, the
sworn enemy of cant, to make high-sounding offers in
the firm confidence of their being rejected! for (she went
on) it is in no jesting, or yet "half-jesting" manner,
that you tell me my hand is free.' The fatal quotation
followed: 'If there be any other — you do not mean
whom I love more — but whose Wife, all things considered, I would rather be, you call upon me as my
Husband (as my Husband!) to accept that man.' Due
comment seems impossible, but Jane added: 'Dearest,
dearest, it will take many caresses to atone for these
words!'

From this heart-searching crescendo her letter glides
gracefully down, a succession of conciliatory para-
graphs gradually restoring their accord until complete
sympathy is resumed by the time it reached her signature. Before the end, however, she indulged in one
gentle rebuke. 'There needs no apprenticeship (she
told him) to train me to disinterestedness of heart.' It
prefaced her woman's logic, where the heart reasons
differently from the head. 'If you love, cease, I be-
seech you, to make me offers of freedom; for this is an
outrage which I find it not easy to forgive.' He had
been right in his facts, but wrong in his interpretation
of her feelings. The feelings are the facts to a woman.
The heart is not the head to a man.
    Since

> Love is not love which doth not sweeter live
> For having something dreadful to forgive,

the pair were brought still closer after this misunderstanding had passed. He mended matters by asking
her if she would marry him straight away even into
beggary, and, with the fact of feeling thus satisfied, she
said Yes, were it not for an obstacle of a different kind.
'Should I do well to go into Paradise myself, and leave
the mother who bore me to break her heart?' Mrs.
Welsh was still hoping for a nominal separation, and,
since she could not live with Carlyle's family, he and
Jane must live somewhere, say at Edinburgh, where
Mrs. Welsh could be within reach. But Carlyle, who
was unable to make inquiries on the spot, now feared
that Edinburgh would prove too expensive, and this
was one reason why he hoped that Mrs. Welsh, on her
departure, would lend them the old home at Haddington for a year. He could 'see,' but not 'feel,' the
reasons which made Jane oppose this suggestion; just
as it seems odd to us now that he should have thought
that inexpensive houses on the fringe of Edinburgh
had all been snapped up.

The gay passages in his letters are precious from their rarity. Here is a glimpse of the meaning of happiness to him: 'Here,' when his work (at Scotsbrig) and hers (in his fancy) were over for the day, he imagined 'tea put on the table, and a circle of glad faces was to gather round it, and there we should sit and talk, or I should read, and play with your black locks; for you were then my own to all eternity, and no other man or woman had any part or lot in your true bosom but myself.' While adamant that the man must be head of his household, which he could not expect Mrs. Welsh, if she joined them, to accept, and agreeing with the poet that 'man must be pleased, but him to please is woman's pleasure,' he knew the nature of woman to conquer man 'not by her force but by her weakness, and perhaps (the cunning gypsy) after all to command him by obeying him.' Nor about Mrs. Welsh had he, even unpleasant, illusions: 'I know her perhaps better than she thinks, and it is not without affection and sincere esteem that I have seen the fundamental structure of her character, and the many light capricious half-graces half-follies that sport on the surface of it.' Mrs. Welsh had another tie beside her father with Templand, for Jane's aunt also lived there, and would need Mrs. Welsh when Jane's grandfather had died. Dr. Fyffe was after the Haddington house, and was so close a neighbour that his presence, as an old admirer of Jane, was one of the reasons why she could not endure the thought of living at Haddington after her marriage.

The passage in which Carlyle declared that 'wives are supported . . . on all incomes from £14 a year to two hundred thousand,' and in which he drew her attention to a certain hedger at his door who, with his wife, formed one of 'the most enviable families on the earth, on the produce of fifteen pence' a day, is worth a second's glance. The truth which he urged was true, but he was not pressing her to share the life of this exemplary hedger. People are happy because they suit each other, not because they possess a fixed amount of property external to themselves; but, in order that they may suit each other, they must have similar habits, standards and tastes. Thus there will always be something in Nature against the marriage of a duchess with a dustman. It is doubtful if love can exist happily between persons of widely different habits, though the love that endures for a night might waylay any pair in the world. We use a word like love in several senses, and Carlyle, who knew this as well as anyone, has been charged with an inhuman proposal where no more than a forcible illustration was meant. He was reasonable from his own point of view: 'A house in Edinburgh...I should like infinitely better than Haddington; but not having it, and having the other, I should be a fool, it seems to me, if I determined otherwise.' Right, again, in his confidence that he could earn his own living and something to spare for a friend in need, his insistence seems tedious to those who have not undergone his discipline. Carlyle simply could not understand that an income by right of property becomes, to those who have had it, a right as natural and as human as an income by right of work. Jane was the product of one tradition, he of another. The propertied are generally less happy than the self-supporting because fruitful activity is a need common to both, and the satisfaction of this need is not pressed upon propertied people. He had the root of this simple wisdom in his bones, but, while the wisdom is distasteful to all whose eyes have not been opened to it, we want also, with the root, the flowers, and Carlyle's thought was, mainly, a vegetable garden.

The concluding letters show on both sides a nervous tension, the worse for the long years that had preceded the approaching marriage. Jane put it wittily when she wrote: 'My head and heart are in an endless whirl which no words can express. In short this marriage, I find, is like death: so long as it is uncertain in its approach, one can expect it with surprising indifference; but certain, looked in the face within a definite term, it becomes a matter of most tremendous interest.' It was five years since their first meeting, and eighteen months since she had held herself engaged (January, 1825), a whole year since they had spoken face to face. Their practical difficulties diminished when Miss Welsh reported that 21 Comley Bank, Edinburgh, was vacant, and we have read her description of its rooms. The thought of their home warmed him, and he wrote back in reply: 'Here are two swallows in the corner of my window that have taken a house (not at Comley Bank) this summer; and, in spite of drought and bad crops, are bringing up a family together with the highest contentment and unity of soul. Surely, surely, Jane Welsh and Thomas Carlyle, here as they stand, have in them conjunctly the wisdom of many swallows!' He passes to a lecture upon human vanity, and concludes: 'Beloved pupil, art thou not afraid of the wonderful lectures thou art fated to encounter from a husband so didactic? Or is it rather by (curtain) lectures that thou purposest to instruct *him*?'

The purgatory of expectation soon engulfed them both, and the fatal moment, which is the heart of all romance, when they would be publicly Proclaimed, as the banns are called in Scotland, gave rise to many shrinking expressions in their letters. The move from Haddington was accomplished during August, and made Jane exclaim: 'I wonder that among all the evils deprecated in the Liturgy no one thought of inserting *flitting*. Is there any worse thing? Oh no, no! From flitting, then, Good Lord deliver us! — and from some other evils best unfolded in all their length and breadth when we meet. And when will that be?' She added:

'The house at Comley Bank is at length completed, and looks pretty and convenient enough; certainly nothing like so commodious and elegant as the one I have left; but *all* things considered, likely to answer much better. So here are two steps in the business happily taken. The last is the worst of all; — would to God it were over also!' He, too, had been ailing, now that the labours of translating German romances were over; and, not for the first time, he considered himself to be bad instead of ill. His affection overflows into tender words, and hers are troubled by the thought that nothing good can be said in 'such horrid circumstances.' Mrs. Welsh had gone to Edinburgh to make some vital purchases, and to order the 'white gowns.' This news provoked a charming reflection: 'Besides you know it would be a bad omen to marry in mourning. When I put it on six years ago, I thought to wear it for ever. But I have found a second Father, and it were ungrateful not to show even externally how much I rejoice in him.'

If she dreaded the banns and the ceremony, she dreaded public inspection thereafter even more. This was why she shrank from travelling the fourteen miles from Templand to Comley Bank in the stage coach, and insisted on a private chaise, and would not hear of her brother-in-law, John, accompanying them 'in such severe circumstances!' The thought of 'that odious ceremony' caused her head to feel faint and her body to shudder. There is always a maiden somewhere, even in a woman of the world. Carlyle tried to hide in the pages of Kant's *Critique of Pure Reason*, as if in the corner of a chaise with drawn blinds, and, when he peeped beyond it, was frightened by visions of Session clerks, tailors and post-keepers, without whose prosaic aid even the flight to Edinburgh could not be arranged in due form. He saw that they were growing nervous, and encouraged her with the desperate reminder that, after all, 'many people have been married before now.' He begged for one concession: 'That you let me by the road, as occasion serves, smoke three cigars, without criticism or reluctance, as things essential to my perfect contentment. Yet (the impending husband added) if you object to this article, think not that I will break off the match on that account; but rather like a dutiful Husband, submit to the everlasting ordinances of Providence, and let my Wife have her way.' He called her 'a wicked gypsy, but one whom I see not how I am to do without.' The words are worth quoting because they show how love was teaching him to speak.

Preoccupied with the local gossip on her 'situation,' Jane sought to correct its forebodings by sending a defensive description of her future husband to her aunt, Mrs. George Welsh, in Dumfries: 'A hundred chances to one, they would not tell you he is among the cleverest men of his day; and not the cleverest only but the most enlightened! that he possesses all the qualities I deem necessary in *my* husband, a warm true heart to love me, a towering intellect to command me, and a spirit of fire to be the guiding star of my life.'

Indeed, at this moment, when she turned to him, her fears were of terrible trifles: 'When I read in your looks and words that you love me, I feel it in the deepest part of my soul; then I care not one straw for the whole universe beside; but — when you fly from my caresses to tobacco, or speak of me as a new *circumstance* of your lot, then indeed my heart is troubled about many things.' She hoped that his sister, little Jane, would join them, once its mistress had grown accustomed to her new home. She begged to be allowed to teach her cousin Phoebe German in accordance with a promise already made. She added, for his consolation, 'my aunt tells me she could live forever with *me* without quarrelling — I am so reasonable and equal in my humour.' It was Carlyle who called this last letter 'the last speech and marrying words of that unfortunate young woman': a joke in her own vein, but no description of hers. The final note of their letters shows excitement, but not foreboding. He ended simply by saying: 'My last blessing as a lover is with you...my first blessing as a husband...is at hand.'

The one who can do without usually gains his bargain, and we should be losing the genius in the lover if we did not gather from this correspondence that Carlyle, however predisposed to matrimony, was the less dependent of the two.

PART TWO
MARRIAGE OF AN AUTHOR

How inexpressibly comfortable to know our fellow-creature; to see into him, understand his goings-forth, decipher the whole heart of his mystery: nay, not only to see into him, but even to see out of him, to view the world altogether as he views it; so that we can theoretically construe him, and could almost practically personate him; and do now thoroughly discern both what manner of man he is, and what manner of thing he has got to work on and live on!

THOMAS CARLYLE: *Essay on Biography.*

CHAPTER FIVE

EDINBURGH: EARLY MARRIED LIFE AND WRITINGS

I

THE name of Craigenputtock farm has become a symbol for the early married life of the Carlyles, but, as we know, their first home was at number 21 of a row of houses called Comly or Comley Bank on the north side of Edinburgh. It was small; compact, furnished with pieces from Haddington, and had been prepared under the trained and skilful eye of Mrs. Welsh. They remained at Comley Bank for two years, a time sufficiently long to leave no doubt in the mind of either. Indeed, before the honeymoon is over, the fate of any engagement is known. Three weeks are enough to dissipate a sensual passion; to reveal a born bachelor; to expose a feminine snare. The love that can survive three weeks of married life is proved to be sterling, whatever troubles may lie in store for husband or wife.

To very innocent and unsophisticated people, the first surprise on leaving church or registry-office is to discover that there has been no mysterious change; that no one feels any different after the ceremony; that the ring seems not to rest on any right, and the signature to represent no new fact in experience. Newly married women are often as shy of showing their encircled left finger as a freshman is of appearing before dusk in his Cambridge gown, and the sensation of not being able to say good-bye may be as strange as it once had been to be alone together. The Carlyles had begun with a long drive in a carriage from Templand, and this journey, horridly shy as Jane had felt under the eyes of the ostlers, may have accustomed her to the company of her husband, for it is an old saying that there is nothing like a journey to reveal the temper of a companion. According to the more human habit of that day, they drove straight to their new home, already familiar to Jane who, almost till the last moment, had been there, helping her mother to prepare it.

Jane set about her new duties with zest. They evoked the practical energies of her nature. The time was to come when she would almost enjoy the worst extremities of domestic redecoration, if only because they made such excellent materials for comic narrative; and it is one of the oddities of fate that a being so dependent on activity and company should have been forced, partly by ill-health but largely by the conventions of her day, to waste years upon a sofa, doing nothing. Her principal occupation, apart from her husband, was to write letters. Without occupation she was wretched, and only in practical affairs could she carry activity to its conclusion. Letter-writing suited her artistic temper to perfection, for each letter is an independent creation. It can be as long or as short as the writer chooses. It can be begun, or dropped, at any moment. It is the lyric of prose, the thrush's overflow of feeling, and the art-form of a good letter is infinitely less exacting than that of a sonnet. In the works of the imagination Jane was not creative enough to complete anything larger than a bird-like letter. Though she talked well, and, unlike Elizabeth Barrett, did not only talk on paper, yet she did not take her chief pleasure in the spoken word. The born correspondent finds writing no irksome labour, and, however much Jane entertained the long stream of visitors, who came chiefly to enjoy the talk that they heard from the two Carlyles, yet a day to her was a wasted day in which she had written to nobody. One suspects that she talked for practice, that she passed through the post

JANE WELSH CARLYLE
By Samuel Laurence (about 1838)

the best of her sallies, and that the good things in her letters were never composed in order to be repeated by word of mouth. A wit like Wilde, to whom writing was laborious, proceeds in the opposite way. He would roll a phrase many times on his tongue, and be content with the laughter that came back to him, before the discovery that a man could no longer live by witticisms forced him to turn his sayings into dramatic dialogue. Jane was to suffer from solitude. She may easily have been bored even by books, but she had one great advantage over the born talker: only prostration deprived her of company. The best of all company to an imaginative person is the imagination itself, and to such nothing in this world is more companionable than a pen, so long as it is running smoothly. A person alive enough to write enchanting letters, but unequal to a longer script, cannot, however, exhaust the energies of nature by correspondence. The whole charm of correspondence is to be a casual occupation. Even Horace Walpole was builder, collector, and printer half his time; but very lively people have more energies than the pen of a correspondent can spend, and so it is no surprise that Jane's body was as active as her mind, nor that the girl who had loved to do carpentry proved an excellent domestic manager.

We are too familiar with the deserted invalid, with the vivacious or querulous correspondent — not to mention, moreover, the ample scope of the modern woman to occupy herself in undomestic ways — to recall without an effort the frustrated but energetic and capable young woman whom Carlyle had married. We forget that a hundred years ago, ladies, as Miss Elizabeth Drew has proved by the aptest of quotations from forgotten instructions,[1] were '*taught* to be incompetent amateurs'; that, in Jane's time, all proficiency

[1] *Jane Welsh and Jane Carlyle*, by Elizabeth Drew, pp. 201–14 (Cape, 1929).

was unladylike; that the duty of young women was to be unoccupied, and the duty of young wives to be obsequious; that ability, and still more intelligence, in women were defects to be hid; that to listen was more becoming than to talk; and that the admitted tedium of this vapid existence could be properly relieved, in the absence of children, only by religion, or by the tending of an elderly invalid, always provided, even so, that no initiative had part in it. It is pathetic to read how every change was rung upon ineffectual satisfactions, but against the law that imposed futility there was no appeal. By moving, on her marriage, to a house that was less pretentious than her mother's, Mrs. Carlyle actually widened her domestic horizon. There was more that needed doing, and, unless she had married an aristocrat of exceptional social tastes, she would, by marrying above her circle, have entered on an existence altogether less absorbing than was opened to her in this small suburban house at Comley Bank. No wonder she was happier once married. As a married woman, she had more feathers to her wings.

With his wide sympathies and his peasant traditions, Carlyle necessarily identified the ladylike with the silly, and it was inconceivable to a man whose parents were living on a farm that a wife should be helpless. If he was at one with the ideal that a woman must be biddable, and must minister to her husband in all his moods, he never identified this lot of woman with incompetence. All the women whom he had known, except the wealthy and wasteful Mrs. Buller, ran their own households, and took a pride in running them well. As usual, life was only human at the two edges of the social scale, and, for another fifty years, the would-be ladies of the middle class were to remain, of all human beings, the narrowest and the most miserable.

To say nothing of their real affection for each other,

there is solid ground for the happiness that runs through the letters written by both husband and wife from Comley Bank. Carlyle himself called the house 'a perfect model, furnished with every accommodation that heart could desire.' Of his wife, he told his mother: 'She ... loves me with a devotedness which it is a mystery to me how I have ever deserved. She is gay and happy as a lark, and looks with such soft cheerfulness into my gloomy countenance that new hope passed into me every time I met her eye. In truth I was very sullen yesterday, sick with sleeplessness, nervous, bilious, splenetic, and all the rest of it.'

Mrs. Welsh was the recipient of similarly satisfactory confidences: '... be of good cheer! You would rejoice to see how much better my husband is since we came hither. And we are really very happy. When he falls on some work we shall be still happier. Indeed I should be very stupid or very thankless if I did not congratulate myself every hour of the day on the lot which it has pleased Providence to assign me. My husband is so kind, so in all respects after my own heart. I was sick one day, and he nursed me as well as my own mother could have done; and he never says a hard word to me unless I richly deserve it. We see great numbers of people, but are always most content alone. My husband reads then, and I read or work, or just sit and look at him, which I really find as profitable an employment as any other.' No doubt, both were anxious to reassure their parents, but each letter rings true. The date, therefore, becomes interesting. Jane wrote hers, almost to a day, within three months of her marriage. These two letters are call and echo.

The social life of which Jane had often dreamed began at once, as this early letter shows. Carlyle already had a few distinguished friends in Edinburgh. Her Wednesday evening tea-parties — they dined at four in those days and neither accepted nor sent invi-

tations to dinner — were quite enough to tempt them.
Sir William Hamilton, John Wilson (Christopher
North) of Blackwood, De Quincey, Francis Jeffrey of
the *Edinburgh Review* were, sooner or later, among her
visitors, and to them she appeared as surprisingly
agreeable as Carlyle had proved questionable to the
narrow Haddington clique. Mrs. Welsh, now more
than relieved, sent a sum of sixty pounds about Christmas. This was, very gratefully, declined. It was work
that Carlyle wanted. Though he had presented his
father with half his savings, for the Bullers had not
stinted their son's tutor, and writing, so far, was a
stand-by rather than an income, Carlyle settled as
a married man in Edinburgh with £300 in the bank.
Writing for the Reviews was more congenial than
being a dominie, and better paid than the drudgery of
translating for the booksellers. Moreover, as Irving
had once pointed out, translators were not only badly
paid but anonymous, whereas, at that day, a man, as
both Sydney Smith and Macaulay discovered, could
become famous through a single contribution, and the
enormous success of Scott was proving that a man
might live in prosperity through authorship alone.
Therefore, though Carlyle wished to deserve fame no
less than to receive it, the most useful and promising
card that he brought with him to Edinburgh was a
letter to Francis Jeffrey.

This was presented in February, 1827, when the
volumes of German Romances were off his hands, and
while he was dallying, unhappily, with a 'didactic
novel.' Jeffrey's diminutive and nimble figure with
the bright-black eyes had long been familiar to Carlyle
in his visits to the law-courts, and, at the end of an
hour's friendly and vivacious talk on everything under
the sun, Carlyle left with the reflection: 'The man is so
immersed in law, otherwise we might become friends.'
Two definite promises were made at this interview: an

introduction to Sir Walter Scott on any morning that Carlyle should go to the Courts, and the possibility of work on the *Edinburgh Review*. 'We must give you a lift,' said Jeffrey, and so their long friendship began.

The days at Comley Bank followed a regular routine. After breakfast with his wife, Carlyle would retire upstairs to the little drawing-room, where the unfinishable (but posthumously published) pages of his novel stared him mournfully in the face. About two, he would go for a walk, often toward the sea-shore or into the streets of Edinburgh, before returning for dinner at four o'clock, after which they would read 'learned languages' together until coffee (unless it was a Wednesday when they were at home to callers) stimulated them to further talk or reading until it was time to go to bed. 'You would wonder (he wrote) how much happier steady occupation makes us, and how smoothly we all get along.' Dr. John Carlyle was an early visitor, so Jane was not always alone during the seven hours between breakfast and dinner, and the day would sometimes end with Carlyle taking a stroll in their tiny garden, meditating gratefully on his home, under the stars.

In April, 1827, Mrs. Welsh, whose tenants at Craigenputtock were in arrears with their rent and unsatisfactory in other ways, paid a visit to Comley Bank, and, as Carlyle was looking for a farm on behalf of his brother Alexander, it was decided that the two men should visit the place. This was the first time since their marriage that the Carlyles had been apart, and a very affectionate letter from Mrs. Carlyle to her husband survives. The result was that the tenants were persuaded to quit, that Alexander Carlyle was to enter Craigenputtock in May, and the possibility was considered of his brother and his sister-in-law joining Alexander there. The immediate difficulty was want of accommodation, and the neglected condition of the property, which was really over-rented; but Mrs. Welsh was anxious now to see her daughter there, and Jane and Thomas fancied that a country life, to which he was always inclined, might modify their chronic biliousness. A family party at Craigenputtock, after half a year of marriage, was a proposition very different from the plan that Jane had ridiculed during her engagement. Beside, with Alexander Carlyle in occupation of the farm, and with Mrs. Welsh a neighbour anxious to supply some capital if necessary, the Carlyle family, as skilled masons, could be trusted to make any needed improvements to the landlord's house at the farm's door. Health and economy encouraged the change.

With his brother and his mother-in-law satisfied, and a further chat with Jeffrey, Carlyle abandoned his unfinished novel with relief, and set to work to enlighten the benighted inhabitants of these islands on the merits of German authors. His first contribution to the *Edinburgh*, on Richter, appeared in July (1827). This article led to a dinner where Carlyle made friends with Wilson (North) and several others of the same feather, and returned home about four in the morning to find that his young wife had been sitting up for him. So long as people talk about a young man, it does not much matter what they say. To have a reputation means little more than to become a topic of conversation for others. That it should have seemed a heresy in Scotland to cry up anyone but Scott, and that one a foreigner, was precisely the kind of irritation out of which reputation is first made. Jeffrey, who had a Review to edit and who wanted young blood to replace his veterans, was gratified. Mr. D. A. Wilson publishes a note in which Jeffrey said: 'You are a man of genius — proud and happy to know more of you. I fairly tell you that I think your taste vicious in some points, and your opinions of your German idols erroneous.' Such sincerity appealed to Carlyle, and his public career in letters may be dated from this essay.

The closing months of the first year of their married life could not have started more auspiciously for both of them. In July they left town and paid a visit to the farm, where it was arranged that the necessary improvements should be completed in time for them to move to Craigenputtock in May 1828. Another article for the *Edinburgh* was being written, and, when Carlyle approached Jeffrey in connexion with a professorship of literature and moral philosophy then vacant in London, the shrewd little man frankly confessed his doubts. After acknowledging the quality of Carlyle's gifts and learning, Jeffrey added: 'You are, to say it in one word, a *sectary* in taste and literature, and inspired by some of the zeal by which sectaries are distinguished — a zeal, that is, to magnify the distinguishing doctrines of your sect, and rather to aggravate than reconcile the points in which they depart from others.' [1] Jeffrey was always a tonic, and, when he heard with disappointment of the Craigenputtock plan, he observed: 'My impressions, perhaps somewhat selfish, [he got on capitally also with Mrs. Carlyle] are against it. I think it has been your misfortune not to have mixed sufficiently with intelligent men of various opinions, and open and intrepid minds.' Jeffrey also knew that chaff is the most persuasive kind of criticism. Even if Carlyle had not liked laughing, he was usually open to sincere criticism of himself. In a casual sentence from a letter, Carlyle sketches Jeffrey for us: 'There is a glance in the eye of the man which almost prompts you to take him in your arms.'

If the editor of the *Edinburgh* did not want too many doses of Germanic subjects, a kind fate was calling into existence a new *Foreign Review* in London which wel-

[1] *Carlyle to the French Revolution*, by D. A. Wilson, p. 30 (Kegan Paul, 1924).

comed them. Thus Carlyle was now assured of a market for his locally unmarketable German studies.

II

At the present day we turn to these early essays of Carlyle, if at all, in order first to discover the peculiarity of the appeal that German literature had for him. Long before the war, admiration for all things German had begun to seem excessive, though we had a very uneasy feeling that in research, in applied science, in the social organization which had redeemed factory-areas from squalor, that had eliminated the Cimmerian smoke which plunges Sheffield or Leeds into abominable pools of dark and filthy air (in order, to our bewilderment, to convert these industrial excreta into valuable by-products), and that had made the humming acres of Krupps a centre of amenity, the Germans had left us disgracefully behind. Only an academic set, however, still sat at the feet of the Teutonic idol, or believed that in metaphysics, in mastery of historic truth, in racial superiority, Prussia was the head of European civilization. Intellectual courage is not the chief virtue of an Englishman, and the admiration aroused by German thinkers in English men of letters, from Coleridge onward, set a fashion which it became respectable to follow, though, in the nation at large, this fashion often disguised a very natural fear at the successes, in the field and in material expansion, of the policy of Bismarck, the products of Krupp, and the achievements of German synthetic chemistry.

Undoubtedly, Carlyle was the English writer who did most and was earliest to popularize German ideas. Carlyle was not influenced by Coleridge, the unachieved Newman of the English church. Even in German metaphysics Coleridge was seeking not Goethe, not Germany but the Catholic Christ, apprehensible to the intellect through theology, whom the establishment had ignored. Carlyle, who was no churchman, had made his find by himself, and we need not go further here than Goethe for the origin of this fascination. The essays on Goethe, Richter, and on the State of German Literature were written in 1827 or 1828, and it is convenient to begin with the Goethe. In German Carlyle had, then, a specialty of use.

To start thus with Carlyle's writings is not only to start as he started, in due order of time, but to approach the coalfield of his prose by the easiest descent. Here, in these essays of the young man of thirty-odd years, is none of the turgid and fuliginous prose that (as we saw) in certain, and not uninspired, moments would emerge even in his love-letters, and was to be the characteristic of his future style. Here, the style is lucid, restrained, reasonable, ensuing persuasion, and not asking us to dodge our cowering heads from a pen wielded like a chopper, a chopper, even when it struck out golden sparks from the truth when this was hit. There is, too, something engaging in the sight of the dyspeptic Scottish dominie, usually so suspicious of urbanity, holding up to our reverent admiration the character and work of a man completely civilized. Teufelsdröckh may repel, amuse, or somewhat grotesquely attract us. With Goethe we feel no demur, for Goethe was some one whom many could admire beside Carlyle himself.

We note also that Carlyle, trying to unravel the puzzle that, he says, Goethe still presented to English-speaking people, takes the poet, and the form of Goethe's writings, for granted. The substance and the spirit of both are sufficient for Carlyle. This, of course, was his way, and yet to-day are we so sure that it is not the awkward beauty of the style rather than his few and simple ideas that maintain Carlyle's own reputation? — however blasphemous this question may appear to the veterans among his admirers, and however paradoxical to readers who now find his notions humdrum and his eccentricities of language too much like the German brass band of their youth. A critic, when introducing a foreign writer, is entitled to choose his point of emphasis, and Carlyle fixed on the marrow of the man. The mood in which Carlyle was writing is indicated early in his essay, where we find this sentence: 'The wisest, most melodious voice cannot in these days pass for a divine one; the word Inspiration still lingers, but only in the shape of a poetic figure, from which the once earnest, awful, and soul-subduing sense has vanished without return.' A keener intellect would have ended the sentence at the words, 'poetic figure.' The final clause not only revives the atmosphere of Hume, but the temptation of the nineteenth century to take its fashions in new dogmas for certainties. There is much of Carlyle's escape from rustic Calvinism into urban rationalism in these few words. To an extent beyond his ken, the mud of materialism was still on his feet. Moreover, when Goethe, in a testimonial, flattered Carlyle by praising his originality, Mr. D. A. Wilson, though a hero-worshipper, remarks: 'There was almost nothing new about him, and even the eccentricities of his style were mimicry.' From such a source this criticism is to be weighed.[1]

Having touched on the mood in which he approached Goethe and the Germans, we must note that his indifference to the artistic form of the German poet was not, in fact, indifference to form itself. On the contrary, it was a preference for the formless, for exuberance, *sturm und drang*. Otherwise, as J. R. Lowell has shown succinctly in an excellent criticism, the dominie who found no artistic example in Goethe

[1] *Carlyle to the French Revolution*, by D. A. Wilson, p. 46 (Kegan Paul, 1924).

would not have surrendered so easily to the extravagance of Richter, whom, by the way, De Quincey
also preferred. This surrender is interesting, for if we,
too, confine ourselves to the marrow of Carlyle, we are
surprised to find that one so reverent of virtue should
have been blind to the virtues most wanting in himself.
Of these, to retain his favourite moral category, temperance was the sum. Fortitude was his all in all. In
these early essays, moreover, there is a core of sweetness, a humour as tender as a rough man's caress.
Time was to show the suburbanity of supposing moral
purpose to be the prime quality of a work, as if the root
were more than its flower, as if the foundations did not
exist for the sake of the house, but the house for the
sake of its foundations. Carlyle disdained the habit of
perfection, on the provincial assumption that violence
is more trustworthy evidence of force of character than
restraint, and that indulgence in volcanic moral explosions shows more heroism than habitual obedience
in a thousand little things. In a soul open to grace,
holiness is but health in its perfection. So, too, in the
art of letters. That style which has been called the
sanctity of literature, is a habit of obedience to perfection so fastidious that it will admit nothing of the
ego that cannot be purged away, so that the vessel of
language shall be transparent as a lamp wherein form
and substance are as inseparable as the flame is from
a lighted candle. But criticism without charity is
corrupt.

The reasons for this defect in Carlyle are glaring.
Fate had weighted the scales against him. We do
better to remember the enormous disadvantages, the
clay in his blood, the Calvinism in his head, the dyspepsia in his stomach, which he overcame, than the
graces which remained beyond his utmost struggles.
The defects are mentionable because, in these early
essays, there is promise of a quality, and absence of a

mannerism, not destined to be fulfilled. Mr. George Moore's convenient distinction between Folk and Culture, between Gothic and Greek, is illustrated by Carlyle and Goethe. Gothic was more than Folk, because it created a perfect set of forms for a Folk-convention. Carlyle was Folk, but not Gothic. Even the classic of Romance he came to disdain. The reason why the temperance of these early essays was abandoned, why the sweetness turned sour, the laughter harsh, and the humour to railing is mainly a problem of biography, to be considered at a later date. For the moment, the wild rose of Annandale does not deserve its other name of canker, and we can enjoy its fragrance without the sorrow of remembering how short the day of the briar rose must be.

The passages from *Werther*, quoted by Carlyle, are poignant: indications of the inner life that he had been bringing to his reading of the novel; and all reading, to this tormented soul, was part of the autobiographical adventure by which he, even more than most young men, was seeking to discover the nature of his ego in order to transcend it, to thrust it without by defining it from the *outside*. It is worth notice, in an age obsessed by print, that, while the act of composition had set Goethe free, Carlyle was only set half free by reading Werther's sorrows. This is a capital instance of the waste that attends the passing of wine from one bottle to another, of the full good that comes from the practice of the arts, and of the partial and limited good that comes from the enjoyment of them. It seems to be a universal law that we can only accumulate vitality by spending it; and, because there is more spending in the creation than in the consumption both of spiritual and material things, so the joy of creation can never be passed on in its fullness; and the most sympathetic reception of the ideal spectator, say of a picture, or of the ideal reader of a book, cannot confer upon a consumer a tithe of that liberation of soul which has gone to the completion of a masterpiece. An English wit once put it prettily: 'I cannot [he wrote in an essay on some controversial theme] expect you (the reader) to agree with every word I have written, because I cannot expect you to spend as much time in reading my words as I have spent in writing them, or to know the world as I know it.' If the young Carlyle could learn but a fraction from the German novel which first revealed him to himself; if the author whom he idolized, even in the book of his nonage, was still in a state of grace beyond his understanding, then we must not entertain exaggerated hopes of the educative power of good books.

It was (dare one say, naturally?) the serenity of Goethe that Carlyle reverenced: a complete man, he called him, a man the full master of himself. Far off, like a fixed star above him, Carlyle discerned Goethe, serene but remote. In the rays from that altitude a serene reverence was born. The idea of this essay is sweet. Its foundation is solid. We observe, however, Carlyle alive to, but unmoved by, the fusion of substance with form in Goethe. Carlyle was ready to acquire, if he could, the wisdom that shone so serenely; but his perception of the unity of the whole is intellectual, not imaginative. The classic simplicity of the German poet begets no emulation in the Scotsman. We find a mental appetite for it. Psychic appetency is not there. Goethe was the sign-post, rather than the way, by which Carlyle came to German literature; nor was the English poet yet born who could have warned him, as this poet was to discover late in life, of an essential difference. 'Long I mistook seeing the end for being in the way.' The way was provided for Carlyle by the violently contrasting Richter.

For the most revealing of these early essays, for the essay, indeed, which is also intrinsically the best, we must turn to that on Jean Paul Friedrich Richter, an essay akin to the opening pages of the *Life of Schiller*. The Goethe, timely, courageous, and helpful as it was, good as it remains, is yet ill-defined, vague, half-fumbling, half-unrealized. His hero is still too near to Carlyle to have become capable of 'recollection in tranquillity.' The halo, dimly descried about Goethe's head, is not distinguished from the haze of its aura. Nor is the reason hard to find. The two men were of different temper. Even if the Dark Angel had assumed the same form for both of them, the German Jacob had closed with his adversary, and pinned him till he had been compelled to bless; while the Scotsman had been only capable of defiance: an act previous to the bout, in which the wrestlers have not closed. Carlyle was not, and was not destined to be, like the Hellenist, a complete, serene, and wise man. He was intended rather to show how far an incomplete, unquiet, ill-balanced man could hope, by honest struggles, to find some accommodation for his difficulties. None need despair who is familiar with Carlyle. If, indeed, in the rhythm of human history, mankind was descending a slope at the time of Carlyle's birth; if the change from the crest to the trough is not yet over, and if, therefore, unhealthy souls are as typical of to-day as more whole-some tempers were in the communion of the thir-teenth, and as more splendid individual specimens were familiar in the fifteenth, century, then, for many, an heroic struggler against the tide of his time may offer a more apprehensible character than any victor. As a child is a child's best companion; as the ill are more compassionate to the ill, and the healthy more wholesome to the healthy, so, perhaps, the best physi-cian for our day is rather one who has suffered from our complaint and who has carried our burden. If so, in England at least, where the limbs are vigorous but the heart is sick, Goethe may have to wait longer than

Carlyle before he shall be rediscovered.[1]   Greek literature slept for a thousand years, and might have
offered little to the ages of faith. Carlyle need wait no
longer, probably, than another century, until, that is,
the anti-Romantic Movement, now visibly rising, in
its turn shall have come full circle at the end of another
hundred years; the watchword, from being (as we
hear) back to Dryden and to Pope and even to
St. Thomas Aquinas, may have changed to back to
Carlyle and Richter, back even to Victor Hugo!

Carlyle, the man of many parts, could not assimilate
the whole of Goethe. This can be clearly seen when
the style of the essays on Goethe and on Richter are
compared with one another. In the first, Carlyle
gives the faith that is in him. He fails to give sufficient,
sound, and convincing reasons for that faith. The
result is that he seems to be writing round his subject
rather than upon it: to cry 'lo, see,' and, when the reader
asks 'see what? ' to repeat his enraptured exclamation.

The essay upon Richter, on the other hand, is as
clear as noonday. Like a hound slipped from the leash,
Carlyle, with one bound, is on the scent of his quarry,
and he does not swerve until he has run his wayward
beast to ground, under our feet, in its own earth, where
the pursuer proves no foe but a happy, friendly, contented companion. Richter and Carlyle were two of a
kind. Carlyle's sympathy is perfect; his detachment
that of a lover to whom the flaws in the beloved are
very dear. His response is spontaneous. The temper
of the twain is one. Carlyle's essay on Richter is probably the best criticism, of equal scope, that any foreigner has written. Writing about Richter, he is seeing
his own image in a German soul, and few delights are
keener to a foreigner fond of travel. Carlyle loves the
molten lava of Richter's smouldering prose, so like a

[1] Cf. Goethe's *Faust*, by F. Melian Stawell and G. Lowes Dickinson,
1929.

swell at sea in its ever-changing and amorphous shapes. He is indulgent to the very slaps and buffets of these waters. He enjoys being unexpectedly drenched from a wave that seemed to be subsiding; to lurch and to laugh; to be uplifted; to be thrown. Like an ancient mariner in a squall, Carlyle, we feel, is at last in his element. He is indulgent to the very scum on the surface of Richter's books; to their far-fetched titles; their medley of content, their erratic discursions from the main theme; their grotesque humour, their substantial earnestness; to the prophetic but night-marish visions, sib to his own. We do not need to look for Carlyle in the qualities of Richter's work. Carlyle is as much on their surface as a school of porpoises at sea, and as happy in his tumbling. It is impossible *not* to think of him while he writes or quotes.

Thus, the best criticism of this essay is quotations:

Genius will reconcile men to much. By degrees, Jean Paul began to be considered not a strained crackbrained mixture of enthusiast and buffoon, but a man of infinite humour, sensibility, force and penetration.... His friends he must have loved as few do.

... the whole is one tissue of metaphors and similes and allusions to all the Provinces of Earth, Sea, Air; interlaced with epigrammatic breaks, vehement bursts, or sardonic turns, interjections, quips, puns, and even oaths. A perfect Indian jungle it seems; a boundless, unparalleled imbroglio; nothing on all sides but darkness, dissonance, confusion worse confounded. Then the style of the whole corresponds, in perplexity and extravagance, with that of the parts.... often the panting reader toils after him in vain; or, baffled and spent, indignantly stops short, and retires, perhaps for ever.... There are rays of the keenest truth, nay steady pillars of scientific light rising through this chaos: Is it in fact a chaos; or may it be that our eyes are of finite, not of infinite vision, and have only missed the plan?

... an intellectual Colossus ... a humourist from his inmost soul.

Humour is a sort of inverse sublimity; exalting, as it were, into our affections what is below us, while sublimity draws down into our affections what is above. The former is still rarer, and, as a test of genius, still more decisive.

[After Shakespeare, *not* here sovereign, Swift, Ben Jonson], Sterne follows next; our last specimen of humour, and, with all his faults, our best; our finest, if not our strongest.

Unite the sportfulness of Rabelais, and the best sensibility of Sterne, with the earnestness, and even in slight portions, the sublimity of Milton; and let the mosaic brain of old Burton give forth the workings of this strange union, with the pen of Jeremy Bentham!

The beaten paths of Literature lead the safeliest to the goal; and the talent pleases us most which submits to shine with new gracefulness through old forms.... All this is true, and Richter must lose of our esteem in proportion, [but these faults, allied to his best merits] are little likely to be imitated.

In his *Dreams* there is a mystic complexity, a gloom, and amid the dim gigantic half-ghastly shadows, gleamings of a wizard splendour, which almost recall to us the visions of Ezekiel.

An intense and continual faith in man's immortality and native grandeur accompanies him.

He has doubted, he denies, yet he believes.

Time has a strange contracting influence on many a widespread fame, yet of Richter we will say that he may survive much. There is in him that which does not die; that Beauty and Earnestness of soul, that spirit of Humanity, of Love and mild Wisdom, over which the vicissitudes of mode have no sway.

Richter will live, Carlyle thinks, with our own Sir Thomas Browne, and Hooker and Taylor, 'like a cluster of date-trees, with its greensward and well of water, to refresh the pilgrim, in the sultry solitude, with nourishment and shade.' Well, if the temperamental attraction is understandable, we may also note the spell that German literature has often cast on young Englishmen, even of Gallic sympathies. Turn from the young Carlyle to the young Meredith, and ask

yourself whether, if we owe the rare essay on the Comic
Spirit to Molière, do we not also owe the Shaving of
Shagpat, the Aristophanic laughter that delighted in
the Great Mel and in Richmond Roy, the lumbering
periods of the prose, like thunderclouds split with
lightning, something even discernible in such poems as
the Nuptials of Attila and in the great symphonic ode
in honour of the South-west Wind, to Meredith's
youthful schooling at Mannheim? The truth, possibly, is this: the German tongue looks, even without
its spines of Gothic letters, rough and prickly as a por-
cupine to English eyes; and, when spoken, its gutturals
sound harsh and rasping to our ears. The revelation
of its music comes through singing. At this moment
I do not vividly recall a chorus in Wagner's operas, but
eight years have not effaced the memory of the choral
songs that are sung in course of the Passion Play at
Ober-Ammergau. The memory that abides is of a
language which, far from being harsh, gave to its
abundant consonants the rich quality of vowels, so
that, just as Italian is more melodic to the eye than to
the ear, when read to oneself than when heard spoken
or sung, so, conversely, German, rough to the glance,
and harsh in conversation, opens its harmonies chiefly
to the singing voice. Can it be that the harmony
further from the surface, the harmony that hides from
all but loving eyes, is, once recognized, proportion-
ally dearer? If so, Carlyle may have reflected, in his
own English, a beauty beyond the appreciation of all
not as deeply versed as he in his German models.

The essay on Richter, however, must not lead us
astray. It may, in truth, have been the essay which
gave to Carlyle the most personal pleasure in the
writing. The most useful of the three, that on the
State of German Literature (1827), best tells us why
German literature meant, and was to continue to
mean, so much to him. No better, wider, more per-

suasive introduction, of equal brevity, to German letters could be imagined. Its historical survey has prevented it from growing out of date. We see the future historian finding himself as the vivid descriptive artist of past epochs.

As he had praised the colours on his own palette in the rolls of paint in Richter's prose, so he begins, in this third essay, to criticize some of his own foibles in Franz Horn, the German literary historian. 'His stream of meaning, uniformly clear and wholesome in itself, will not flow quietly along its channel; but is ever and anon spurting itself up into epigrams and antithetic jests.'

In answer to a Frenchman's question: Si un Allemand peut avoir de l'esprit? Carlyle replies 'who was it that gave to mankind the three great elements of modern civilization: Gunpowder, Printing, and the Protestant Religion?' Is it only, or mainly, the passage of a century that provokes a smile of irony at these words? Carlyle thinks that 'perhaps something better than *esprit*' was to be found among the Germans. He did not take a view of Voltaire to be compared with that of Blake, who hated him.[1] Carlyle was little attracted by the French. It is not indifference, however, but charity that makes us reserve our complete confidence from a Calvinist who cannot be just to a Catholic and, therefore, to an anti-clerical; for what can such know of French history? — even less can we think of a French Catholic who fails in justice to the author of the *Institutes*, another Frenchman. It is enough here to remember that Carlyle was displaying the virtues of an

[1] Cf. p. 159 *ante*: 'Crabb Robinson would also visit Blake, and his record of their conversations preserves the fine saying about Voltaire: that he was commissioned to expose the natural sense of the Bible, and that he told Blake: "I blasphemed the Son of Man, and it shall be forgiven me, but my enemies blasphemed the Holy Ghost in me and it shall not be forgiven them."' (*William Blake*, English Men of Letters series, by Osbert Burdett, p. 179.)

underrated Germany to a world that, he thought, had overestimated France.

If he shrank from the wit of Jane Welsh, he naturally shrank from Voltaire's, and yet the 'good works' of the philanthropist of Ferney might surely have suggested some of the constructive seriousness that lay in the wittiest of mankind. Let us remember that the wit of Voltaire could even inspire masterpieces in other people, that his practical benevolence remains an example of the height to which private statesmanship can go. Many visitors to the Louvre find their way to the Victory of Samothrace, nobly enthroned above the steps in front of it and between the two flights of stairs that flank its sides; still more pass round it on their way to where the Venus of Milo stands, in easy majesty, at the end of the long gallery which, like an avenue of sculpture, draws their eyes to her at its far end; but few, in comparison, are drawn to the *Comédie Française* for the sake of Houdon's masterpiece. Yet the statue of Voltaire which dominates the salle of the famous theatre is the most vivid piece of portrait-sculpture between Michael Angelo's figures of the Medici and Rodin's figure of Balzac. Voltaire, leaning forward in his marble chair, is more alive than life. The simplified folds of his robe seem to flow with intelligence; the left hand that rests upon the chair is in no marble sleep. It is a careless hand, caught between one movement and another, and only when we raise our eyes to the forward-peering face, alert with interest, as if to listen were to think and to think were to forestall, do we realize that each hand is, actually, a point of rest in the composition. Once seen, Houdon's statue of Voltaire seems the genius of French comedy, even in the *Théâtre Française* itself. It effaces, for more than the long and unforgettable first glance, even the effect of Molière; as Molière is subsumed by its vitality, so the music of Corneille and Racine appears to be subsumed in the beauty of the statue as a statue. Houdon was a fine artist, but, with Voltaire for his subject, he surpassed himself. The man who could inspire a statue more alive than life must have possessed a vitality of which the wit whereby he is best remembered could have been no more than the incandescence of his mind.

If Carlyle had been less suspicious of wit and intelligence, if he had had the biographer's grace to seek the finer justice in those types to which he was temperamentally least drawn, if, on the congenial ground of religious seriousness, he had had Blake's power to discriminate between the unholy spirit that Voltaire was searching and the Holy Spirit in Voltaire that directed his arrows, Carlyle would have given more than a passing glance at the genius of France embodied in the bony little figure, blazing with intelligence, electric with nerves. The contrast that it offers to his German heroes would have thrown *their* characteristic virtues into a higher light. Carlyle could paint the contrast between his admirations and his hatreds. He was inclined to neglect the contrast between one kind of virtue and another. Contrasts were his strength: distinctions eluded him.

Gunpowder is physical; printing is material; the Protestant Religion was a moral protest at its root. Have either of these admitted inventions done more for the human spirit than the *esprit Gaulois*? Carlyle thought that the contribution of the latter had been fully, if not over fully, appreciated; yet a witty Frenchman himself might be the first person to ask if *esprit* is ever appreciated enough, if, indeed, France herself has not rather held the flame than fed the candle. It is here, in making the case for German letters less balanced than it need have been, that Carlyle becomes more the advocate than the critic. In this German pasture he was taking a holiday from the un-serious, as he took a holiday from her wit in the love of his wife.

In these essays we note good things of the sort not usually associated with their eventually famous author. For example, he defines a pedant to be 'a man who mistakes his own contrasted individuality for the type of human nature, and deals with whatever contradicts *him* as if it contradicted *this*'; a critic to be one who transposes himself 'into the author's point of vision [to make] a survey of the author's means and objects as they lay before himself, and a just trial of these by rules of universal application'; best of all: 'art is to be loved, not because of its effects, but because of itself: not because it is useful for spiritual pleasure, or even for moral culture, but because it is Art, and the highest in man, and the soul of all beauty. To inquire after its *utility*, would be like inquiring after the utility of a God or ... the utility of Virtue and Religion.' The latter-day pamphlet on *this* theme is not included in Carlyle's later volume of that title. With Ruskin intervening on the opposite side, it was left for Whistler to affirm it, and Whistler's lecture obscures the simple truth by associating with it an extreme view of the individualist doctrine in order to lay the earnest Ruskin, whose fate it was to advance the most doubtful doctrines of beauty in the most musical of poetic prose, by the heels. In these essays there are flashes of discernment that seem to have been flashes, and no more. The seeds of Carlyle's more familiar gospel, and of some prejudices that became pronounced, are more apparent.

He compares French influence, 'a baleful incubus,' with the 'far nobler mind of Germany,' in spite of his gratitude to Madame de Staël. He defends German letters from the charge of bad taste, from 'displaying, in particular, a certain wild and headlong temper, which seizes on all things too hastily and impetuously; weeps, storms, loves, hates, too fiercely and vociferously, delighting in coarse excitements, such as flaring con-

trasts, vulgar horrors, and all sorts of showy exaggeration'; and he clinches his defence ingeniously: 'Two
nations that agree in estimating Shakespeare as the
highest of all poets can differ in no essential principle,
if they understood one another, that relates to poetry.'
Then comes a passage that remains, alas, of general application to poor old England; an argument that we
cannot escape, a fact that we cannot deny, a fashion
more worthy of Philistia than of Great Britain:

The German authors...are considerably better situated
than our own. Their booksellers, it is true, cannot pay as ours
do; yet, there as here, a man lives by his writings.... No case
like our own noble Otway's has met us in their biographies;
Boyces and Chattertons [and Mary Webbs and James Thom-
sons!] are much rarer in German than in English history.
But farther, and what is more important: From the number of
universities, libraries, collections of art, museums, and other
literary and scientific institutions of a public or private nature,
we question whether the chance which a meritorious man of
letters has before him of obtaining some permanent appointment, some independent civic existence, is not a hundred to
one in favour of the German compared with the Englishman.
This is a weighty item, and indeed the weightiest of all; for it
will be granted that, for the votary of literature, the relation
of entire dependence on the merchants of literature is, at best,
and however liberal the terms, a highly questionable one. It
tempts him daily and hourly to sink from an artist into a man-
ufacturer; nay, so precarious, fluctuating and every way unsatisfactory must his civic and economic concerns become,
that too many of his class cannot even attain the praise of common honesty as manufacturers.

Since Carlyle's time, the merchants of literature have
been enlarged. To the publishers of books we must now
add the editors of great newspapers, who open their
columns regularly to literary journalism. A minor, and
at last almost self-supporting, literary activity is now
establishing itself by this means. The average quality of
this work is happily higher than its reward, and we all

owe too much to it to be ungrateful. Nevertheless the
work is fitter for young apprentices than for ripe pro-
fessionals; it is, for the most part, precarious; it is very
largely underpaid; and its effect upon its votaries is unfortunate. I have known a few of these writers; have
done some of their work myself; have known and
watched the progress of many more. Despite admiration for their quality, wonder at their endurance, envy
at their skill, to say nothing of personal affection for
friends and a lively appreciation of the good fellowship
that distinguishes them, I can think of none who has
not fallen short of the writer that he might have become if he could early have escaped from the drag of
this ghastly occupation. It is the destiny of such to attempt, in order to live at all, more than can fairly be
asked of him; to be always hurried; to do by the clock
that which can only be well done when time is second-
ary; to know a little of many books; to know none well
that he has not known before he started; to read too
much; to reflect too little; to know that sciolism will be
accepted for scholarship, readableness for style; to be
unable to decline work for which he has either relative
ignorance or personal distaste; to put speed before quality; to fear conciseness; to banish the idea of leisure
from his world; to cultivate competence as the highest
of literary virtues; to write when he has nothing to say;
and, when he has, to be unable, from want of time, to
say it with all the beauty, and lucidity, and brevity of
which he would otherwise be capable. Fleet-street is
like a whale that swallows many Jonahs, and unfortunately it does not regurgitate them whole; half the artist
in each remains, a journalistic chyme, in the whale's
belly. If the great Sainte-Beuve himself, in the princely
condition of having a whole week in which to prepare
one weekly essay, groaned under the devastating regularity of that burden, how shall others, of less vocation
and with many times his load, hope to survive without

self-injury? The only remedy is higher pay with more exacting qualifications, and the latter are such as would elude any inartistic test. Indeed, in the England which enables its principal literary weekly journal to *boast*, with shocking justice so far as figures go, of 'an average circulation exceeding 30,000 copies,' in a population of forty millions who have had the benefit of half a century of State education, what remedy can be found? There is none, except that recommended by Carlyle: to follow the example of Germany and endow a number of posts that could be offered without disgrace to our younger men of letters. Only so can the tragic line of our Chattertons and Mary Webbs be intercepted; our Blakes be saved from isolation, and ourselves be spared the spectacle of a Wilde in plush knee-breeches, a youthful Shaw in 'rational dress' courting the attention of the town. English letters have survived in spite, and not because, of our sacrificing everything to popular talents, and of our heaping on the second-rate the rewards that are the complement of a Thomson's despair, a Chatterton's suicide. This passage in Carlyle's essay has lost none of its pertinence in a hundred years.

The excellence after which the Germans strove, Carlyle tells us, was 'a certain clear, light, unaffected elegance, of a higher nature than French elegance, it might be, yet to the exclusion of all very deep or genial qualities.' He defines this rather vague attribution as follows:

They resemble English writers of the same, or perhaps an earlier period, more than any other foreigners: apart from Pope, whose influence is visible enough, Beattie, Logan, Wilkie, Glover, unknown perhaps to any of them, might otherwise have almost seemed their models. Goldsmith also would rank among them; perhaps in regard to true poetic genius, at their head, for none of them has left us a Vicar of Wakefield; though, in regard to judgment, knowledge, general talent, his place would scarcely be so high.

We should have to take down some dusty volumes from our shelves to appraise this verdict, and we feel on more solid ground when Carlyle affirms that it is in 'the practice or science of criticism' that his Germans excel. By this he meant that they had passed beyond questions of style and the inference of a poet's nature from the qualities of his poetry, to poetry's very nature; from the methods of a man to 'the more mysterious mechanism [by which] Shakespeare organized his dramas, and gave life to his Ariel and his Hamlet.' This, he concludes, is 'the task of criticism as the Germans understand it': a far higher task, we are assured, than 'the systems of Boileau and Blair.' To these critics, poetic beauty was underived (a divine madness as Plato fancied), and Carlyle contrasts their assumption with the English theory, 'from Hume to Alison,' that proceeded from externals. Fichte is especially praised, indeed, for having postulated a Divine idea in the universe, of which men of letters were the interpreters to their fellows, forming a kind of priesthood of the Muses, that third order at which Newman hinted, and which Lionel Johnson even dramatically attributed to Newman's talk.

According to Carlyle, traces of that ethereal vision were discernible in our own poetry of the Elizabethan age, and still irradiate Shakespeare's *Tempest*. He held that this light had become eclipsed for us, and commended Tieck, Richter, Herder, Schiller, and particularly Goethe, 'combining French clearness with old English depth,' for uniting once again the Real to the Ideal in a contemporary poetry not to be matched outside Germany. With us, there had been 'a partial abandonment of poetry in favour of political and philosophical Illumination.' Bentham was enthroned upon Parnassus, and the abracadabra of utilitarianism was the respectable philosophy of the day. He then passes to a not very satisfactory defence of mysticism, the second count in the charge against the German writers, as bad taste and extravagance had been the first, and explains that the popular difference between Kantism and cloudy cant is small, however ridiculous. German philosophy is defended by the argument advanced on behalf of German criticism: 'The Kantist, in direct contradiction to Locke and all his followers, both of the French and English or Scotch school, commences from within, and proceeds outwards,' and the works of Dugald Stewart are declared to be 'the best preparation for studying those of Kant.' In those days, one was either a mechanist, with Hume, or a mystic, with Christianity. A disquisition follows on one of Patmore's favourite texts:

> 'Who search for truth and do not start from God,
> For a long journey should be shod.'

The final conclusion is this: 'That in the opinion of a Kantist, the French are of all European nations the most gifted with Understanding, and the most destitute of Reason; that David Hume had no forecast of the latter; and that Shakespeare and Luther dwelt perennially in its purest sphere.' With the caution that, to-day, we should write Reason where Carlyle wrote Understanding if we are to appreciate the distinction in his mind, his position in respect of German literature is easily intelligible. Indeed, the science of criticism can never be very scientific because words change their meaning in this way.

We have spent some time on these early essays, because it is ever best to make a famous writer's foundations clear; to begin at his beginning; and, incidentally, to treat those of his writings which, superseded by more celebrated productions, have become with time dwarfed, or less known. Beside, even in men of smaller stature, the earlier writings contain the later in germ, and it is sometimes an accident of circumstance, a question of biography, which tendency shall develop, and which be arrested. Carlyle had been defining himself to himself in these early essays, had seen his own reflection in a German looking-glass, was discovering his talent for descriptive history, and only now needed to compose a spiritual autobiography in order to cast out the ego that tormented him. Established in the Reviews of Edinburgh and London, he was now set on the literary path that lay ahead. Through the stages of despair, of dominie, of Edinburgh Reviewer, he had become a writer of promise on his move to Craigenputtock.

III

While these and other essays, on Werner and the like, were being written, the last months that the Carlyles spent in Edinburgh ebbed away. The time was mainly memorable for its human interests, for visits from De Quincey, an elfish little creature whose five feet were 'mostly legs' so that 'he resembled a pair of tongs.' [1] Mrs. Carlyle, who grew fond of him, said 'what wouldn't one give to have him in a box and take him out to talk.' Carlyle sketched his appearance: 'A most gentle and sensible face, only that the teeth are destroyed by opium and the little bit of an underlip projects like a shell.' De Quincey would bring his children of an evening to Comley Bank, and when the children departed and De Quincey fell ill in his lonely lodgings, Mrs. Carlyle found him, brought him to her house, and nursed him till he had recovered. That Mrs. Carlyle should love the elfin creature was natural in a woman of her motherly instincts and with her zest for conversation, but it was fine of Carlyle to forget De Quincey's assault on *Wilhelm Meister* and also to take him to his heart.

Mrs. Carlyle could always make friends with the

[1] *Carlyle to the French Revolution*, by D. A. Wilson, p. 39 (Kegan, Paul).

men; with the women she was not equally successful. Her numerous past and present friendships with men were idealized rapidly in her imagination, and it is amusing to find Mr. Wilson declaring that Jeffrey only made himself so agreeable to conserve his friendship with Carlyle himself. Though Mrs. Jeffrey and Mrs. Carlyle disliked each other as only women can, one fancies that Jeffrey did not find his diplomacy at all disagreeable. In fact, Mrs. Carlyle had some temperamental affinity with her romantic and flirtatious friend, Miss Jewsbury, a spinster who, failing to find a husband, threw restraint and decorum to the winds whenever an unattached gentleman appeared. The contempt that her conduct aroused in Mrs. Carlyle was sincere, because Jane, with a better head and a finer taste, could indulge a similar propensity without making herself ridiculous. The professional Aspasia, with wit and brains, is revolted by the amateur antics of a foolish man-hunter.

It was in Edinburgh that Mrs. Carlyle tasted, for the first time, the sweets of the intellectual society that she valued, for which, in some sense, she had married, and in which alone she could shine without self-reproach.

CHAPTER SIX

CRAIGENPUTTOCK AND 'A WORK OF GENIUS'

I

'NO such frightful place' was the verdict of Jane after she had been installed some three months at Craigenputtock. 'The solitude' she went on in a letter to Bessy Stodart 'is not so irksome as one might think. If we are cut off from good society, we are also delivered from bad; the roads are less pleasant to walk on than the pavement of Prince's Street, but we have horses to ride, and, instead of shopping and making calls, I have bread to bake and chickens to hatch. I read and work, and talk with my husband, and never weary.' On these horses we must pause for a moment.

Carlyle had alluded to the precarious health of his wife in his home-letters from Edinburgh, and had hoped that riding 'a smart pony' would make her fit again. According to his latest biographer, however, the last medical evidence available during her lifetime suggested to her doctors 'that, from her early teens, she had suffered from an internal trouble peculiar to her sex, which riding would make worse.' [1] A partisan of hers would say that the medical charge preferred, on no good evidence, against the husband was now being changed, by his admirers, into a parallel charge against his suffering wife. A biographer of the childless pair will admit the probability of some physical defect in one of them, and will be content to see what support Mr. Wilson's contention has, since the rumour about Carlyle's impotence has no sufficient evidence to support it. On the minor matter of general health, they

[1] *Carlyle to the French Revolution*, by D. A. Wilson, p. 50.

clearly suffered, equally, from bad diagnosis and disastrous medicines.

The entry of Jane into practical housekeeping had begun by easy stages. Edinburgh was the gentle slope by which the problems of Craigenputtock were reached. At Comley Bank Carlyle had been obliged to be very careful about his diet. Jane began by baking bread. She used to say that her first attempt at brown bread was made with awe. After she had mixed the dough and watched it rise, she sat opposite the oven-door feeling, as she told Miss Jewsbury long after, like Benvenuto Cellini while he overlooked the placing of the cast of Perseus in the furnace. When, at last, the oven-door was opened, and the loaf appeared, brown and crusty, light and dry, she felt very proud and delighted. For greater mysteries, she preferred an artist's solitude. The same friend tells us that once, when a suet pudding was in hand, she beguiled the servant out of the house, locked herself into the kitchen, weighed and measured like the amateur she was, for your born cook 'judges' only, and behold! the pudding looked good and round, like the earth at the end of God's labour upon it.

At Craigenputtock, one was almost entirely self-supporting: no shops, no supplies in emergency, no easy remedy for oversights at the eleventh hour. Everything depended upon foresight and preparation, and every housekeeper will know what that means. At Craigenputtock a yard divided their dwelling from the farmhouse. The contents of the Carlyles' larder were all alive. A cook there had often to become her own butcher, and she or her maid milkman and digger of spuds. A horse, a cow, some fowls, some swine, were the housekeeper's principal resources. Except in extremity of weather, the tending of a live larder can be very good fun. Jane's exaggerated anecdotes are by no means all tragic. Indeed, her imagination could not have invested her recollected endeavours with so much life if her imagination had not already vivified them in her practice. Even the solitude was an artistic creation in her memory. The house stood on a moor, shaggy with rocks, and a steep green hill rose behind it. The stillness, Jane said, was so intense that, when she went out of her door, she could hear the sheep cropping the grass, as they looked at her with innocent wonder. Her red-letter day came once a week, with the arrival of her letters. Other days had surprises and excitements of a different kind. Of the countless stories that her memory preserved, two give a picture of her life in summer and in winter.

In the height of summer she once asked a farm-hand to fetch her a bottle of yeast. The fellow returned, scared and empty-handed. When Jane asked him what had happened, he said that he would do anything lawful to please her, but begged not to be sent on such an uncanny errand again. The stuff in the bottle had worked and worked till the bottle flew out of his hand, and had 'gane into a ditch' where he had left it in terror. When the weather or the absence of a messenger made it impossible to send to Dumfries for butcher's meat, she would cast her eyes upon her poultry: a breed of long-legged hens, and then, with a long rod in her hand, would advance into the yard, to point out those ready for killing, feeling herself the while, she said, like Fouquier-Tinville pricking his list of the condemned. We must rather share her sympathy for her hens than that of those who say that Craigenputtock was her scaffold.

In winter matters could be frightful enough, but even the worst crisis of a housekeeper is not a tragedy. The following story, here condensed from Miss Jewsbury, is so vivid and so human in its physical distress that countless other town-dwellers who have tried the country in the winter, will feel that it has happened to themselves.

One hard winter, Grace, the servant-girl, gone for a day's visit to her home, was held up by the snow and could not get back. The next morning, therefore, Jane was up early to light the fires and prepare breakfast. With the ardour of inexperience her quick eyes noticed that the elaborate steel-grates in the house were in need of scouring. She made this her first task, and then searched for food for the fire. Indoors there was none, and this meant crossing the yard to an outhouse. But the front door, which led to the yard, refused to open. It was frozen. She called Carlyle, who with his utmost force burst the ice, whereupon a snowdrift, six feet high, fell into the hall. Carlyle found a spade, dug a path to the wood-house, fetched the fuel, and then departed. While the fire was drawing, the elements of breakfast had to be fashioned into food, the bread made, the butter churned, the coffee ground. All this was successfully accomplished, and, fortified by the meal, Jane then started on the house, for the return of her servant was evidently very doubtful. In her absence, the un-milked cow was a perplexing problem, for the farmer's wife could not be asked to lend a hand after the first day, and its melancholy lowing compelled Jane to go to its relief. She had had no experience of milking cows, but at length her caressing fingers were rewarded, and she used her persuasive voice also to coax its milk into her pan.

The snow lay; the servant could not travel; and gradually Mrs. Carlyle, emboldened by success, attacked even more ambitious tasks. She had tidied the house, cleaned the brasses, but had hitherto quailed before the large kitchen, which, by now, badly needed to be scoured. With two pans of hot water beside her, Jane knelt on the floor and began her scrubbing. She started near the hearth, and described a large clean circle about the armchair, summoned Carlyle, and asked him to light his pipe and remark her progress. He regarded her, we are told, benevolently, and, from time to time, gave her words of encouragement. Half

the huge floor was soon cleaned, when a mysterious
gurgling arrested her, became louder, was followed by
a plop on the fire, whereupon a thick stream of oily
black fluid poured from the chimney, flooded the floor,
and with unerring instinct obliterated with its ooze the
large patch that she had cleaned, by which time the
fire itself was totally extinguished. The fierce fire that
she had made to heat her water had melted the snow at
the chimney's mouth, and had brought down in spate
the soot below it. This reverse was too much, and Jane
burst into tears. That same night, the absent Grace
returned, after incredible efforts, to clasp Mrs. Carlyle
in her arms, and, between laughter and tears, to say:
'O my dear mistress, I deemed ye were dead.'

A glimpse of her domestic strategy in an emergency
must complete the picture. One day the postman
brought a letter from Lord Jeffrey, saying that he proposed to bring his family, and some visitors, to Craigenputtock. Though he had written in good time, the
weekly post only delivered his letter on the morning of
their arrival. The larder, naturally, was unequal to this
sudden call. Mrs. Carlyle, therefore, mounted Larry,
galloped to Dumfries, and was home with the necessary
supplies in time to welcome her party of visitors; and we
may believe Miss Jewsbury when she adds: 'There was
no trace of her thirty-mile ride except the charming
history she made of it.' A storyteller's faculty can rob a
crisis of its terrors in anticipation of the effects that these
offer to his art. Carlyle demurred to some details
in Miss Jewsbury's recollections, in which he thought
the tragic emphasis to be misplaced, but his second
thoughts upon them were warmer than his first, and
there is no doubt that they preserve the spirit of the
original teller and of her adventures. Even the stroke
which brings the author before us, comfortably seated,
pipe in mouth, and uttering encouraging words to his
kneeling spouse, has the tender irony of the handy wife

upon her less practical husband, and there is as much affection as humour in the contrast.

A country life, moreover, offers to townsmen exquisite pleasures, and the stories that survive are by no means all of tragi-comedy. Larry could work in harness, and we hear of long drives at night between Templand or Scotsbrig and Craigenputtock, when the pair, happy in their companionable solitude, would conclude a day's journey under the stars, sometimes lost in the beauty of lonely moor and shimmering sky, sometimes in trepidation of the dark, when Carlyle's hands upon the reins seemed less reassuring than Larry's animal prudence. In his absences to London, she would sometimes make these long journeys alone, and was once benighted, having lost her way and come full circle to her starting-point. It is abundantly clear that her life in this lonely spot was a nursery of some happy memories, even though many of its experiences were exacting at the time. Carlyle's own verdict upon this phase of Jane's married life was this: 'The saving charm of her life at Craigenputtock, which to another young lady of her years might have been gloomy and vacant, was that of conquering the innumerable Practical Problems that had arisen for her there.' Mental stress does not come of such things to a capable young woman. If there were any signs of it at this season, they would have arisen in connexion with her husband. What was happening to him upstairs, while Jane was abundantly occupied about the house?

He looked back on this time himself with the satisfaction that solitude and productive work furnish so fully to an author. 'I found (he recalls in his Reminiscences) that I could do fully twice as much work there in a given time, as with my best effort was possible in London — such the interruptions etc. Once, in the winter time, I remember counting that, for three months, there had not any stranger, even a beggar, called at Craigenputtock door. In summer we had sparsely visitors.'

His work was his companion, the best that any writer can have; but housekeeping is the drudgery, not the satisfaction, of a normal wife and would-be mother. The nursery is her study, as his children are his dreams; and, after three years of marriage, Mrs. Carlyle was childless still. The more we are assured that Jane was never long without domestic help, the more we are asked to believe that no unduly arduous duties were laid upon her, the more insistently we ask how far her moments of leisure could be satisfying? A writer, baulked by some sterility of achieving his work, would hardly find complete content in an overflowing nursery. Suppose him condemned to the drudgery of research or even of translation, would games with his children entirely content *him*? Jane was a sympathetic listener to Carlyle's writings; his future was as the future of a favourite son; his moods as preoccupying as the ups and downs of infancy; but he was, at best, but half an infant to her heart, and it is the youngest child, the latest baby, that is a mother's satisfaction. The intellect is a man's toy, and women watch us playing with ideas instead of rattles: only, we are less dependent on them in the later game. It is this independence of them that makes all the difference. The appeal of appeals to a woman is the appeal of complete helplessness. Their centre of gravity must lie in another, and they are jealous of the very work which makes a man independent of themselves. The lot of an author's wife must always be exacting: that of a childless one can be cruel. When a woman happens to be half an artist, she is torn two opposite ways. When she is not but married to an artist, only children can supply the double loss of dependence upon herself that an artist-husband means.

This situation, fundamental as it was, was further complicated by extraneous, but inalterable, circumstances. Carlyle's marriage had eased his burden, but it had not relieved him entirely from his moods nor cured his chronic dyspepsia. He was certainly better since his marriage, but he was neither changed nor cured. An artist or an author will always labour under some difficulties of temperament, and his health, as a rule, will be precarious, if only because he lives so much upon his nerves. An even greater problem is that of the temperament called artistic, because this last has not the outlet and relief of productive work. Mrs. Carlyle was one of its victims; her health was always precarious; and she was a disappointed mother as well. Even in the early happiness of her Edinburgh days there had been some ominous symptoms. The major satisfaction of her new existence was teased by some invisible want. In the middle of February 1827, a contented letter to her mother contained the following clause:

'*Alone* we are never weary. If I have not Jean's enviable gift of talking, I am at least among the best listeners in the kingdom, and my husband has always something interesting and instructive to say....With "all conceivable implements for ladies' work," with books, with a piano, though neither my playing nor my singing seems to give Mr. C. much delight... it is my husband's worst fault that I will not, or cannot, speak. Often when he has talked for an hour without answer, he will beg for some signs of life on my part, and the only sign I can give is a little kiss.'

This is an odd avowal for a contented young wife whose conversation was distinguished for wit and sprightliness, and it is made at a time when the wistfulness of accomplished wedlock ought to be merging into hopes of the motherhood that should lie beyond. Plainly, Mrs. Carlyle had not enough of the right kind to do, and the triviality of her makeshifts ought to have been giving way to the genuine satisfactions of maternity.

In some degree, therefore, the physical activities demanded of Jane at Craigenputtock must have proved a relief, for, on the whole, she was more active than studious by nature; and the social activities of a Madame Récamier, the ideal solution for her with a nursery in the background, were not within reach. At the same time, however, as she was more occupied with practical problems, she became lonelier in other ways. Carlyle now had a bedroom to himself, because he suffered from sleeplessness and the slightest sound disturbed him. By day, he also began to withdraw into himself. At Craigenputtock she could no longer sit and watch him, for he not only wrote alone, which is understandable enough, but preferred to think alone, and sometimes took his dinner alone also. An intelligent woman soon learns that there are moods in which the best service that she can render to a writer is to leave him in his solitude. The times when he is unproductive, when his ideas will not take shape, when his imagination is fallow, make all familiar company exasperating to him. He does not want to be watched in this banality of mind. The ego that can be driven out by productive work returns to plague him, and, miserable in his own esteem, he shuns a near spectator of his misery. To appear in his household at such times is involuntarily to become a domestic spectacle; to answer harshly when he does not feel harsh; to appear bored with others when he is only intolerable to himself; to be thought irritable when he is only self-exasperated; to be condemned for silence when he would give anything to be able to speak. After one of these exposures he will return to his lair more wretched than ever, and the single consolation offered by his own room is that none will suffer there from his sufferings, or remark the unhappy contrast of his condition with their own. After weeks of such numbness, when self-solitude has become unbearable, and the desire to be taken out of himself may be intense, he may have grown incapable of attempting the remedy, shun outside society and even refuse agreeable invitations, because, unless the experiment prove successful in all respects, its failure will have made his ineptitude worse than before.

At Craigenputtock, Carlyle had all that he most needed, except the unattainable company of his muse. For the moment, she had withdrawn herself from him, and he had the horror of being left face to face with the ego whom his Review-writing had scotched but not killed. With all outside him a desert, he was driven to brood on his disease; for the ego is a disease worse than the Promethean vulture, since it is Prometheus preying on himself. To objectify the subject that should be used only as a transmitter, unconscious of its own part in the rays that it receives and should refract; to force a paralysed hand to describe the state of paralysis, to make Satan cast out Satan, is the hardest task of all. Yet the attempt must be made, or the mirror will displace its image, the paralysis will pass from the hand to the brain, and the ego will murder its proper master. It can be vanquished only by being cast out; and the attempt explains why so many of the early works of genius are real, or disguised, autobiographies. Faith is the will in action. The wretched being must walk on the waters. He must work a miracle, or sink for want of faith. He must confide in his enemy, or be confounded by him. Carlyle had to define his enemy imaginatively in the pages of a book. He was filling with ideas, but they lacked an image or container.

Duties are so much easier to recognize than to fulfil, that we may leave him to his problem, how to tackle the impossible, while, with her own help, we watch Mrs. Carlyle's reactions at this time. The best record was made thirty years later, when other bitternesses had intervened and when her imagination had lost none of its faculty for dramatic description. Allowing for some heightening of the lights and blackening of the shadows, the following words show at any rate how she saw herself in this part:

It is not the greatness or littleness of the duty nearest to hand, but the spirit in which one does it, that makes one's doing noble or mean.... I had gone with my husband to live on a little estate of peat-bog.... Further, we were very poor, and further and worst, being an only child, and brought up to 'great prospects,' I was sublimely ignorant of every branch of household knowledge, though a capital Latin scholar and a very fair mathematician. It behoved me, in these astonishing circumstances, to learn to sew. Husbands, I was shocked to find, wore their stockings into holes, and were always losing buttons; and I was expected to 'look to all that.' Also it behoved me to learn to *cook* — no capable servant choosing to live at such an out-of-the-way place.... So I sent for Cobbett's *Cottage Economy*, and fell to work at a loaf of bread.

Paragraph follows paragraph as the memory revives, and it was Mrs. Carlyle's way to dramatize herself and her situation, for she was too nearly an artist to throw away the best of her effects. To reduce her narrative to history we can call in the aid of Jeffrey's impartial eyes. He was a friend of both the Carlyles, had, as we have seen, suggested that his family should pay them a visit, had eaten the dinner that she had helped to cook, heard the story that she had made of her thirty-mile ride to and from Dumfries, and had watched her play her part as hostess afterward. On his return home, he wrote to Carlyle as follows:

Take care of the fair creature who has trusted herself so entirely to you. Do not let her ride about in the wet, nor expose herself to the wintry winds that will, by and by, visit your lofty retreat ... and in the meantime be gay and playful and foolish with her, at least as often as you require her to be wise and heroic with you. You have no mission on earth, whatever you may fancy, half so important as to be innocently happy. [From D. A. Wilson's biography.]

Amid her various activities, 'sitting here companionless' was her reiterated phrase, a phrase that recurs in ordinarily happy letters. Her husband wrote or wrestled in his room for much of the day, and would take exhausting rides, for he was a believer in violent exercise, till dinner, after which he would read Spanish with her till tea, and then continue his work alone, whether writing or reading, sometimes disappearing into his brother's farm for his last smoke. Thus he had at call another man's company. She had neither such a woman's, nor a child's. It was only human of her to cling the closer to her husband because she was deprived of richer ties, and the letters that she wrote when he was absent breathe a lover's passionate tenderness. His replies are no less touching, but then, beside her, he had his children in his work. It is always harder for a man to be everything to a woman than for a woman to be everything to a man, for of the two he is mentally more independent. She finds herself in others. He is much more self-absorbed, and self-contained, and blinder to needs of which, being a man, he has next to no experience. Unless he is a victim to jealousy, he does not want to be wanted, except occasionally. If he has any work to do, he wants to be undisturbed. The wish of a woman to be wanted is a wife's or mother's development of the girl's desire to be desired. Thus, in married life, the natural wants of husband and wife are exactly opposite, and, if they have no children to bridge (as nature intended) this difference, there is likely to be trouble. It will fall first on her and may remain a puzzle to him until he discovers, most probably too late, its explanation.

At this critical stage in the married lives of the Carlyles, their biographers present us with two conflicting pictures. The apologists of the lady emphasize the shadows in her existence. The admirers of Carlyle wash all the shadows out. The suggestive facts, however, can be stated briefly. The Christmas of 1829–30 was severe, and Mrs. Carlyle had to go to bed with a bad sore throat. Fearing diphtheria, Mrs. Welsh hurried over from Templand to nurse her daughter, who, though disappointed of presiding over the dinner on New Year's Day, for which a fatted goose had been provided, shortly recovered. It has been said that her health was never the same after this attack, but that seems to be an exaggeration, especially since, in our opinion, physical illness was not the marrow of her troubles. A month later, in a letter to Miss Stodart, Mrs. Carlyle said: 'It is well we have meat and fire "within ourselves," otherwise we should live in hourly apprehension of being snowed up, and consequently starved to death without even the mournful alternative of "eating our own children."' Was this very grim joke entirely fortuitous? An artist's jokes are dangerous because he exaggerates, instead of concealing, the pinch in his shoe.

The chief events in the quiet year that followed were the death of Carlyle's favourite sister, Margaret, and another visit from Jeffrey, who again saw the condition of Carlyle and used a skilful pen, in the friendliest fashion, to criticize the limitations of his situation, his writings, and his creed. As autumn drew on, Carlyle wrote to his mother: 'The wife and I are very quiet here.... These are the greyest and most silent days I ever saw. My broom, as I sweep up the withered leaves, might be heard at a furlong's distance.' The next event was the summoning of Jeffrey to London, where he became Lord Advocate in the new Government, enlivened his friends with the buzz of the town, but did not disguise that he was being as much harried by affairs as they, or one of them, might be by excess of country solitude. To live by writing for the Reviews, even when they will print fifty pages and will pay as generously as Jeffrey, is to stave off rather than solve the problem of living, and so Carlyle, with a book finished at last, resolved to scrape together fifty pounds and see what he could do with the publishers in London.

His departure, at the beginning of August 1831, was a severe trial to his wife, whom not even the most accommodating of biographers can imagine at Craigenputtock *without* him. On the other hand, if he was to support her anywhere else, it was clear that he must make this journey. The headaches to which she was subject now became acute, and in the spring of 1831 she wrote to her sister-in-law Jean: 'I have been in bed all day with a headache, and am risen so confused and dull that, for your sake as well as my own, I shall keep my speculations — news I have none....' This is not an isolated symptom, for we have Carlyle's own recollection of her later state on the eve of his journey, which a loan, pressed upon him by Jeffrey, enabled him to undertake. The night before he started, Carlyle remembered to have lain on the sofa in the drawing-room, with Jane, the packing done, sitting by the table late. Her thoughts issued in the words: 'about to part; and who knows for how long, and what may have come in the interim?' 'These words [wrote Carlyle] had a guise of sport, but were profoundly plaintive in meaning.' 'Courage: only for a month,' he answered, but there was more behind. We now know that she thought herself to be with child and to be parting from him at a time when she was wanting his presence more than ever.

These are the lights and shadows that the facts cast upon the picture: a gradation of tones, precious in its humanity, but by arbitrary selection or partisan emphasis easily marred. Noting only the physical facts, but passing over the mental, the human situation, the implications even of some sentences in Jeffrey's letters, Mr. D. A. Wilson writes of Jane at this period:

She was often sick, but not beyond what her mother could treat.... There was chronic biliousness, female troubles, and 'nerves,' the usual consequences of neglecting bodily work and upsetting the natural balance of mind and body. Her mother hoped for pregnancy.... Her daughter had inherited from the father's side a tendency to tuberculosis, and so she had to be richly nourished. A thin diet would make pregnancy likelier, but might bring on the dreaded consumption. ... Thanks to her (mother's) advice and attendance, the six years at Craigenputtock may be said to have given Mrs. Carlyle a stock of health which carried her to her old age.[1]

Since we know what her health was to be, this is rather hard on Craigenputtock. What is the use of meeting one exaggeration by another, of Mr. Wilson being nearly as 'reckless' as 'Mr. Froude'? The interest of Jane's condition is that it was no extraordinary fate; and, even with a legend to overthrow, Mr. Wilson, an apostle of good sense, must know that the commonest problem of feminine 'nerves' is not stated fairly by referring all its factors to 'neglecting bodily work.'

II

The manuscript that Carlyle carried to London in August 1831 had occupied him for the previous twelve months, and it was (he recalled) at Templand that the idea of *Sartor* came to him in the symbolism of a philosophy of Clothes. No more appropriate spot could be imagined, for Mrs. Welsh, who now lived at Templand, had always been the pride of her dressmaker and the envy of her women friends. He was not the first to use this symbol; it had also been in his thoughts for some time; but the thought became an image at Templand, and the image shaped conveniently into a book.

Consider how much the idea can be made to cover; how all shams can be grouped under its skirts; how all fine aspirations can be compared to figures still unfitted

[1] *Carlyle to the French Revolution*, by D. A. Wilson, p. 96.

with their vesture; the old humorous idea of mankind, suddenly stripped of its pretences; the new fantasies that it opens to the imagination; the variety, the expansion, the excuse for going on when the imagination is busy, for stopping when the fancy flags! Mental ideas, physical ideas, political ideas are equally fitted for the chalk and tape-measure of a clothes-philosopher. He can cut and shape them as they come: from the Universe which is the garment of God, to the coat-tails of gigmanity; from the robes of officialdom to a Bolshevist's red tie or red cap. Carlyle, who had been an enormous reader, had lately learned much, through Jeffrey, of the world of procedure and affairs; the Reform Bill controversy was raging; there had been another revolution in Paris; he had taken to the study of the profit-and-loss economists, and had found their dismal science funny and absurd. Unusually full of varied matter, the form came to him suddenly at Templand, as if Mrs. Welsh were to prove after all, to him even, an inspiration by her clothes.

Jane's verdict on the book: 'a work of genius, dear,' has become an inevitable quotation. How far is it true?

Sartor Resartus is one of those books which will always be mentioned respectfully but which is really read and liked by comparatively few. Its ideas are simple, familiar, true, and widely neglected: the sort of ideas over which it is easy to yawn. Its humour is genially clownish, its language often grotesque, but its occasional beauties are extraordinary. There are passages that glint and glow like gems still in the rough, after but a few turns of the lapidary's wheel, enough to show that they are male gems, and of fine water. We can liken this writing, again, to clusters of pale garnets on the boughs of the red hawthorn, with sharp spines about them, and abundance of green foliage sprouting from the twisted arms that spread from the stem, short and rough with its wrinkled bark, grey and bitten with the winter winds, but dusted here and there with green and yellow. Certain chapters, that on Symbols and that on Natural Supernaturalism, have seemed inspired to some critical writers, while others have been drawn to the basis of solid good sense that here became articulate with such difficulty.

In style the book is an example, at the opposite and rustic end, of the impassioned prose that De Quincey also contributed, with urbanity and scholarship, to the Romantic Movement. The form is whimsical, in the capricious English manner. The substance, a critical intellect will feel, is the foundation from which a man of Carlyle's quality should have started: not to which he should have won so painfully at the age of thirty-six. The truths which are rudely hammered: the necessity of work; the vanity of happiness; the presence of mystery; the wisdom of silent acceptance; the insight given by love, are marred by much denunciation of their opposites, as if even now, Carlyle had not surrendered to his own gospel. Did he ever learn the simple fact that it is better to love good than to hate evil? The biographer sees in the book a spiritual autobiography, and the liker of his kind a proof of the height to which sincerity and perseverance can carry a man beset with every kind of inner difficulty. We seem to see a rustic preacher struggling on to solid ground out of an enormous bog. The stars are reflected in the water-pools about him, and the man himself becomes a symbol of humanity struggling after intelligence: tragic, beautiful, and as lonely as, against the material forces of nature, is that other eternal and bent figure, stiffly following the plough. Why was all this so unnaturally difficult; what were the inhibitions that gave impediment to his very speech? Carlyle seems to have had more to unlearn than any man of equal intelligence. He was an inspired peasant who missed becoming a great poet: a strange cross between two temperaments and two traditions, in which the shepherd used his crook for a pencil, and the scholar his pen like a spade.

The book, therefore, is a grotesque medley, illumined by beautiful passages, and it also shows one typical weakness of the great man. He could touch people, bore people, annoy them, exasperate them, but he could not make them either blush or wince. For all his railing, Carlyle never hit hard enough to be hated, was never really on the unpopular side. The things that he denounced were those that people liked to hear denounced, even when they had no intention of abating their allegiance to them. Of the cant that was ridiculous he freed himself: of the cant that was respectable he was not free. Just as sinners enjoy nothing so much as an eloquent sermon on the torments of the damned, so many an Englishman is secretly flattered when told that he is a shopkeeper, a philistine, a moral coward and a hypocrite: he knows these charges to be true, but he associates them with the things for which he really cares: riches, business capacity, freedom from civil commotion, the outward respect of his humbler neighbours. He is convinced that beauty and strength do not go together; that the less imaginative he is the richer he will remain; that practice and theory are better when rigidly separated; that he can go on his own way most quietly if he professes whatever is most fashionable, and that this profession is all that is needed to enable him to hold his head high in the world; that, as good artists and writers will still go to their work without reward, only an unbusinesslike nation would wish to pay them; that the denunciations which his conduct excites, if listened to respectfully, will enable him to add the virtues of humility and tolerance to his other blessings, without his pocket being a penny the worse. The only thing that he dreads is popular initiative, but the chance of this has long died under the oligarchical government to which Englishmen have been accustomed since the days of the Tudors; and obedience is so natural to an Englishman at home that he can safely trust his poorer neighbours to suppress any attacker of abuses before he is required to interfere.

Had Carlyle come down from general denunciation to particular abuses, from abstract charges to precise exposures, he would have had a much warmer reception, and like Sydney Smith, shall we say, might have been execrated instead of honoured till he reached old age. As it was, he provoked no more than boredom and impatience, and when his *Sartor* was praised in America by Emerson, and his reputation in Germany began to flow back, England soon relented. Indeed, she is generous to every artist who can live down some years of neglect successfully. She reserves several places for popular preachers of 'unpopular truths'; and the office of king's jester, happily now kept in check by our extraordinary law of libel, survives, and is the more esteemed because it entails no charge upon the Treasury. Carlyle, unlike Byron, was inclined to beat about the bush.

From these obvious considerations, which explain why Carlyle's outspokenness led him into no danger of martyrdom, it is pleasant to turn to the qualities of the book that are more often remembered. The following unforgotten sentences are from *Sartor* at its best:

Ach, mein Lieber, said he once at midnight, when we had returned from the coffee-house in rather earnest talk, it is true sublimity to dwell here. These fringes of lamplight, struggling up through smoke and thousandfold exhalation, some fathoms into the ancient reign of Night, what thinks Boötes of them, as he leads his Hunting Dogs over the Zenith in their leash of sidereal fire? That stifled hum of Midnight, when Traffic has lain down to rest; and the chariot-wheels of Vanity, still rolling here and there through distant streets, are bearing her to Halls roofed in, and lighted to the due pitch for her; and only Vice and Misery, to prowl or to moan like nightbirds, are abroad: that hum, I say, like the stertorous, unquiet slumber of sick Life, is heard in Heaven. Oh, under that hideous coverlet of vapours, and putrefactions, and unimaginable gases, what a Fermenting-vat lies simmering and hid. The joyful and the sorrowful are there; men are dying there, men are being born; men are praying, — on the other side of a brick partition, men are cursing; and around them all is the vast, void Night.

This is less than half of the long passage which makes much of the third chapter of *Sartor Resartus* like a nocturne of music on the theme of a city at night. If it be contrasted with, say, the opening chapters, wherein much is written but little is said, we see that Carlyle's prose becomes wordy whenever it is not descriptive. A brooding mind which seizes ideas with difficulty, which has more depth and weight than edge, labours its thoughts as if they were rocks in its progress, while it will flow easily between the green banks of description and reflect like a clear river whatever images may be cast upon its surface from the clouds or birds that cross over it, or from the houses, trees or people that it passes by. The less musical passages are emphatic in assertion or denunciation, or else humorous and grotesque, yet even here the seriousness with which the ideas are regarded makes the writing less humorous than Rabelais, less fantastic than Sterne. *Sartor Resartus* will never be loved as much, as disinterestedly, as *Tristram Shandy*: Teufelsdröckh is less human than Uncle Toby. To those who like it, the book will mean too much to be enjoyed for its own sake; and those who are more critical of its value will prefer a lighter touch for their ideas, a tone of greater levity for their humour. *Sartor* is scarcely a masterpiece in either kind, but it will always be cherished by those who, like-minded with its author, are Puritans in grain without having lost their imaginations or their sense of humour.

The classic simplicity was beyond Carlyle, but his humour saved him from being a Romantic who took himself too seriously. Even his humour was apt to be timid: otherwise he would have seen that the catastrophe which he predicted, should mankind be stripped of clothes, would not survive longer than the shock of novelty. Artists, models, actors, and athletes, boxers and bathers, quickly discover that the modesty imposed by the wearing of clothes is artificial; and we come to suspect its decency as soon as we have become accustomed to the appearance of the human form. There is nothing immodest in the human body. Anyone who has made the comparison knows that the immodesty lies in the clothes, and that indecency consists not in wearing nothing, but in wearing very, very little.

To reasonable arguments of this kind, to criticism addressed to the intelligence, *Sartor Resartus* would be an easy prey; but then the book was not addressed to the mind, but to the feelings, and objections of this sort do not really apply. Carlyle had been accused of mysticism when mysticism was a term of contempt, and his object was to expose the shallowness of the rational and prosaic outlook. Hume he had left behind. Bentham had never attracted him. The political economists of his day seemed to him as superficial as their new science. A Calvinist by upbringing, Carlyle preserved a Puritan's sense of duty, which seemed to him far more worthy of reverence than a philosophy of profit-and-loss. To gain the whole world and to lose your own soul was to make a bad bargain, whatever your profits and pleasures might be. His rationalism had deprived Carlyle of belief in the literal truth of certain fables, in signs and marvels that might be superstitious, but he was poet enough never to have lost his sense of wonder at the universe and in man's strange destiny on this earth. He knew that wonder to be at the basis of human existence, that reverence was natural to man, and that in attempting to fulfil the duty nearest at hand there was a satisfaction that the search for happiness could never give. Both his father and Faust had taught him that much. Money-grubbing, as an end or occupation, could only satisfy people who were only half-alive, and they must be enlightened by appealing to feelings and to instincts far deeper than formal reasoning or cold logic could reach.

The aim of *Sartor*, then, was to appeal to these instincts and feelings, to recall the wonder and the reverence that a shallow philosophy and commercial activity were trying to ignore. In this, the book was certainly successful. Its sincerity excuses many faults; its humanity suffuses its humour and its mannerisms. The Puritan version of the Romantic gospel is a remarkable confession. Carlyle had lived his book before he wrote it, and the thin disguise between himself and his hero enabled him to see himself in some perspective, and to make his ideas more persuasive than they would have been if presented in the naked unpopularity of a direct challenge to his readers. We feel, indeed, that a man must have lost almost everything to have had to labour so painfully over the alphabet of good sense; but there is abundant promise of descriptive narrative in the best of these pages, and the glances at history and the little discussion on hero-worship [1] reveal the historian groping toward his appointed work.

III

When Carlyle left for London with the MS. of *Sartor* in his pocket, Mrs. Carlyle was starting the fourth autumn at Craigenputtock alone. His affectionate letters show him sympathetic and responsive. In the first he wrote, 'delightful it was.... on opening my trunk to find everywhere traces of my good "coagitator's" care and love. The very jujube-box, with its worsted and

[1] Book III, Chap. 7, 'Organic Filaments.'

darning needle, did not escape me; it was so beautiful that I could almost have cried over it.' A week later, in reply to her letter he said: 'I see poor Craigenputtock through it, and the best little Goodykin sitting there, hourly meditating on me, and watching my return.' He tells her not to 'fret herself, and torment her poor sick head. I will be back to her; not an hour will I lose.' Apart from the discouraging reception of *Sartor*, Carlyle was not very happy in London, and the thought of the sympathy, perfect in all but one respect, that he had had to leave behind in lonely Craigenputtock made him say: 'Standing on a kind of basis which I feel to be of adamant, I perceive that, of all women, my own Jeannie is the wife for me; that in her true bosom (once she were a mystic) a man's head is worthy to lie. Be a mystic, dearest.' With his book completed, the separation from her was bearable, but for the time being she had nothing while her husband was away.

There is more than one indication of her state. Rather than wait for her letters, she would ride over to Dumfries and back to forestall the postman. There were now no kinsmen at the farm, until Carlyle's mother sent over Alick and Jean to relieve Jane's solitude. Thanking her for this thought, Jane wrote: 'I think I must soon have worked myself into a fever or other violent disorder; for my talent for fancying things...had so entirely got the upper hand of me that I could neither sleep by night nor rest by day. I have slept more since they came.' As his stay in London was to be extended, for *Sartor* was still without a publisher, it was decided that she should join her husband, who had now been repaid the money that he had lent to his brother, John. Carlyle also was feeling the strain acutely. 'Why [he wrote to his wife] should a man, though bilious, never so nervous, impoverished, bug-bitten and bedevilled, let Satan have dominion over him? Save me! save me, my Goody....' In this plight, he had only an 'untoward lodging-house' to offer to her, but, side by side again, they were spared the worst.

Mrs. Carlyle arrived on October 1, 1831, and remained till the end of March. On the whole she enjoyed the change, the talk, the people, but her health prevented her from accepting many invitations. Instead she had visits from Jeffrey, Allan Cunningham, Lockhart, Mill and others, but her husband continued to be 'hag-ridden,' and in addition to his disappointment over the rejection of *Sartor*, the death of his father on New Year's eve was a severe blow. The magazine-editors were more friendly than the publishers, and after six months Carlyle decided to return to Craigenputtock, where he could live more cheaply than anywhere else, and meantime to support himself by writing for the Reviews.

This return looked like defeat, and the voyage from Liverpool to Annan was a sore physical strain on Mrs. Carlyle. Carlyle's reaction made him wrap himself in solitude, and his wife who, like most women, was better able to bear real suffering than a man, did her best to be responsive by concealing or minimizing her own troubles. The extent of the strain on her nerves Carlyle scarcely recognized at the time; his indigestion and his gloom were too insistent. She put a brave face on it in her letters. 'It is the stillest, solitariest place that it ever entered your imagination to conceive, where one has the strangest, shadowy existence. Nothing is actual in it but the food we eat, the bed one sleeps on, and praised be Heaven, the fine air one breathes. The rest is all a dream.... For my part I am very content. I have everything here my heart desires that I could have anywhere else, except society.... My husband is as good company as reasonable mortal could desire.' At the same time she watched the swallows building under the eaves of her house, and preparing to bring up a family.

She made a little poem on them which she sent to Jeffrey. 'Would I were such' is the last line.

The summer of 1832 was complicated by the sudden dismissal of a servant who could not quickly be replaced, and Mrs. Carlyle, leading, as her husband confessed, 'a dull life' beside him, began to complain of 'prolonged bad health and worse spirits.' The winter spent at Edinburgh was scarcely a success. Carlyle admitted to being languid and bilious, and was finding both Edinburgh and Craigenputtock no longer suitable for him. One odd result of the silence of the moors was to make the smallest noise at night intolerable to both of them. On the journey back, in March 1833, Mrs. Carlyle became definitely ill, and had to spend a week of misery and influenza at Templand with her mother, whose own health was now failing. The briefest indication of her condition is the apology that Jane sent to Bessy Stodart in July 1833, for an unanswered letter. 'I wrote to no one; had enough to do in striving with the tempter ever present with me in the shape of headaches, heartache, and all kinds of aches, that I might not break out into fiery indignation over my own destiny and all the earth's.' Carlyle himself was almost in despair, and the effect of each upon the other can be imagined.

Since Carlyle, wrapped up in himself and depending upon his work and its recognition for support, withdrew into himself in these dark hours, the only hope for his wife, absolutely dependent, in the absence of children, upon him, lay in some amelioration of his condition. They seemed to be revolving in a vicious circle, when suddenly one Sunday evening in August 1833 a strange carriage arrived at Craigenputtock. It had brought a young American, still with his reputation to make, who had made the journey in order to meet the author of certain articles in the Reviews. The young man, Ralph Waldo Emerson, was later to write an account of his visit in *English Traits*, published in 1856. No doubt, any likeable person would have been welcome, but Emerson quickly won the heart of his host and hostess. He remained for twenty-four hours, and left behind what Mrs. Carlyle afterward called a day of 'enchantment.' He records that Carlyle was finding his solitude tedious; he could 'not help congratulating him on his treasure of a wife.' Such company was bound to be a blessing, but this first evidence of the effect of Carlyle's writings upon the outside world was hardly less so.

The gleam of light soon passes, and the winter that followed was not free from disappointments, since two attempts on vacant professorships were unavailing, and in his mood of depression Carlyle fancied that Jeffrey could have used more influence than he did. That Carlyle should have tried for these posts is a sign of his downheartedness, since he never sought for appointments when his work was going well. Matters were growing intolerable, and the only change it was possible to make was to say good-bye to Craigenputtock and to make a bold move to London. The language of both on their present plight was free from ambiguity. He wrote of bolting from 'all these sooty despicalities' and made unrustic references to 'draggle-tails of byrewomen, peat-moss and isolation, exasperation and confusion.' She spoke, even of the impending change, with 'diseased indifference. There is a sort of incrustation about the inward *me*, that renders it alike insensible to fear and to hope,' and concluded: 'It seems as if the problem of living would be immensely simplified to me if I had health. It does require such an effort to keep oneself from growing quite wicked, while that weary weaver's shuttle is plying between my temples.'

Carlyle led the way in order to find a house, and reached his old lodgings in May 1834. Early in June his wife joined him and they took possession of the house in Cheyne Row which was to be their home for life.

Much comment has been made on these Craigenputtock days, but they tell their own story, and the story is spoilt if it is exaggerated. A tormented and self-centred man is not the same as a selfish one, though the effects of his character may be nearly as trying to other people. Carlyle had the imagination to see the point of view of another if his concern was that of an historian or a biographer, but he was apt to miss a human situation under his own roof, and his letters probably make more sympathetic reading than his daily conduct. As the head and the prop of his little household it was natural that the initiative should lie with him, but it is impossible to deny that she felt the loneliness and isolation long before he felt them, and that (very soon after he had felt them) he determined to move. This self-centredness would not have mattered nearly so much if Mrs. Carlyle had had some one beside her husband to return her solicitude and affection. As things fell, she was wholly dependent upon him and Nature's unkindness rather than he must be blamed for the abnormal situation that resulted.

CHAPTER SEVEN

CHELSEA AND THE FRENCH REVOLUTION

I

THIS year 1834 was a turning-point, in three directions, in their story. The remoteness of Craigenputtock was left behind that Carlyle might find an ampler life and more society in London, where, we must also note, the serial publication of *Sartor*, in the pages of *Fraser's Magazine*, was being completed in August; and, before the month was out, Carlyle had begun work upon the *French Revolution*. This was a subject that had been possessing his imagination for many months; and, as yet, though fresh and alarming in the memories of Englishmen, it had found no English historian, was little more understood or intelligible to them than is the Russian Revolution at the present day. The opening years in Cheyne Row concern the growing London life on which the Carlyles were embarking, and the writing of this History, a momentous task, for, should it prove a failure, it would force Carlyle (he said) to abandon literature and to try his lot in some other occupation, or in America whither so many, on both sides of the Border, had begun to emigrate.

On the whole, they made a propitious entry into London. A cab, piled mountain-high with luggage, bore them to the house, and Chico, the canary, who had 'sung by sea and land' all the way, 'struck up his lilt in the very London streets whenever he could see green leaves and feel free air.' The house in Cheyne Row (then number 5, now 24) had attracted Mrs. Carlyle from his description, and her feelings responded to its massive wooden staircase, its abundant

cupboards, the dressing-rooms attached to the bed-
rooms, and the high wainscoting; while Carlyle
thought with pleasure of the little private garden at its
back, where he could walk unobserved in his dressing-
gown and light his pipe, the smoke from which, when
indoors, he had generally to enjoy on the hearth lest
any of it should fail to be drawn into the chimney.
Bessy Barnet, the 'romantic maid,' was in attendance,
and they were not left neglected by their friends. The
nearest to them was Leigh Hunt, a picturesque, if
somewhat dilapidated, neighbour who liked to escape
from his own home for a chat, and amused them by
copious advice and abundant, if not always judicious,
goodwill. They liked him, and were sorry for him with
his queer neighbourly ways, but his wife became rather
an embarrassing neighbour. In towns, the neighbour
is a peculiar species: ever at hand, usually on the
watch, as full of chatter as a bird and, like a bird, ever
ready to borrow. Poor Mrs. Hunt was constantly in
need of neighbourly assistance. Her household was
irregular, and its needs imperfectly supplied. In emergencies, which were frequent, she would borrow from
Mrs. Carlyle, and she crowned her requests on a famous occasion by asking for the loan of a fender.
Still, this degree of dependence was not immediately
reached, and the Hunts were not unwelcome during
the weeks in which the Carlyles were settling into their
new home.

John Stuart Mill, the earliest of the disciples of whom
Carlyle had begun to feel the need, who had already
lent him many French books and had sent to him the
gleanings of his own observations in Paris, was a frequent visitor, and in their walks together the subject
of the French Revolution was discussed at length. In
the evenings Allan Cunningham would often drop in,
and, whatever may be said of the tempers of Carlyle
and his wife, they were never without friends, and

could plant themselves nowhere without these friends reappearing. In the wider social world, Mrs. Buller and Mrs. Austin were their first hostesses, though routs and set dinners were attended rather with curiosity than enjoyment. On the whole, from the very first, it was the little circle that began to group itself about their own house which most contented them. In Cheyne Row the choicer spirits found the quality which the Carlyles themselves, for a long time, missed in general society.

In spite of the discovery of a new subject worthy of his best, and of the friends who lightened his leisure or helped him to understand its nature and to find his materials, Carlyle was soon in one of his despondent moods. He had good circumstantial reasons for anxiety. The move to London had been made with a few hundred pounds against the future, but also at a time when, through the publication of *Sartor* in Fraser, editors were beginning to fight shy of him. It was a bad time for radicals. The passing of the Reform Bill had provoked a reaction. Every one, except a few extremists, felt that it was necessary now to call a halt; and the slightest tendency to oppose abuses, to help those in dire need, or even to champion education, was visited with the sly vengeance of good society. Editors are particularly sensitive to such currents of opinion, and when the style no less than the opinions of a contributor are unpopular, we must not be too severe on the editors who were holding back. To the contributor himself, the outlook was serious, for his only real capital was his brains and his goodwill. At the end of July, after his first month in London, Carlyle makes a clean breast to himself:

Nothing can exceed the gravity of my situation here. 'Do or die' seems the word; and alas! what to do? I have no confidant. For five days together I sit without so much as speaking to anyone except my wife. Mood tragical, gloomy, as of one forsaken, who had nothing left him but to get through his task and die. No periodical editor wants me; no man will give me money for my work. Bad health, too (at least singularly changed health), brings dispiritment. Fears of beggary, etc., besiege me. On brighter days I cast these off into the dim distance, and see a world fearful, indeed, but grand: a task to do in it which no poverty shall hinder.

We can sympathize with him, and the phrase 'no confidant' need not mislead us. Having made the experiment of transferring himself and his wife to London, he could not confide to her the responsibility of his inevitable decision. To very few of his friends would any man confide it. If the future was to be saved, it must be saved by Jane's husband himself. On a huge, obscure and unpopular subject, how could he hope for much success? He was still puzzled about it, and, as its outlines began to drift across his imagination, he found himself dreaming of 'a work of art.' A work of art from such a chaotic subject and from the hand of such a dubious author seemed unlikely, especially if his future depended upon its recognition and success.

He needed an encouraging word from outside himself, an unpremeditated word or it would be humiliating. The word came in the first of Emerson's letters, with praise of *Sartor* for its burden. Carlyle, a very human and lonely person, craved response, for the pride of proud men, and he was a proud peasant, is the reverse of their need for sympathy. A pure artist, if that convenient term may be used, can work alone, as Maris did, since his work is really the worship of beauty, as independent of approval as a flower, but it is not so with the preacher, with the Blake or the Ruskin, who would also teach. There was the stain of the preacher in Carlyle, and the preacher must have some response, some disciples. The proof that Browning was a purer artist than has always been remembered is that he was indifferent to this need, and continued to write unrecognized, without lamentation. There are animals that live alone, and animals that live in flocks, and to note the distinction is to criticize neither. Carlyle was nearly at the end of his resources when the writing of the *French Revolution* began.

Such a crisis, as usual, called out his desperate hope and energies, and the book soon began to grow under his hand. On the first of September 1834 the opening pages were written. As he became absorbed in it, his spirits rose. At the end of the month, he wrote to his brother, Dr. John: 'It shall be such a book: quite an epic poem of the Revolution; an apotheosis of Sansculottism! Seriously, when in good spirits I feel as if there were the matter of a very considerable work within me.' The under-dog, the rebellious servant, Carlyle's favourite figure, was to have his prose epic at last. This return of vitality is one of the welcome incidents in Carlyle's life, for, though it could not have been isolated, the records of such productive moods are few, and there is no doubt that his history of the French Revolution was written with more enjoyment than any of his books. We feel happy, too, when we hear of him declining to write for *The Times*, on the kind suggestion of John Sterling's father, then editor. The poet of Sansculottism would not have been happy on *The Times*, and the editor, too, might have had his embarrassments. With the work going well through the winter, and Mill on hand to second its progress, the clouds cleared. When a writer is happy with his proper work, he has no temptation to worry about his material future. His plans for the book enlarged as he went on. Before Christmas it was shaping from one into two volumes.

Meantime, Mrs. Carlyle, though the winter was cold, was also having her distractions. In September, when the taking of the Bastille was about to be exultantly described upstairs, Edward Irving suddenly appeared at her door on horseback. He gave an appreciative glance at the room in which she was sitting, and, with more kindness than accuracy, exclaimed: 'You are like an Eve, and make a little Paradise wherever you are.' It was his first and his last visit, for his health had given way under the strain and excitements of his preaching, and the holiday he was about to take had been too long postponed. In December he was dead. To the last Carlyle had tried to save Irving from himself, and even now was doing his best to persuade Irving's friends how precarious was the life of their hero.

Irving was not the only old friend who now came Mrs. Carlyle's way in London. Near by, she had 'a brother and sister, the most intimate friends I ever had in East Lothian.' These were none other than the Rennies. The faithless George was now a sculptor, and before long to become a Member of Parliament. With the remarkable attraction that Mrs. Carlyle had for many men and for several women, another regular visitor was Eliza Miles, whose mother had kept the lodgings in which the Carlyles had stayed during their visits to London. She became so devoted to Mrs. Carlyle that she had wished to return to Craigenputtock as her servant, but had been dissuaded in one of the graphic letters that contain Jane's reflections on her life there.

The casual visits of friends, however, do not fill existence, and it was now plain that Mrs. Carlyle's hopes of motherhood were to be disappointed permanently. Her favourite brother-in-law, Dr. Carlyle, was fond of prescribing for her an activity that should 'fill your whole mind,' but good diagnosis could not supply the remedy. In a letter to him at Rome, where Dr. Carlyle was this winter, she complained of loneliness, and said that she was not so well off as she had been when he had been walking and reading Italian with her at Craigenputtock. Their days followed the now familiar rule. After breakfast at nine, Carlyle wrote till two; dinner and a walk filled the afternoon, and then he would return to read with his wife or work again as the mood took him. She was therefore dependent on her friends for society and amusement, though Carlyle of course saw more of her than of anybody else. It could scarcely have been other than a rather empty existence. Housekeeping which does not involve children will never fill a married woman's life, and the more intelligent she is the less satisfaction does she find in it. Miss Drew's reminder of the straits to which Victorian women were reduced for occupation should always be borne in mind, and there is a complication in being an author's wife that is too much overlooked.

Most husbands do their work away from home, and the consequence is that necessity rather than the husband is usually blamed for a wife's solitude in a childless marriage. With a writer or an artist a similar loneliness may be felt, but this is more trying when the man is under the same roof, for invisibility is harder to bear than enforced absence. Many of Mrs. Carlyle's letters ache with an exasperated solitude, whereas, at the other extreme of occupation, the wife of a sailor will take his absences for granted and endeavour to adjust her whole life to a necessity wholly impersonal. When an author does appear he may not be good company, and if he should be moody his appearances will be the aggravation of disappointment, instead of its relief. The more devoted to him Mrs. Carlyle was the more certain she was to feel some disappointment in her destiny. No admiration for his work, no reading day by day of his MS. as it advanced, neither care for his health nor attention to his whims could fill a heart that Nature had intended to be a mother's.

At the turn of the year, Carlyle was making steady
progress. He was feeling himself the master of his task,
and saw that his book could not be completed in less
than three volumes. The second volume was started in
February 1835; his mental machinery was running
smoothly; and he told his brother that he was more
sure of himself than he had felt for a long time. A preliminary advertisement appeared in the March number of Fraser, and the happy author even hoped that
he might finish the work in May. His only worry now
was the attitude of the magazine editors, to whom he
was looking for current work and ready money. All his
future depended on this book, for he confessed rue-
fully: 'It is now some three and twenty months since I
earned one penny by my craft. I have been ready to
work, abler than ever. To ask able Editors to employ
you will not improve but worsen the matter. When
want is approaching one must have done with whims.'

II

The first volume, now known as Part I, concluded
with the book upon the Insurrection of the Women,
and the trusty Mill, who had been following the subject with intense interest, asked if he might borrow the
MS., to read it as a whole at leisure. Mill's circumstances at this time were curious. We all know the
pale, thin, distinguished, doubting, cloistered-looking
face in Watts's portrait: a bookish, bachelor face if ever
there was one, with nothing romantic there unless intellectual dreams. Already known for subtlety and
logic, Mill had been busy resolving his own doubts,
and had made some stir in the world by his tentative
conclusions. News of these had impressed a certain
Unitarian clergyman who numbered among his con-
gregation a married lady much busied with her mental
difficulties. She was a Mrs. Taylor, who found her
husband dull because the respectable man could pro-

pound no answers to the various 'questions' that beset her. Even the clergyman did not feel equal to her need, so, as he knew Mill, he referred Mrs. Taylor to the philosopher, and implored Mill, in 1831, to go and see her. Mill knew and cared nothing for women and was very disinclined to go, but in the end he was persuaded. She turned her dark, black eyes upon him, and the sleeping man in Mill suddenly awoke. He was thrown completely off his feet by an emotion hitherto beyond the range of his experience, and not all the philosophy in his composition could resist Mrs. Taylor's dark eyes. Mill proved to be the solution of her difficulties, and to the astonishment of all his friends, he found a consoler and guide in Mrs. Taylor. Gossip was busy with the pair, and at last Mr. Taylor himself approached his wife about it. She replied roundly that nothing in the world would induce her to renounce this friendship, so the married pair quietly separated, because Mr. Taylor did not wish to involve his children in any scandal. The result was that Mrs. Taylor retired to Kingston-on-Thames, where Mill would join her at week-ends in order to continue their philosophic discussions in convenient privacy.

This arrangement had been pursued for some time when Mill borrowed Carlyle's MS., which he took and left at Kingston in order to spend his Sundays over it. The MS. attracted the attention of Mrs. Taylor, who sat up late over it one night, and left it in a heap on the nearest table in the sitting-room before retiring. There the housemaid saw it the next morning, when it looked like a pile of waste paper, which she promptly threw upon the fire. All, except a few tatters, was burned.

Mrs. Taylor, it is said, received the news with equanimity, but Mill, naturally, was overwhelmed. The next day, March 6, 1835, he made his way to Cheyne Row and knocked on the Carlyles' door about tea-time. His staccato rap was familiar to the pair, but, when he was shown into their room, he looked like the figure of Death. For the moment Mrs. Carlyle thought that he had gone off with Mrs. Taylor. There was a cab at the door, and, scarcely able to speak, Mill gasped out a request that Mrs. Carlyle should go down and talk to the lady outside. Carlyle, not knowing what the matter could be, took Mill by the hand and led him to a chair. Then the news was told, except that Mill laid the blame upon himself. The lady in the cab drove away, unconfessed and without entering. Before that pale face reproaches were impossible: Mill, looking like the ghost of an idea that had committed suicide, seemed on the verge of taking his own life, and Carlyle, with the tenderness that lay deep in his nature, listened with his wife for three mortal hours to the poor man's inextricable misery. They did their best to comfort him, and to conceal from him how serious the matter really was. At last Mill rose to go. When the door had shut upon him, Mrs. Carlyle threw her arms about her husband's neck, and they comforted each other like two children deserted in the dark. They had a long talk together, which culminated in Carlyle's determination: 'It shall be written again.'

The fate that he had defied in the past had never delivered a blow so terrible as this, and there can be little doubt, from the agonized night that followed, that Carlyle's peace of mind over his work was *never* the same again. The next day he wrote a courageous and comforting letter to Mill, who immediately sent a cheque for £200, of which Carlyle retained half, enough, he said, to reimburse him for the cost of living while the burned pages had been written.

Telling Emerson that he was writing the *History of Sansculottism*, and that his 'best hope' was only 'to be scolded and reproached,' Carlyle added significantly: 'I suffer also terribly from the solitary existence I have all along had; it is becoming a kind of passion with me, to feel myself among my brothers.' The preacher had not yet found his following. The tension of his proud nature could only be relieved by the fellowship that is the better part of genuine fame. 'It is certain' remarked Professor Teufelsdröckh 'that our own belief gains infinitely the moment we have convinced another mind thereof.'

III

Carlyle found himself with this History of the French Revolution. It provided him with a basis of reality, of fact. In the orthodox beliefs that he had shed, and in the German poetry and philosophy that he had studied, he had only been substituting mental clarity for mental fog, and, not having really an intellect of the first order, he could only see in Goethe a healthy man. He could not find in him, or take from him, the basis and foundation of this health. By circumstance and temper Carlyle was drawn to the downtrodden and to the strugglers, to the men who had surmounted difficulties rather than to those who were born free. He had the bad Protestant habit of setting merit above virtue. The witness of health, for him, was the price at which it had been purchased. He was less inclined to 'consider' the care-free 'lilies of the field.'

Moreover, men and not ideas were his primary concern, and history appealed to him because it could be considered the 'essence of innumerable biographies.' Somewhere in history, therefore, he had to find the assurance, the evidence, for his natural-supernatural beliefs; for the superiority of reality over shams; of sincerity over pretences; of work over worldly rewards; even upon this earth, of a day of reckoning. The French Revolution, he remarked, 'has done more to reconcile me to reality than anything else.'

Protestantism overthrew the Universal Church for

the Bible, and Carlyle, having outgrown Bible-worship, looked for his Divine scripture in History. Plato, for example, had never meant anything to him; and a cloud-capped mind, uneasy in a world of ideas, must find somewhere in immediate fact the palpable witness that to it is indispensable. Carlyle had, moreover, the Puritan conscience: a sense of the evils surrounding one, with the peasant's sole reaction, to protest. Thus, he was unable to appreciate the French genius in its flower, while he was well able to respond to the mass of an oppressed nation. Somewhat puzzled, he observed: 'French authors even of genius seem to get along comfortably without any *conscience*, or even feeling the want of one.' Yet the Puritan conscience is really a disease, or, more precisely, the condition produced in a good conscience that has been outraged beyond bearing. In *Sartor Resartus* we have seen his imagination respond to the movements of a sleeping city. In the *French Revolution* Carlyle was to become the spokesman of a nation arousing itself from a long nightmare of abuse. With imagination enough to realize the narrow limits of human knowledge, which was Carlyle's notion of a mystic, he was well prepared to write the epic of a human movement in rebellion against institutions that had outlived their usefulness and had been disastrously abused.

The book, he truly said, was more like an epic than a history, and his aim was, while being true to facts, to render the emotions under which the Revolution was begotten and carried out. Here his talent for human delineation and for descriptive narrative had free play. Whatever may be said against this volume, none can deny that it is instinct and pulsating with life. The men, the crowds, the movement, seem to pass under our eyes. He could get under the skin of a man, or into the passion of a mob, and follow them into action. Even when his portraits, say of King Louis or of

Robespierre, are ill-drawn, it is the understanding not the vitality that we question.

In a man with a talent for generalization, impatient, however scrupulous, with details, it is remarkable how few and simple are the facts by which he pins his history to the ground. Our emotion is so stirred that we overlook the gaps and condensations in the story. The actual events related in Carlyle's *French Revolution* are hardly more numerous or examined than the chapter-headings. His whole energies were spent on fattening these events into a living tissue. A fact suggests to him the state of mind that it produced in the chief actors and spectators, and the mass of activities which any collective policy involves is lost in the excitement of the decision. He can, indeed, disperse his imagination over a crowd of men. He has none of the talent by which a writer who is interested in organization can bring the machinery of administration or of an army before us. Here, too, the unorganized or the self-organized means more to Carlyle than the planned and the disciplined. A riot is more comprehensible to him than a battle. The revolutionary armies, and the great battles by which the Revolution itself survived, have no place in his pages. In this flood of emotion, if we miss anything it is the absence of that grip on 'a situation' which comes to a man, whether soldier or statesman, who has had personal contact with affairs. Carlyle, like Nietzsche, never sat on a committee. The wonder rather is how much life he could imagine from books. Turmoil rather than order was the reflexion of his own soul.

A fault in the book is the absence of contrast. The narrative, the interludes, even the connecting passages, are keyed so high that when it reaches moments of fierce activity there is no margin, and the high notes, seeking to stretch themselves, sometimes collapse into discords.

It is best to think of it as an unforgettable picture, and not to scrutinize too narrowly the quality of the minor effects. If we do the latter, for all the excitement of our reading, we become restive under this incessant appeal to our emotions, as we stir below a public speaker whose rhetoric, however excellent, suggests our feelings rather than our enlightenment to be the object of the man. It is a common error that, once the feelings alone have been touched, a quickened conscience and a right activity will follow; but the imagination is more exacting, more aristocratic, than that. The incisive speech of Parnell did not pass with his presence from his hearers. Its effect can still be felt because it was as strict as steel. There was no reverberation in his periods, but, even on the printed page, the lucid argument rings like iron on stone. None could wriggle away from it. Even Gladstone was converted in the end. The effect of such speech is to be independent of any kind of audience. In the House, as in Ireland, attention to Parnell was involuntary. The style of Carlyle, on the other hand, will always appeal most to emotional people. He has written a history of poor men for their poor brothers. The superlative edge of an aristocratic intellect, which can compel the attention of *all* sorts and conditions of men, belongs to a different type of mind. Possibly his book, on the kind of audience which was every author's before the Education Acts were thought of, would have produced a deeper effect if the Sansculottism of its author had been less apparent. He said somewhere that to 'arouse into activity' was the 'best effect' of any book. In England we divorce our theory from our practice, and have lost the memory of violence for so long that, to this extent, we have lost also some contact with reality. The books that arouse Englishmen into activity are like Bunyan's, addressed to the inner life and to the individual soul. England is chiefly rich in private, personal revolutions.

In any case, the best that a Bunyan of historians could produce is to be studied here. With the sympathies of most of his readers running counter to the Revolution and to his own, Carlyle tried to address their feelings by displaying the soul of the suffering French populace. Indeed, the tattered prose of his book resembles, in this respect, the march of the women of Paris to Versailles. It is one of the best examples of his method, better, I think, than, for example, the account of the taking of the Bastille:

The Art of Insurrection was an art needed in these singular times: an art for which the French nature, so full of vehemence, so free from depth, was perhaps of all others the fittest. Accordingly, to what a height, one may well say of perfection, has this branch of human industry been carried by France, within the last half-century. Insurrection, which Lafayette thought might be 'the most sacred of human duties,' ranks now for the French people, among the duties which they can perform. Other mobs are dull masses; which roll onwards with a dull fierce tenacity, a dull fierce heat, but emit no light-flashes of genius as they go. The French mob, again, is among the liveliest phenomena of our world. So rapid, audacious; so clear-sighted, inventive, prompt to seize the moment; instinct with life to its finger-ends! That talent, were there no other, of spontaneously standing in queue, distinguishes, as we said, the French People from all Peoples, ancient and modern.

Let the Reader confess too that, taking one thing with another, perhaps few terrestrial Appearances are better worth considering than mobs. Your mob is a genuine outburst of nature; issuing from, or communicating with, the deepest deep of Nature. When so much goes grinning and grimacing as a lifeless Formality, and under the stiff buckram no heart can be felt beating, here once more, if nowhere else, is Sincerity and Reality. Shudder at it; or even shriek over it if thou must; nevertheless consider it.

Throughout, Carlyle must endeavour to forestall the opposition of his readers, by substituting an alien emo-

tion for their own. Familiar with his book, having
accepted the Revolution, having moreover also accepted, with our lips at least, the republican and
Egalitarian creed of its shapers, we are apt to forget
how desperate an enterprise was that of Carlyle one
hundred years ago. Even to-day, is any passage in the
French Revolution so famous or so familiar as Burke's
lament for the passing of chivalry, his sympathetic
picture of the fallen queen? It is true that Burke was
the finer artist, a far greater master of the harmonies
of English prose, but is it only to his art, only to his
music, that the English soul answers by some echo
from its deeps? Are we really so susceptible to the
beauty of our mother-tongue as to place the crown of
our applause on Burke, whose doctrines we profess to
have repudiated, and to give respect, with critical qualifications, to Carlyle — the approving champion of
democracy? I think it doubtful. Carlyle was fulminat-
ing against the English, aristocratic grain, and his
style has suffered, to our taste, from the ragged associa-
tions that it arouses.

It becomes, then, very necessary to consider his style
with scrupulous fairness, admitting, as we should, that
English prose, for all its vagaries, is finally judged by
some obscure sense of a classical standard: a sense too
latent to have produced any classical tradition, too
weak to maintain the classical standard even when it
has chanced to emerge, but not too feeble to withhold
something from all highly idiosyncratic experiments,
nor too flimsy to place beyond changes of taste the few
simple writers that we have.

To begin with, Carlyle was a self-educated rustic,
with a passion for study that had to look beyond his
home for all its food. There was no background of
literature behind him. His foundations were entirely
in the soil. He had also practical ambitions, and, even
as late as the time when the fate of the *French Revolu-*

tion was hanging in the balance, was still wondering whether he should not become an engineer, that is to say, a mason (like his father) with a professional knowledge of mathematics. The self-taught man, like the self-made man, brings to his achievement an energy, even a freshness, with a genuine respect for fact that is often found missing in the descendants of educated people. But, if the loss is very far from being all on his side, if he can often beat them at their own game in the study and can bring a quality to his writing with which it would be hopeless for them to compete, yet his victory is purchased at a price: the highest merits must be accorded to him, but he does not quite reach virtue. If genius were inherited, the son of such a man would reach it, but virtue, the health of manliness, is not acquired in one generation. Virtue (save in poetry) can never be self-originated. Its best quality cannot be self-acquired. It is the child, not the creature, of effort; the flower on a stem that budded long ago.

Early hungry for languages, Carlyle's linguistic knowledge, and for the reading of books in other tongues this was extensive enough, was absorbed by one who had no proper language of his own. Scots is a beautiful speech; we do not need Burns to prove it; but even this speech was not pure or native to Carlyle, since his Dumfries idiom was not that which he found even in Scottish writers, in Hume, for instance, or in Walter Scott, not that, either, which was current in educated Edinburgh. Between the cottage on the moor and the parlour in the city there was an initial gap. Lowland speech and Hume's written English are virtually separate tongues, and Carlyle came to Greek and Latin, to German and Italian, without the stamp of an English of his own. He wrote, and probably thought, in a mixture of polyglot, in part the product and in part possibly the cause, of a certain inarticulateness peculiar to him. Under the influence of Goethe the thoughts begin to clear, but (as we have seen) the dominant influence was that of Richter, in whose murk and lightnings, both of soul and of speech, was a quality congenial to Carlyle. He found in Richter, as it were, an example which would justify him in developing his natural bent. There were no such examples in Scotland.

It is scarcely necessary to add that Carlyle was a natural Romantic, and, putting all these facts together, we have to ask not whether the style of the *French Revolution* is good English, but whether it is a genuine original, whether, in fact, it is right Carlylese. There is no doubt about the answer. The style of this book fits the nature of its author like a glove. Nothing, before or since, is strictly comparable to it. It passes the Romantic test! Even the prose of Meredith, a man also mainly self-educated and himself the product of a confusion of class, though it owes, in its turn, something to a schooling in Germany, turns out, on close examination, to have only a surface similarity. It would be more just to say of these men, and would tell us more about them, that both were Romantics who composed eccentric narratives, than that both fell under German influences in their youth.

In Carlyle's day a Romantic was still in an awkward position. Blake, even the Lake poets and De Quincey, had scarcely yet established themselves as models. Where then, we ask, was Carlyle to turn at home for a prose that should satisfy his peculiar hunger? Hume was too simple, too dry, too sceptical, too much tutored for him. Even Sterne was too discursive, too humorous. The great prose-writers who then dominated letters were Gibbon and Johnson. Carlyle, while recoiling, rather provincially, from Gibbon's footnotes, though apparently left undisturbed by the monkeyness of Sterne, always cherished Gibbon. He said that Gibbon's History was a kind of great monument from the past. You traversed a great stretch of time in Gibbon's majestic pages, but only the historical imagination that the two men possessed in common bound the pair together. In standard and in influence Dr. Johnson was the great exemplar.

Johnsonian prose, however, respond to it as we may, and the excellent idiom of his recorded conversation makes us much less aware of the antithetical balance of Johnson's prose than we should be with Boswell wanting, was, historically, the grand style in its decay. The apparatus of seventeenth-century prose, the age of music, had lost most of its harmony to become in Dr. Johnson's writings a convention, a deportment. The organ-music of the great Anglican divines, of Hooker, of Andrewes, or of Sir Thomas Browne, had passed away. The weaknesses of eighteenth-century prose show the artifices of the grand manner, and the 'grand manner' is the imitation of the 'grand style.' Mrs. Meynell has traced to Gibbon's nodding moments the later mannerisms of the solemn leading article: to Gibbon's double negatives the style that Dickens caricatured in the speeches of Mr. Micawber. She suggests, from examples,[1] the origins in Gibbon of Mr. Micawber's 'emotions of no common description' (when he dwelt upon the past). Since Swift and Addison were respectively too terse and too urbane to serve Carlyle for models, and since he could not find in Burns the prose he needed, Carlyle naturally turned to the home of *sturm und drang*, and enjoyed, for its own sake, the incongruous mixture of a Teutonized English.

As we miss in the history the sense, apart from the emotion, of affairs, so we miss in this style the absence of assertiveness, the classical simplicity. The Romantics have had their shrewd thrusts at classical writers,

[1] *The Second Person Singular*, by Alice Meynell.

and a decayed classicism is depressing indeed; they have (as their way is) quarrelled furiously with one another. The test of unromantic criticism is to be just to the vagaries that are little to its taste.

A writer like Carlyle might fancy that, once the sincerity of his originality has been fully conceded, criticism has nothing more to say. Let us see. Is it really so much to admit the individuality of an individual? Is there not something in the curious fact that English writers, to whom every liberty is granted, whose waywardness is indulgently called our English way, yet fare differently with posterity in proportion to this waywardness? Addison is rarely praised. He excites no feelings, yet he is cherished in quietness by those who have an ear. Swift, a master of strict prose, was somewhat romantically bitter, for his savage indignation has lost something of its edge for us, and yet that lucidity which shrank from nothing abides, as if it comprised all qualities in itself. Congreve and Gay wrote prose that has only to be rediscovered, even to an ordinary audience in a theatre, to show the independence of classical simplicity from decay. The homeliness of Bunyan's or Pepys's prose is so happy as to seem artless, and of its immortality there is no doubt. These are among our prose classics, and the small band, as each century passes, receives perhaps two, at most, recruits. Froude has now changed places with Carlyle in the pillory reserved for husbands and biographers. Carlyle did not admire *Julius Cæsar: A Sketch*; yet, when the matter of pure English is in question, the beautiful lucidity of Froude's prose, at its best, in the long run will save several of his histories from the faults of their historian. If our sense for simplicity were not deeper than we often suppose, we should not allow, as we do, our original writers to toss up and down in our esteem, eclipse succeeding vogue, and revival eclipse, while Bunyan and Addison, Swift and Congreve, Hawthorne and Froude, free alike from acclaim and misprision, stand as quietly as the stars, waiting to be read and, once read, remaining above our disputation.

Carlyle, even to the warmest of his admirers, can never stand above controversy. If he should cease to excite feelings, he would cease to be read, and, along with many writers of his kidney, he must be prepared for ups and downs, rejected when current taste is unromantic, exalted when the romantic fervour revives, and chiefly enduring as an historian whom later historians dare not neglect, an historian whose pages, even to unsympathetic students, remain a permanent protest against musty research, archivist-hunting, inhuman politics, and narrative dullness. He may well be content with such a fame, for it was precisely this which he had determined to deserve; and we must add also that the 'scientific historians' who followed him have failed, in his unexplored and complicated field, to convict him of any serious inaccuracy. The latest historical judgment of him that I have seen declared Carlyle to be 'one of the most accurate historians' who ever wrote. Again, with no experience of violence or of revolution, he recognized the note of Reality as a man recognizes his national anthem in a foreign land. Books can never take the place of personal experience; they never initiate a movement of men; the ground must be ready for them, the emotions be already stirring before they can become a centre of activity, a rallying point. Thus, if the *French Revolution* did not accomplish in England that which the books of Calvin or Rousseau accomplished in Switzerland and France, the reason is no fault in the Scotch writer. He was endeavouring to create a mood that was unknown, alien, and hateful to his fellow-countrymen. To have made the French Revolution intelligible to them, to have communicated something of the mood which initiated and sustained it, needed an inspired writer. Carlyle set out to perform a miracle, and he succeeded.

Where the current of opinion was with him, in making history a romance, in the mutual admiration of the northern protestant peoples, in the existing ties with the Germans, who had lately been our allies and had supplied a German dynasty to the English throne, Carlyle confirmed the tendencies, and established the Teutonic fashion. Treated in the romantic spirit, and what is more romantic than to act upon a sublime creed, the French Revolution was a possible subject in the eighteen thirties. It needed a magician, however, and in Carlyle that magician was found. We now need his like for Bolshevik Russia.

IV

Even to read of the burning of this manuscript appals; but there seems, too, a fateful appropriateness in the fatality. If a man cultivates a certain virtue, we expect him to find more occasions than his neighbours to practise it. The explorer is in character should he be devoured in the tropics or be frozen to death within a few miles of the North Pole, and by some mysterious sympathy we attract the hazards of our choice. Carlyle could boast of a desperate courage. He was inclined to the belief that he must write against the grain, and fate ordained that this prince of disaster should suffer the worst extremities in its power. By triumphing over them Carlyle gained enormous merit; we cannot doubt that his prayer was answered: only, if it had not been the wrong kind of prayer! For the moment the disaster unnerved him, and his work came to a full stop. He felt paralysed. One of those great readers, men who are most at home between the covers of a book, for whom the written record is a more vivid experience than the thing recorded, and literature less the channel than the very stream of life, Carlyle turned to the novels of Marryat and to Dante's *Inferno*, as it were under their eaves to build again. He had to recapture the mood in which work was possible before he could begin to work at all. He took strenuous exercise, roaming the London parks, probably to enable him to sleep, and about the beginning of July, four months after the catastrophe, the subject had captured him again. When the new first part was shown to his wife toward the end of September, she declared it to be an improvement on the former version. He would admit no more than that it was not very much worse.

It may have been a coincidence, but meantime Mrs. Carlyle had fallen ill, and when Mrs. Welsh arrived to nurse her, and was prepared to stay till the end of November, Carlyle went off to Scotland for a month, and was probably glad of the solitude. He was in no holiday mood, but it was better that he should go away, and desire to return, than linger in industrious misery in Chelsea. When he came home he set to work with such tenacity that by the end of April 1836 the second volume was completed. We can guess the strain upon him throughout this winter from one of his remarks: 'A little black speck dances to and fro in the left eye like a signal of distress.'

A man generally too proud to seek others but needing friends, and even disciples, Carlyle was not left alone at this time. His wife was proving an attractive hostess. Young men also began to arrive with letters from Emerson in their pockets, and when the now devoted Mill introduced Godefroi Cavaignac the little stream of foreign exiles from France and Italy began. It was Cavaignac who told Mrs. Carlyle that she would be 'French soon,' and the Cheyne Row circle was quietly establishing itself. Cavaignac was followed by Mazzini. While his work was advancing steadily, Carlyle needed to be amused in the evenings, and his wife, in the absence of callers, was finding in this foreign colony ample material for the narratives that she told and he heard with equal pleasure.

In July he had begun Part III, and his wife then went to stay with Mrs. Welsh, by whom she was petted to exasperation since she complained of being given everything but the things for which she asked. She sent by post an amusing account of her experiences with her mother, who probably also found some difficulty with her child. When Jane returned to London on the first of September, Carlyle was able to boast that he had recognized her trunk on an omnibus in Fleet Street, and his pride in this alertness is amusing.

Before the end of the year his book had gone to the printers.

'Thank God, it is done, Jeannie. What they will do with this book none knows, my Jeannie lass; but they have not had for two hundred years any book that came more truly from a man's very heart; and so let them trample it under foot and hoof as they see best...'

'Pooh, pooh, they cannot trample that,' she answered, and it was the best assurance that he could have.

The year 1837 began in fog and drizzle, and Mrs. Carlyle was a victim to influenza more than once. Her own share in the troubles of authorship is described to Sterling with characteristic vivacity:

The rag-taggery of printers' devils drives one from pillar to post. Quelle vie! Let no woman who values peace of soul ever dream of marrying an author. But this I observe to you in confidence; should I state such a sentiment openly, I might happen to get myself torn in pieces by the host of my husband's lady admirers, who already, I suspect, think me too happy in not knowing my happiness. You cannot fancy the way he is making with fair intellects here. There is Harriet Martineau ... and Mrs. Pierce Butler ... and then there is a young American beauty.

Allan Cunningham's comment is also interesting: 'Carlyle [he said] will be very well and happy enough if he gets a little more fame.'

The *French Revolution* brought this to pass, and a review by Mill, which has been called courageous in its welcome, hastened the recognition of a book the vivid qualities of which were, in truth, more likely to be quickly felt than slowly discerned. With this volume Carlyle established his reputation, though he had not yet left anxieties behind. In the same summer as that in which Queen Victoria ascended the throne, the Jeremiah among her prophets found his audience.

CHAPTER EIGHT

A LION AND HIS WIFE

I

AT first sight the victory over circumstance seemed to be complete. Carlyle had not only rewritten his book in the teeth of disaster, and shown that his determination was equal to any burden, but he had also increased his reputation, and there was no longer any doubt that the world would listen to him. For most men this would have secured repose, and it should have inaugurated a happier life for Carlyle and his wife. It was, however, at this time that their inner distresses began to become pronounced, and the ensuing years are a quaint mixture of increasing outward prosperity and of unceasing inward disquiet. It would be easy to exaggerate the situation: to present Carlyle, with his moods, his ebullitions, his hatred of any commotion, his failure to find a quiet room in a house where there was no noise and where all was ordered for his comfort, as the author of caricature; to present his wife as merely the tragic victim of a ludicrous temperament. The spectacle suggested by the enormous correspondence that has been printed could readily be termed farcical in its extravagance and tragic in its foundation, but either view is that of a spectator content with the superficies of a situation, both human and understandable but complex in the extreme. A situation is a stage-picture: the participators are conscious of very little but the tension of their own nerves.

If Carlyle, at this time, compared his circumstances or the quality and the reception of his work with the condition of affairs at the date of his marriage eleven years before, he had every reason to be thankful. He had defined his own attitude, found a fine subject, created a style as personal as he could wish, and forced the world to accept him. The outward obstacles had been overcome, and the writer's control of his medium was no longer in dispute. Those who had been inclined to shake their heads over his marriage had forgotten their hesitations. He was still in love with his wife, and she with him. Of all this he could hardly be conscious: why should one be specially grateful for the normal satisfactions of men? It was here that the shoe still pinched him. He had had more difficulties than other people. From that distant day when he had flung defiance at the skies he had not ceased to be 'bedevilled,' and it seems as if the spirit of defiance had been all that he had gained from that moment of Pyrrhic victory. The determination to fight against his mysterious inhibitions had overcome them on every occasion, but it left the enemy no weaker than before. He was in the position of a general who wins a series of encounters in an endless guerilla campaign. The castor oil that he consumed for his liver, the strenuous exercises that he never spared, could not bring order into his digestion or peace to his mind. He was still inhibited and hag-ridden, a troublesome companion to himself.

This condition, no doubt, helps to explain why the annoyances that could be controlled bulked so largely in his consciousness. It was not only an indication of frayed nerves. The palpable enemies had to be furiously denounced because the impalpable eluded him. His troubles were psychological and interior; even the work in which his energies found an outlet brought him small peace of mind. Carlyle was the unhappiest of authors. The condition that is periodic with many writers, that is persistent with some, was a chronic condition with him; but, though the morbid symptoms were pronounced, there was a core of health and vitality, and the genius, choked and thwarted in its issue, was really to be seen not in the struggles to which it was condemned, but in an underlying simplicity and gaiety, an abounding humour as unquenchable as itself. He wrote, truly, that he would have been one of the merriest of men if he had not been one of the most sickly. Because the lighter and the healthier side of his temper has left no equal record, it must not be overlooked, for in its absence he would not have kept his friends, nor would it have been possible to live with him. Genius *is* the gaiety of life.

Mrs. Carlyle had foreseen the difficulties in his path, and she knew that the worst of them were congenital. Her reasons for disquiet were that she had been disappointed of children, and, in the consequent loneliness, and helplessness to help her husband, she was deprived of the companionship that comes from sharing troubles. The more he was in need the deeper was his isolation; and, when matters were at their worst and they sought change in separate holidays, the return to which they both looked forward so sincerely would often bring them no nearer than they had been before the holidays had begun. Love can reach a soul which is the victim of external misery, but it cannot reach a soul that is the source of its own unrest. In this disappointment love is wounded in the act of giving, which is its life, and the effect of this rebuff is to produce some of the symptoms that distress it in its object. In its effort to find the right offering, the key that should open the dividing door, any seeds of jealousy will be nurtured, and the wife who is disappointed of children is apt to be jealous: through concentrating on one a feeling that nature intended to be dispersed. His nature could not be at rest, and hers suffered probably the more because their mutual affection did not solve their troubles.

The *French Revolution* had brought Carlyle to the eve of a popular success, and this was assured when, against the grain, but for financial reasons, he undertook to become a public lecturer. The best of his lectures survive in his printed works, and can be conveniently considered among them, thus allowing us to glance at the lecturer and his wife during what proved to be the turning-point in his career.

II

Between 1837 and 1840 Carlyle delivered four series of lectures, beginning with six on German Literature and ending with those on Heroes and Hero-worship. According to his own account, he was 'agitated, terrified, driven desperate and furious,' and his wife was sufficiently apprehensive of a breakdown not to attend the opening lecture. The course was, however, a success, and his opening diffidence is said to have commended him to his audience, who were struck by his handsome face, his earnestness, his blue eyes and his ruddy complexion. Moreover, he treated them well in that he did not read his addresses but delivered them as speeches with, at most, but a few notes in his hand. His nervousness was unconcealed, and, despite the increasing number of his hearers, he suffered from sleeplessness and indigestion throughout the course. The lectures were given at Willis's Rooms, and before a fashionable audience, among whom was Harriet Martineau. She heard them with admiration, became friendly with the Carlyles, and was one of the first admirers to cause Mrs. Carlyle a twinge of jealousy. In May 1838 we find the latter writing:

I took one glimpse of him (just one) as he came on the stage, and to be sure he was as white as a pockethandkerchief, but he made no gasping and spluttering as I found him doing last year at the *fourth* lecture.

A year later, she was writing to her mother:

To-morrow is the last lecture-day, thank Heaven. Unless

he can get hardened to this trade, he certainly ought to discontinue it; for no gain or éclat that it can yield is compensation enough for the martyrdom it is to himself, and thro' him to me. — To appearance he has got through the thing this year much more smoothly and quite as brilliantly as last year; but in defect of the usual measure of agitation beforehand, he has taken to the new and curious crotchet of being ready to hang himself after, in the idea that he has made 'a horrible pluister (mess) of it.' No demonstration of the highest satisfaction on the part of his audience can convince him to the contrary... Very absurd.[1]

His writings gave him hardly more satisfaction, and it was probably already becoming clear to both of them that he was to remain tormented to the last. Whether he was isolated in his study, or on holiday in Scotland, he could never escape from himself. No one has used words as pronounced as his own. In 1840 he wrote to John Carlyle: 'The absence of ill-fare and semi-delirium is possible to me in solitude only. Solitude indeed is sad as Golgotha, but it is not mad like Bedlam.' The saving clause in all this vehemence is the pleasure that his imagination took in describing his condition; and, if the whole house was thrown into commotion because he had mislaid something, by objectifying his condition of nerves he evoked a drama that would appeal to his sense of humour because the effect was out of proportion to the cause. Some of his wife's sallies at these times could restore sunshine very quickly. Moreover, his enjoyment was as hearty as his explosions. He liked society of a congenial kind, and very much to see his wife shine also in the eyes of others. The sociability and the goodwill in this household were no less genuine than the tension, but to none under its roof was it a centre of peace. Physically and mentally health was precarious.

The letters that they exchanged when absent from

[1] *New Letters and Memorials,* 179.

one another are unmistakably affectionate, and absence convinced them that separation was no remedy.
In reply to one of his, his wife wrote:

I said to myself that you were no better than when you
left me, and all this absence was gone for nothing. I wanted
to kiss you into something like cheerfulness, and the length
of a kingdom was between us, and, if it had not, the probabil-
ities are that, with the best intentions, I should have quarrelled with you rather. Poor men and poor women! What
a time they have in this world, by destiny and their own
deserving. But, as Mr. Bradfute used to say, 'tell us something that we do not know.'

She was also away at this time, and continued:

I long for home, and to be putting it in order for your
coming... O, my darling, we will surely be better, both of us,
there again; effervescing even, don't you think so?

The pathos of their situation was that love was not
enough to make it happy.

While Carlyle was engaged with these lectures, and
suffered a crisis of nerves — 'the ruin of his whole
being,' his wife called it, through having to serve upon
a jury — he was dallying with the idea of Cromwell,
and, with *Past and Present*, so to speak, in the wings, his
wife penned a couple of dialogues that she sent to
Sterling. These could be interpreted subjectively, and
because, perhaps, they suggested such an interpretation she expressly told Sterling not to read between the
lines. As an example of her authorship they are dis-
appointing, and convince us that she was really a letter-
writer first and last. She certainly made the most of
the society that came her way, and it is pleasant to
catch a glimpse of one of her happy adventures.

Early in April 1839, she wrote:

To-day gone a week the sound of a whirlwind rushed
through the street, and there stopped with a prancing of

steeds and footman-thunder at this door, an equippage all resplendent with skye-blue and silver, discoverable through the
blinds, like a piece of the Coronation Procession, from whence
emanated Count d'Orsay!... Happily it was not one of my
nervous days ... and a sight it was to make one think the mil-
lennium actually at hand, when the lion and the lamb, and all
incompatible things should consort together. Carlyle in his
grey plaid suit, and his tub-chair, looking blandly at the
Prince of Dandies; and the Prince of Dandies on an opposite
chair, all resplendent as a diamond-beetle, looking blandly at
him. D'Orsay is a really handsome man, after one has heard
him speak and found that he has both wit and sense; but at
first sight his beauty is of that rather disgusting sort which
seems to be, like genius, 'of no sex.' And this impression is
greatly helped by the fantastical finery of his dress ... but his
manners are manly and unaffected, and he convinces one
shortly that, in the face of all probability, he is a devilish clever
fellow.

This lively description occurs in a delightful letter to
her mother. These letters give no indication of the
difficulty that they found in living together. Jane's
self-reproaches when Mrs. Welsh died in February
1842 show the exaggeration of grief. Jane had idolized
her father and was devoted to her mother, but she was
impatient of caprice and Mrs. Welsh in little things
could be exacting, though, when she was really needed,
as in times of illness, her instability disappeared.

Mrs. Carlyle would take advantage of her husband's
holidays to have the house done up, and, as he had
more than the average man's dislike of these upheavals,
had he been present, he would have been more a hin-
drance than a help. In July 1843 she undertook the
task quite cheerfully, as two sentences from her letters
to him will show. 'You *do so* hate commotions that this
house gets no periodical cleanings like other people's,
and one must make the most of your absence.' Again:
'The early rising, and the shower-bathing and the
having something to look after agree with me wonder-

THOMAS CARLYLE IN 1839
Drawn by Count D'Orsay

fully: the degree of heat also is exactly to my needs. This and the other person drops in and asks if I do not feel lonely.' It was not the work that she minded or even the responsibility, but when Carlyle returned in one of his moods and would perhaps throw everything into disorder, she felt deprived of her reward. What was the use of all her little plans and activities if they had no soothing effect on his disquiet? He was very largely unaware of the effect that he produced upon others by his thoughtlessness, and, though this egoism is not the same thing as deliberate selfishness, it can be no less hard to bear. Selfishness is a form of indulgence, but the egoist is himself a victim, and feels himself to be a victim, to his disease. Carlyle's caprices could be appalling, but he was not selfish in intention, only blind.

A pleasant picture of the pair about this time is given by M. Rio in a passage quoted by Mr. Wilson. 'I don't know a man in London whose talk is so genial as Carlyle's.' 'His Scotch accent did not bother me so much as last year. As for his wife, the expression of her features is the best imaginable.' And again, 'The difference between them, in manners and appearance, and particularly in accent, suggests a difference in class. But when the conversation becomes alive, this man with the rugged face and plebeian accent seems to grow into a giant, and shows that he belongs to the very first quality of nature's noblemen.'

III

No doubt the fashionable crowd that came to hear him lecture was partly moved by curiosity, but, when the spell that he could cast in private converse began to show itself as he warmed to a public harangue, his rugged eloquence itself asserted the fascination that folk will always have for culture once the audience feels its own superiority to be in doubt. The last course survives in one of his most popular books, for in *Heroes* and *Hero-worship* many have found the outlines of a secular religion, and the very title has appealed to the schoolboy latent in us all. The intellectual content is very simple. On the basis that 'the history of what man has accomplished in this world is at bottom the History of the Great Men who have worked there,' typical examples of the prophet, poet, priest, man of letters, and king are made the subject of biographical sketches. We are told that a man's religion is not to be confused with his professions of faith, but is indicated by the assumptions that move him to action, and that all men whom the world has held in respect have first been conscious of the mysteriousness of the universe and have then surrendered themselves to the idea of duty, in obedience to that which lies behind all the formulas. Thus sincerity becomes the first of virtues, and the hero is he who, looking 'through the shows of things into things,' has the courage to act on his convictions.

These words are taken from the essay on Mahomet, partly because this choice of a hero was the most surprising to his audience, who were more familiar with 'our current hypothesis that he was a scheming impostor,' and partly because the essay contains one of Carlyle's few arresting observations: 'They wrong man greatly who say he is to be seduced by ease. Difficulty, abnegation, martyrdom, death are the *allurements* that act on the heart of man.' It is worth quoting because it provides us, rightly, with the answering thrill that the dreary doctrine of duty, duty, almost quenches. Like most people of Calvinistic origin, Carlyle fell short of the truth that it is better to love good than to hate evil. The Catechism may talk gravely of our duty to God and to our neighbour, but the two inspiring commandments which summed up both the law and the prophets never mentioned the

word duty at all. The chill element, the quality that
can make Carlyle dull, was his blindness to grace and
to the joy of right doing, and yet who ever imagined
a hero going sadly or dutifully to his death? The
Christ that has been the wonder of the world outside
orthodoxy is a lovely fountain of spontaneous virtue.
The Man of Sorrows was a conception of the Old
Testament, and those who see no further are those sin-
ridden people who would give to Good Friday the
precedence over Easter Day.

The nineteenth century with its belief in progress
was beginning to worship Man himself, and Carlyle's
gospel of hero-worship was the form that the tendency
expressed in Comte's philosophy took over here. It
was not his fault that people were encouraged by
Carlyle to worship men rather than the spirit that
these had been inspired to teach or work for; but his
view of history is open to the criticism that the failure
of mankind to follow its leaders has played a much
greater part than they. If you believe in the comforting notion of progress you have no motive to observe or reflect, whereas a more detached mind is
equally impressed with the heights of individual
achievement and with their want of effect upon mankind at large. From the point of view of the hero, between one age and another there is very little to choose.
While, therefore, Carlyle has the same story to tell
about each of his heroes, who indeed are nothing but
barely distinguishable versions of his ideal, the Struggling Man, the doctrine of progress remains unaffected
in his mind, and thus it is to his narrations, his little
pictures of high character, that we turn. As a thinker,
he had only the doctrine of sincerity; as an historian he
is not a guide to be trusted, but as the vivid painter of a
certain special type of character, a sort of projection
of his own, he is excellent — so long as he will be
reasonably brief.

As an example of his art, the little sketch of Luther is happy, though, like all Carlyle's portraits with the possible exception of Burns, it is partial in the extreme. Wherever the imagination of Carlyle discovered the Struggling Man, the verdict, the very lights and shadows, are a foregone conclusion. The hypochondria in Johnson and in Cromwell appeal to him, as reflexions of his own. He even goes so far as to say: 'Nay, perhaps the sorrow and nobleness were intimately and even inseparably connected with each other.' Some of his criticism of the Johnsonian style is pertinent to Carlyle's: 'sometimes a tumid size of phraseology not in proportion to the contents of it'; or, again, 'a fundamental mistake to call vehemence (here he was speaking of Rousseau) and rigidity strength! A man is not strong who takes convulsion-fits; though six men cannot hold him then.' In this lecture, on the Hero as Man of Letters, occurs the sentence that has proved such a boon to publishers and booksellers: 'The true university of these days is a Collection of Books.' Only a very bookish person could have let that tempting fancy stand without any qualification! We are in no danger of being deceived by it now. The universities with a tradition of scholarship and judgment to maintain, with a society in which discussion and knowledge are not presumed to be divorced, now stand as a check, however inadequate, on the flood of printed matter which has the outside world almost at its mercy so long as still more books are to remedy the confusion books have caused. We must not look to Carlyle for ideas, for criticism, for reflexion. He had next to none of these. His intellectual foundation was a simple platitude, and his literary genius may be judged from the capacity he had for investing this platitude with the air of discovery, and for persuading the world that sincerity and the like were not merely uncommon virtues but, actually, unrecognized truths! Only a born writer could have found so much to say about so little, but clarity and conciseness are intellectual, not emotional qualities, and Carlyle, like other popular preachers, was vehement and excessive, vague and well-intentioned, repetitive and eloquent, on what are and always will be popular texts. He hammered hard at moral abstractions. He gave to his readers the sensation of embarking, without danger, on a terrific moral crusade. The book really belongs to homiletic literature, using familiar historical figures to emphasize the moral virtues most congenial to the author's mind. Carlyle is in the succession of John Bunyan, but in place of allegory we have history, though the Heroes are really a single conception, the earnest Man of Action, which perhaps Carlyle himself was — in his dreams.

The lectures, having proved a fashionable success, made Carlyle more widely known, and the growth of his reputation is seen in the fact that, here and there, it was thought worth while to attack him. On the one hand he was becoming an inspiration to young men, and a literary force in the universities; on the other he seemed to some of their elders a dangerous influence, for nothing is more disquieting than a respectable champion of subversive views. It is true that his criticisms were all abstract; no man or institution was threatened by him, but apprehensiveness was widespread and anything was feared that might give countenance to the underlying discontent in the country. Manchester's satanic mills were rising in their might; the fate of the Corn Laws was in the balance; and education itself was deemed a danger to be watched very suspiciously.

When, therefore, Carlyle in 1840 did the great public service of agitating for a semi-public lending library in London from which members could borrow good books, he encountered some opposition. Was not the suggestion an implied attack on the British Museum, and would not the proposed new facility for study necessarily encourage discontent? Everyone knew the inconvenience of reading in a public library books that could not be borrowed or taken away, but was not the inconvenience itself a useful check on the desire for knowledge? Was it not, on the whole, better that books should be difficult of access, and, as in Gibbon's day, confined to those who could afford to spend large sums of money on purchasing them? If Gibbon had not been rich, he might never have written a book that many sensible people deeply regretted. Nevertheless in 1840 that invaluable institution, the best friend that English authors have ever had, the London Library, was started, but it is fair to the objectors to remember that the Hungry Forties had begun. The distress was terrible, and starvation so great that some parents murdered their children to obtain money from the Burial Societies. The aim of those in power was not to remedy the prevailing misery, but to prevent its victims from making themselves heard. Books can contain facts, and libraries by making facts accessible can stir up trouble.

Carlyle also lent his support to the movement in favour of international copyright, and the argument that he used was 'thou shalt not steal.' Though he once made a horse-shoe which was guaranteed not to slip, and was never tired of preaching the necessity of action, he was as unpractical as it was possible to be and always angry when the practical side of life made demands on his attention. If a spring-cleaning drove him crazy, service on a jury almost sent him mad. No one enjoys the waste of time involved by attendance at the Law Courts, but it is amusing to see a public-spirited man so resentful as Carlyle. He was such a problem to himself that any additional demand on his attention was almost more than he could endure.

When one thinks of his attitude to service on a jury, his suggestion, in Heroes, that the best man of letters would make the best rulers becomes quaint. In his abstract way, he was inclined to confuse the 'diversity of gifts' with 'the same spirit,' and a poet like Patmore who without previous training can manage and improve an estate to advantage is less common than the poet who confesses: 'I never could a lost thing find, nor a broken thing mend.' One does not see Carlyle happy in public business or in the management of men. He could describe a revolution admirably, but his practical advice boils down to the passionate assertion that men must 'do the right' or perish. He would not have insisted so warmly on the value of wise leadership if he had not himself felt bewildered by the practical exigencies of daily life. He vociferated his principles with vehement emphasis because their practical application puzzled him woefully. With great gifts for portraiture and descriptive narrative, he cannot be considered a force in the world. The sins of society are a popular text, and the man who denounces them, in general terms, enjoys the double prestige of combining flattery with invective. It is interesting that so bookish a man should have interpreted even men of letters in terms of action. Nietzsche was another example. I think we may say that this insistence was the counterpart of a defective practical faculty in either author. There is something of Carlyle's bewilderment in Rodin's Penseur, who sits puzzled because, with the body of Hercules, he has lost his simplicity, and with the brain of a peasant is perplexed by thought.

IV

In this same decade, when reputation and even money were rewarding the author, who was beginning to be a welcome visitor in great houses, a change for the worse took place in the health of his wife. She had

long suffered from cruel headaches, and had been an
annual victim to influenza and a chronic sufferer from
sleeplessness. All this points to some mental distress or
psychological strain of long standing, and anyone who
looks at the facts instead of at the controversy arising
therefrom will not be hard put to find at least a partial
explanation. This is implicit in her overworked girlhood, in her protracted engagement, in her marriage
with a man of different breeding who suffered himself
from nervous strain and morbid inhibitions, in the
solitude imposed by her union with him, in the absence
of children who, in nature's way, would have provided
the natural outlet and the appropriate remedy. The
most fanatical of Carlyle's admirers cannot pretend
that he was particularly easy to live with. If he were
at all difficult, as even the family who idolized him
found, any woman whom he married would be bound
to share some of his suffering, and, if she were also a
childless wife, the explanation stares us in the face.
The reason why we are told that Mrs. Carlyle was a
precocious victim to 'climacteric melancholia' and the
rest of it, is also plain. Froude's interpretation of the
Reminiscences penned by Carlyle in the extremity of
his grief, accompanied by the later suggestion that
Carlyle himself was impotent, has forced the physical
factors into the foreground; and the most convenient
way of exonerating Carlyle from the responsibility,
which he was over-anxious to incur when his wife was
suddenly taken from him, has seemed, to his admirers,
to be to charge his wife with physical disorder. It may
be said at once that there is no evidence to prove
Carlyle a physical defective; that his own remorse was
clearly exaggerated, since the bereaved widower is as
likely to enhance his sorrow as the lover is to enhance
his joy; and that any physical explanation is far too
gross and crude to explain a situation only controversial because its victims have happened to be famous,

and to have set down with entire frankness some of the feelings that moved them when their strains were most intense. The nomenclature of medicine, the adjectives of partisans, tell us next to nothing. We are confronted with a very human situation, the whole complexity of which is thrown out of perspective if it is either reduced entirely to physical factors or made an excuse for covering either party with excessive blame. The fact that Mrs. Carlyle now asked for a separate bedroom, in the hope that she might sleep better alone, is not at all surprising. She had now been married for some fifteen years. If there had been children, Carlyle almost certainly would have anticipated her. The effect on each other of their characters and circumstances was beginning to tell, and the affection which united them without solving their problems naturally embittered her while she lived and her husband when he had lost her.

Meantime, she was both consoled and hurt when he began to reap the fruits of his reputation. We can sympathize with her womanly jealousy of his growing admirers, with the twinge with which she divined their envy of the lion's wife, with her impatience at the good fortune that they attributed to her relationship, with the mixture of pride and irritation with which she received their requests for his autograph, and their 'inexpressible longings' to be invited to tea. She had borne the burden and heat of the day. These outsiders were only alive to the glory of a reputation. To Carlyle success or neglect could be equally occasions for grumbling, though, as his friend had foreseen, a little more fame was, really, doing him some good.

The friendship which he started about this time with Lady Harriet Baring, afterward Lady Ashburton, like most other things about the pair, has given rise to unnecessary controversy. Carlyle found the lady entertaining; indeed, she bore some superficial resemblance to his wife. He gained distraction in her company, and could meet at her house those of the aristocracy who were most likely to interest him. Lady Harriet was too clever to surround herself with dull people, and made much of Carlyle, who was now a celebrity that many were curious to meet. The distraction that he found on his visits to the Barings is quite understandable, and it was only human that his wife should feel no pleasure that he could be happier with them, at times, than he was at home. His visits to their houses were rarely long but they were frequent, and a heart, like Jane's, starved for affection, since no husband can fill the place of a child, was bound to chafe when any sign appeared that he was slipping away from her, not indeed to any other person, but into an atmosphere other than hers, than his own home. It was hard enough that he should segregate himself in Cheyne Row, where she had no nursery to claim her. It was worse that he should enjoy another household better, even if only by way of distraction and change. He would return from these visits full of his news, and the news could not be very palatable to an affectionate but disappointed wife. Lady Harriet, Jane felt, was filling too large a place in his thoughts, and, as he was no less blind than unfailing in his affection, Carlyle could not understand what the trouble was about. Jane was too well-bred to show social resentment. She was always included in the invitations; she sometimes accepted them; she began by liking Lady Harriet, but, when she discovered that Lady Harriet could hold her own and was as witty as herself, the very gifts of the new friend became exasperating. Carlyle was happier than he deserved to be when his wife's heart was comparatively empty, and that she was not the source of this new happiness explains the jealousy that Jane, always possessive, was too fond of her husband not to feel. Years before, it was less Rennie, than the loss of him,

that she had felt. Carlyle never loved Lady Ashburton; he only liked her, but the evidence of his liking
was more apparent than the evidence of his love, and
the consequence was that Jane was made unhappy by
it. A possessive affection, too, can be selfish. Did he
want to escape from it — sometimes?

Carlyle's own troubles at this time concerned the
difficulty of writing his *Cromwell*, partly because he
always found it difficult to begin and partly because,
keenly alive to the shocking industrial conditions of the
forties, he was anxious to do something for the suf-
ferers, which for him meant to arouse the upper classes
to the actual state of affairs. He did his best by writing
Past and Present, and the distinction of his performance
lay in his being the first author of standing to make the
condition of England a living topic in the educated and
fashionable world.

v

When a writer with a vivid imagination turns from
history to the description of current abuses, he is asking for trouble, and, since *Past and Present* has been
acclaimed a wonderful book for its day, we are bound
to ask why Carlyle incurred no penalty. The reason
was that his peculiar style prevented him from being
read by the poorer classes, that he confined himself in
the main to generalities, and that the remedies he proposed were moral and vague. Even the conditions
that he described were mostly abstract, which made it
easy for sophisticated people, by whom he was being
read, to enjoy his denunciations of Mammonism and
Dilettantism without applying the criticism to themselves. Still, it was a great thing for some of the shocking facts revealed by Reports on Factories, and official
inquiries, and Law Reports, to be made current in
general literature, and the conscience of the propertied
classes was so dead that some direct appeal to stir its

sluggishness was essential. Between the practical manufacturers, content to wallow in their profits, who read
nothing, and the reading folk with some conscience
but no knowledge of business, *Past and Present* became
the sensation of a season, doing little more than to
convince people that commercial principles and religious principles were the negation of each other.
There has been next to no attempt to accommodate
them since, and the slow consequence has been to make
us accept the distinction with a gradually confirmed
sense of despair.

Certain phrases, with which we are now familiar,
came into general currency through Carlyle's book.
The cash nexus, the captain of industry, the name of
Morrison's pills for political nostrums, are the readiest
examples; and the condition of the time can be judged
from the surprise which greeted the assertion that a
fair day's work was entitled to a fair day's wages. The
Duke of Newcastle was horrified when the young
Gladstone said the same thing. Equally startling was
the statement that landlords must 'earn their rent' by
good management. Both these statements may be
platitudes to-day: we no longer deny a formula which
is not expected to apply to business. This explains
why the first and third parts of *Past and Present* have
become somewhat tedious. Carlyle confined himself
to moral formulas, and the world has a sound instinct
that, outside poetry, which is the most personal record
of all experience, abstract formulas are — only sublime.

The book lives to-day by the historical interlude
describing, with the help of Jocelyn's chronicle, how
Abbot Samson reorganized St. Edmundsbury. Though
this is overweighted with Carlyle's moral exhortations,
the Abbey lives again in his pages, especially in those
which he translates direct from Jocelyn's text. It is instructive to compare his own discursions with the moving simplicity of the original chronicle. The chapter

describing the unveiling of the relics of St. Edmund by
night is extraordinarily moving, and the modern author stands revealed as a writer who has lost more
than he has gained by his polyglot education. The
nearest contemporary parallel to him, in origin, simplicity, earnestness, and even opinion, is William Cobbett, and can it be denied that the vigorous simplicity of the style of this son of a Surrey farmer is a
closer reflection of the ideal at which Carlyle himself
aimed than the redundant prose of the Scottish prophet? Carlyle appealed to a sophisticated audience,
Cobbett to anyone who had learnt to read. For the
former, Cobbett was too direct to be agreeable. The
latter would certainly prefer Cobbett if he had received a tithe of Carlyle's praise. It will be objected,
perhaps, that Cobbett was a pamphleteer, and Carlyle
an historian, and that breadth of vision and range of
interest necessarily outweigh the delight of pure English in a narrow field. The argument is not convincing. Cobbett also wrote a history, and it is one of
the wonders of English literature that his *History of
the Reformation* remains so little known. A comparison
of the two writers, however tempting, would carry us
too far. The reason for the neglect of Cobbett's history
appears to be that he was writing against the current
of opinion, whereas Carlyle, for all his bluster, was
really reflecting the tendency, though latent, of his
time. The rising tide carried Carlyle to success, but
we are beginning to realize that his view of history was
more the fashion of his age than an impartial pre-
sentment.

The fashionable villain that he changed into a hero
in his next book, on Cromwell, was a violent reaction
but in the mood of his day. The Protestant nations,
dynastically allied and continually expanding throughout the nineteenth century, were beginning to glorify
themselves and their own history. Carlyle constituted

himself the spokesman of this tendency in England. It had even been as a disguised form of 'protestantism' that the French Revolution itself had attracted him. Once Napoleon had been defeated, Carlyle could assert, without fear of persecution, that the Reformation consisted of three phases, beginning with Luther's action at Wittenberg, followed by Cromwell's at the Great Rebellion, and concluded by the recent Revolution in France. All that we had to do was to overthrow the legend of the regicide, to see in Cromwell the best ruler that England had ever had, and to look for another leader of his type to show us a way out of our present industrial welter. The sympathy that lay deep in Carlyle's nature made it necessary for him to have his say upon the condition of England, before turning to the study of Cromwell in good earnest.

VI

Towards the end of the eighteenth century the legend of Oliver Cromwell had begun to undergo a change; to pass from that of a villainous usurper to the other extreme of a national hero. It was Carlyle's object to complete the transformation, and he set about it in an ingenious way. The abstract method, whether employed to exalt or to vilify a controversial character, soon becomes fatiguing. There ensues a demand for evidence and fact, and it is exceptional if one highly coloured but generalized picture succeeds in replacing another. Whitewash is a poor substitute for tar and feathers, or black for white. Carlyle, therefore, at first puzzled by the bewildering mass of documents and pamphlets relating to this disputatious time, resolved to thread his way through the tangle by fixing on some central character, and to confine himself to documents relating to him. His choice fell upon Oliver Cromwell, the most prominent Struggling Man of the revolutionary epoch. Cromwell, though a much

richer millionaire than a careless reader would discover from Carlyle's book, had several points of sympathy for the son of a Scotch Calvinist farmer. Cromwell was a puritan, a self-made king, a revolutionary,
and a regicide: a Sansculotte who succeeded to the
throne that he overthrew: that rare combination, an
overwhelmingly successful revolutionary. He was
blunt in speech, relentless in action, who moreover, in
the words of another admirer, Macaulay, 'on those
who resisted had made war as the Hebrews made war
on the Canaanites'; in Ireland, 'not a small teasing
tyrant, such as those who have long been her curse and
her shame, but one of those awful tyrants who, at long
intervals, seem to be sent on earth, like avenging an-
gels, with some high commission of destruction and
renovation.' Carlyle's appetite for violence, which is
sometimes the mark of very bookish men in their writings and ideals, and here, again, we think of Nietzsche,
was satisfied in Cromwell, whose red sword, plain
speech, and Biblical idiom were, so to speak, the 'evidence' of his simple sincerity and force of character.
Moreover, he had been much abused by people with
few of his advantages. Cromwell's achievements, however estimated, were matters of history. He had not
yet had a literary monument, however, at all adequate
to his deserts. This Carlyle intended now to furnish,
with the idea of vindicating his character at first hand,
by a collection of his letters and speeches, with no more
annotation than was absolutely necessary to link them
together and to fill the inevitable gaps.

Nothing could appear more simple or straightfor-
ward. Propaganda never wore a more innocent face;
yet, apart altogether from our opinions of Cromwell,
nothing turned out to be more inadequate, and even
likely to mislead. To read Carlyle's volumes by themselves and without prejudice is to be amazed that there
had ever been any controversy about Cromwell. Of

the points most disputed in his career — whether or not he arranged to be excluded from the Self-denying Ordinance; whether or not he was privy to the escape of the King — there is nothing said. Cromwell is presented throughout at *more* than his own valuation; his heroic character is assumed from the very first, and every sentence intercalated by Carlyle takes his subject's virtuous aloofness for granted. Much of the correspondence, part of the speeches, are necessarily trivial, but we are invited to heed them all as the pure and simple gold of a sterling and earnest character. Even if this had been the unquestioned verdict, for which only the documents that formed the evidence had previously escaped publication, it would not achieve either portraiture or history. To offer it, even to a willing public, in the guise of both is a very curious proceeding, and shows how powerful was the presupposition in Carlyle's own uncritical head. All it actually achieves is to familiarize the reader with Cromwell's epistolary style, and to omit, as irrelevant, almost everything else bearing upon the history of the man and of his period. The omissions in the book are disguised by its great length.

Once more, however, as in the history of the French Revolution, Carlyle's power of conveying the confused counsels of men and assemblies in revolutionary times is highly successful. He failed with the Struggling Man, but he succeeded admirably with the bewildered groups and with the atmosphere of halting counsels and confused expectancy. The hapless soldier impatient with the men of talk is also made vivid to us, once Cromwell's experiences with his own parliaments began. It is also a pleasure to read contemporary documents, but Carlyle's treatment of them shows that original authorities may be made as misleading as the more generalized methods of more academic historians. The quotations, however, accomplished the

effect desired, and, as their collection was extremely
laborious, Carlyle received the reward of his industry,
though his method of procedure resulted in a book that
is neither adequate portraiture nor adequate history.
It survives with the aid of his general reputation, and
is rarely challenged by literary critics because it is
much too long for most critics, unless they be historians, to read. The ordinary reader takes it for granted,
and to-day it has become one of those familiar volumes
which are much more often reprinted than read. It is
bought in cheap reprints and in collected editions.

VII

Before we leave this period in the lives of the
Carlyles, the reader should be reminded of the letter
that Mrs. Carlyle wrote to Mrs. Aiken in October
1843. It is too long to quote, but it contains his wife's
detailed description of the turmoil that occurred in
Cheyne Row when Carlyle returned from his travels,
and after three days of content with the household
improvements that had been made in his absence, was
led by the sound of a piano being practised next door
to have back the workmen who had just been dismissed, to construct a new room under the roof and,
when this had been accomplished, to return to his
original library. Mrs. Carlyle's final comment was:
'A man of genius cannot hold his genius as a sinecure!'
The zest of her description and the wit of its close
show that she had not lost her high spirits. To see her
only as a victim to circumstances would be as untrue as
to see only the author of caricature in Carlyle himself.

CHAPTER NINE

TO THE CLIMAX OF FREDERICK

I

THE book on Cromwell was published in 1845, and its success with the public confirmed and extended Carlyle's reputation. Financially, he was more comfortable than he had ever been, but the clouds over his household did not diminish. The tense situation which his married life was becoming only needed some visible reason to reach a climax, and his unwise efforts to encourage an intimacy between his wife and Lady Harriet made matters worse. Mrs. Buller had declared, from the beginning, that the two women would never accord, and the familiar problem is as insoluble to exceptional people as to the narrowest of suburban families. Either Carlyle had to give up his entertaining friend, which was unreasonable in his eyes; or Mrs. Carlyle had to feel left out of the party, to look, in her own eyes, relegated to a lower place. Since he could not be happy without this friendship, nor she so long as it endured, a compromise, which made his pleasure costly to him and exacting to her, was tried, with the usual results. There was a painful altercation between the pair, and they parted in a quarrel. She was paying a visit to Seaforth after an unhappy stay at Addiscombe, and she did not let her husband know when she had arrived. He wrote to her: 'I hope it is only displeasure, or embarrassed estrangement from me, that robs me of a note this morning. Perhaps an unfriendly letter would be worse. Never have we parted so before, and all for nothing! Adieu, dearest, for that is always your title, if madness prevails not.'

There were also little signs of strain and distress, less emphatic but equally revealing. If one of his letters happened to be late, she would grow painfully alarmed. She now grew to attach more than feminine importance to presents and anniversaries. He did his best, scarcely realizing that these things are evidence, and it is constant evidence of constancy that a jealous affection craves. Children, being utterly dependent, cannot help wanting their mothers all day long; a man is comparatively self-contained; an author flies to his books and his work, and a writer with a passion for solitude, however practically helpless, gives no evidence of wanting anybody. The pregnant phrases from her letters at this time reveal as much as the entire correspondence. In truth, Carlyle's want of proportion in many of his writings has set a bad example to many gleaners in this arid field. A birthday present from Carlyle was acknowledged with the words: 'Oh, why cannot I believe it, once for all, that, with all my faults and follies, I am dearer to you than any earthly creature?' In another she wrote: 'I am weary, weary to such a point of moral exhaustion, that any anchorage were welcome, even the stillest, coldest, where the wicked should cease from troubling and the weary be at rest, understanding both by the wicked and the weary myself.'

She had now reached the point when the physical and the mental causes of her condition reacted upon each other. She was revolving in a vicious circle. The years ahead looked interminable, and there is no good reason to follow every detail in a story which is more exceptional in the thoroughness of its record than in the misery or the strangeness of its facts. Troubles with servants and her complaints of ill-health made the year 1846 end in what she termed 'a disgusting history.' Since Nature was mainly to blame, and a woman in Mrs. Carlyle's condition cannot be easy to live with, it is to the credit of Carlyle that he scarcely complained at all. It is true that he had less reason, for, so long as he was occupied, he was absorbed. Mrs. Carlyle was never properly occupied but, no sooner was he in the same condition, than he found it unendurable. Being a man, he complained of the universe. She, being a woman, complained of him. It was now Carlyle's turn to suffer from the vagaries of his companion, which were as unreasonable in their symptoms as they were pathetic in their cause. Sometimes the poor man would take his meals alone, and certainly most women in a small house would consider this to be a slight in itself. While it lasted, it meant his wife's exclusion, and emphasized the isolation of her life. These arid years continued to revolve with little change until 1857, the year of Lady Ashburton's death. Mrs. Carlyle fixed on this lady because she was the most tangible fact on which a nerve-wracked wife could fasten. If Lady Ashburton had never existed, the state of affairs would have been substantially unaltered. The condition of Mrs. Carlyle has been called hypochrondria, but that is the name of a disease, and a disease remains a disease when no simple explanation can be found for it. At one time, she was afraid of losing her reason, and she made her husband promise not to have her 'put away' if this occurred. Sometimes she discussed suicide. Her letters are barbed with small bitternesses: 'So long as I can stand on my legs, he (Carlyle) never notices that anything ails me'; Lady Ashburton is the lady 'to whom all family ties yield'; a reference to her dog Nero enables her to add, 'I am no longer alone any more'; she thinks that to her husband her company is 'useless.' These by themselves suggest a doleful picture, but the desperate expressions of affection are scarcely less frequent. An emotion disappointed of its outlet and its satisfaction is what we find. Carlyle complained so loudly of the trifles that every one has to bear that, being almost silent on this, he has not received much sympathy. He is entitled to his share, since he intended no evil and could not change a temperament very difficult even to himself. Fortune had been unkind, and if there was a radical fault in this marriage it was that the two had come together, for love is not 'enough' without its proper outlets and its natural buttresses. If they had been less fond of one another, and their fortune had been otherwise unchanged, they would both have been spared a great deal.

II

After the publication of *Cromwell*, no book came from Carlyle for five years. He could settle to nothing, and was seething with impatience also at the complacency that prevailed. To be fair, then, to the explosions which filled *Latter-Day Pamphlets*, which appeared in 1850, we have to remember that they were in reaction from the mood which was to culminate in 1851 in the Great Exhibition! It is difficult to realize the commercial jubilation of those days, the extravagant worship of the profit-and-loss philosophy, the insensate blindness to the social misery on which the commercial fortunes were fattening. Some ten years later, Ruskin was to have the reviews closed to him for denouncing this sham political economy, and, if *Unto This Last* has worn better than *Latter-Day Pamphlets*, the exasperation which two such different books display is convincing evidence of the complacent blindness that they were attacking. Carlyle, it is pleasant to remember, was a great admirer of Ruskin's book. The subjects of Carlyle's Pamphlets, such as 'Model Prisons' or 'Stump Oratory' have lost much of their topical interest, and even the denunciation of democracy, common enough of recent years, had staled long before it produced the present discernible reaction. A book whose work is done may outlive its object if it is a masterpiece of style, but no one would choose the Pamphlets as an example of Carlyle's peculiarities at their best. His spleen needed an element of contrast, an historical sketch or a personal portrait, and with him denunciation was a temptation that became wearisome when indulged. The constructive notion that was tempting him, under the general title of 'Exodus from Houndsditch,' was a religion in which men could believe who had lost their faith in orthodox Christianity. Neither the prophet nor his age was ripe for anything of the kind! Browning, Carlyle, Ruskin, well aware where the want lay, were unable to supply it. Coleridge was believed by his disciples to have found a way out, or a form of restatement that would be acceptable. From the first, Carlyle had shown impatience with Coleridge, and when a life appeared of his friend John Sterling, by an archdeacon who bewailed the young man's doubts, Carlyle seized the opportunity to draw a different portrait: if not of a man who had attained truth, at any rate of one who had cut himself clear of errors.

The book was written without difficulty in three months, and, as Carlyle was writing of some one whom he loved, its tone was a welcome change, and its tranquil tenderness surprised everybody. It is certainly one of the least irritating of Carlyle's books, and that is high praise of a style so crusty. No one can ever forget, or fail to enjoy, the description of Coleridge's talk, in which the want of sympathy turns to genial humour because the writer is describing the process, not denouncing the man. Sterling is shown to us as a man in the same intellectual plight as Carlyle, but as a man, of course, more urbane, less inhibited, far less concentrated but more graceful. The book is scarcely a characteristic example of Carlyle's prose, but it is a delightful biography which can be read with appreciation by those for whom the strident prophet is vague, extravagant, a bore. The personal idiom of the author is sufficiently present to flavour the style, and to lend distinction to it, while it is kept in check by the writer's wish to present his subject sympathetically.

We know that this Life was written with extraordinary ease, and the rhythm is happy, the happiest of any in Carlyle's books. Almost any paragraph will serve. The following is the description of the young Sterling — and of how many promising young men inclined to letters will it not remain permanently true:

A voracious reader I believe he all along was; — had 'read the whole *Edinburgh Review*' in these boyish years, and out of the circulating libraries one knows not what cartloads; wading like Ulysses towards his palace 'through infinite dung.' A voracious observer and participator in all things he likewise all along was; and had had his sights and reflections, and sorrows and adventures, from Kaimes Castle onward, — and had gone at least to Dover on his own score. *Puer bonae spei*, as the school-albums say; a boy of whom much may be hoped? Surely, in many senses, yes. A frank veracity is in him, truth and courage as the basis of all; and of wild gifts and graces there is abundance. I figure him a brilliant, swift, voluble, affectionate and pleasant creature; out of whom, if it were not that symptoms of delicate health already show themselves, great things might be made. Promotions at least, especially in this country and epoch of parliaments and eloquent palavers, are surely very possible for such a one!

It is pleasant to catch Carlyle smiling, and the queer collocation 'in all things he likewise all along was' is like the friendly gabble of a turkey on a sunny morning. There is, too, more art in this biography than appears at a first glance, for the materials are slight, nor was it possible to give much evidence of the charm that Sterling exerted personally. His own writings, so far as they are quoted, some letters, some lines from his poems, do not make us wish for more. Sterling, it is clear, was no poet, and his prose, even when he had a terrible personal experience on which to draw, that of the tornado that wrecked his house in the island of

St. Vincent, is undistinguished: a faithful, unexaggerated record of stark fact, thin in the telling. Compare this with the final chapter in which Carlyle seeks to justify this Life of his friend, and has nothing but his affectionate memory for basis, and that thin writing changes into mellow and becomes moving. In the first part, when the interest begins to weaken, the chapter on Coleridge is a welcome interlude. In the second, when the story wanes again, the account of old Sterling, the Thunderer of *The Times*, with his big voice, explosive ways, social pretences, and natural pomposity, fills a blank in the picture. Some one, who writes very like Carlyle himself, is invoked to fix this portrait: 'Sterling rushes into the clubs, into London society, rolls about all day, copiously talking modish nonsense or sense, and listening to the like, with the multifarious miscellany of men; comes home at night; redacts it into a *Times* leader — and is found to have hit the essential purport of the world's immeasurable babblement that day, with an accuracy beyond all other men.' Carlyle seems more at ease with the active father than with the wayward son, but the son was eager, honest and inquiring, and had withal abandoned Holy Orders, a sure passport to Carlyle's regard. As one reads this book, precious because it stands a typical memorial of those many charming beings who have no biography, who achieved little in the vulgar sense except a personality dear to their intimates, one feels that Carlyle might have been much more cold to both the Sterlings if he had not known them personally. The quality of his sympathy is more conspicuous than his verdicts and his judgments, and his imagination is best proved when he indulges it from fellow-feeling. If Archdeacon Hare had not written of Sterling in his capacity of curate, Carlyle might not have been moved to write this biography at all. It was possible to claim Sterling for unorthodoxy, and this

motive flowered into something richer, the affectionate
memoir of a charming friend.

III

A little event, which proved to be of unexpected
importance, was the introduction of James Anthony
Froude to Cheyne Row about this time. It was in
1849 that Froude had made the acquaintance of the
Carlyles through James Spedding. In his record of
this meeting, Froude gives two vivid sketches of the
Carlyles, but a glimpse only of the atmosphere of their
household. We are told, indeed, that Carlyle treated
his visitor 'I cannot say unkindly, but shortly and
sternly,' that 'I saw then what I saw ever after — that
no one need look for conventional politeness from
Carlyle — he would hear the exact truth from him,
and nothing else.' Of exact truth brusque people are
allowed to have the monopoly, since excuses would be
hard to find if they, too, were liable to err. We also
overhear the pair in conversation: 'Carlyle's talk was
rich, full, and scornful; hers delicately mocking. She
was fond of Spedding, and kept up a quick, sparkling
conversation with him, telling stories at her husband's
expense, at which he laughed himself as heartily as
we did.' The page is turned, and there is nothing to
show what impression, if any, Froude formed of the
married life of his new acquaintances. The question
arises because Froude's biography is based upon
Carlyle's own statements and conversations after Mrs.
Carlyle's death, when, disordered by grief, he was
penning his self-accusatory Reminiscences. At that
time, we hear (toward the end of Froude's biography):
'I saw him almost daily.... In his long sleepless nights
he recognized too late what she had felt and suffered
under his childish irritabilities. His faults rose up in
remorseless judgment, and as he had thought too little
of them before, so now he exaggerated them to himself

in his helpless repentance. For such faults an atonement was due, and to her no atonement could now be made. He remembered, however, Johnson's penance at Uttoxeter; not once, but many times, he told me that something like that was required from him, if he could see his way to it.' This public atonement, then, was not a theory formed by Froude, but the view expressed to Froude 'not once, but many times' by Carlyle in the fire of his grief. The place to discuss this will occur later. Froude approached the Carlyles with no preconception except admiration for a man whose peculiarities he was ready to excuse.

IV

The hostile reception of *Latter-Day Pamphlets* had killed any fancy that Carlyle might have indulged for playing some active part in public life, and, though the *Life of Sterling* went into a second edition, the religious papers were unable to forgive the irreverence with which Coleridge had been treated. Carlyle was depressed, for both books had been interludes, and he was most at a loss when he had not any definite work. The philosophy of Coleridge, the religion of Pusey, the political economy of the Manchester school, the 'consecration of commerce' in the Crystal Palace, were all forms of cant to him, and he wanted to escape from them all into the atmosphere of some sincere hero. With his book on Cromwell, he had exhausted his interest in the Reformation as a theme, and John Knox and Luther had ceased to be inviting studies. Some one who was German, protestant, and probably secular, was indicated. His choice fell upon Frederick the Great, and, at the age of fifty-six, Carlyle decided to undertake what in any event must have been a huge, and proved in his hands to be a portentous, task.

The fourteen years which he devoted to his work became known to Mrs. Carlyle and himself as the Night-

JANE WELSH CARLYLE
About 1850

mare of Frederick, the Valley of the Shadow of Frederick, and similar ominous names. In the letters that have survived, and the accumulation is extensive, so that even now it would be rash to predict that finality has been reached, the painful picture has been painted in detail. To reproduce it would require volumes of quotation, and neither the artillery of Carlyle nor the acid humour of his wife invite emulation. In their own kinds they remain inimitable. The essence of the situation was that it endured unchanged for all these years, and all that we can usefully do is to note some revolutions of the wheel that rotated unsleepingly. Both suffered under the strain; it seemed endless; a trial of endurance which, he sometimes feared, would end in his death, and in her insanity. The ebb of his popularity also troubled him.

It was in a mood of characteristic gloom that the preparation of the book on Frederick began. Carlyle had lost hope, he said, and he affected solitude, shutting himself upstairs with his books except for an afternoon ride or a walk at midnight. If visitors appeared before tea, his wife received them. The pair had reached the period of their silver wedding and had now entered the second half of nearly forty years in company. Their affection from the first had had an element of desperation, and now ill-health and disappointment mingled with it to make her somewhat soured and him gradually afraid that there was no remedy for their common troubles. Of these Carlyle's mother was not unaware, for the friendly relations which existed between her and her daughter-in-law were built on candour. In June 1852 we find Mrs. Carlyle quizzing the old lady as follows: 'I am surprised that so good and sensible a woman as yourself should have brought up her son so badly that he should not know what patience and self-denial mean.' In little things the charge was justified, and it was the importance of little things that Carlyle was apt to over-look. That so much affection should subsist with so much strain is the paradox of a situation which now increased in tension as the zenith of their marriage was passed. This is by no means uncommon in child-less marriages, and has only been misunderstood because so few marriages are documented with the thoroughness of the Carlyles. To see it, as this union has often been seen, in isolation, is to mistake its inter-est and to distort its character.

Another domestic earthquake occurred this summer, and to fly from the workmen and their noise Carlyle went to Scotland where he found himself as much hag-ridden as before. Against the grain he decided to go to Germany in order to collect materials for his projected book, and on the first of September 1852 he arrived at Rotterdam. The tour was made in the company of Mr. Neuberg, who was to conduct Carlyle and to remain his faithful assistant, researcher, and amanu-ensis for many years. It must always be remembered that, whatever vagaries Carlyle's temper might dis-play, he was never at a loss for friends to volunteer these services. A later assistant was Mr. Larkin, whose comments on the pair are the evidence of an eye-wit-ness, not to be neglected when the time comes.

Carlyle was abroad till the middle of October, and his letters are a record of 'sleepless, joyless, sad and weary wanderings!' Mrs. Carlyle understood, and told his brother John: 'He cannot conceal that he is really pretty well, and gets sleep enough to go on with more or less pleasantly. I wonder what he would have made of my sleeping accommodations during the last three months.' Her own letters are no less depressed, and the correspondence can have been cheerful read-ing to neither. Both suffered from disordered nerves, but the difference between them was that some of her complaints are more credible because she found ob-

jective reasons less trivial than his. In moments of
crisis her humour gains the upper hand, as in her
spirited account of the visits from burglars which were
made when the smell of paint had made it impossible
for her to shut the windows at night. She took the precaution of sleeping with loaded pistols by the side of
her bed. The first time the thieves got away with the
stuff, but were frightened by the fall of a candlestick
long before they had finished. The second, they attempted the drawing-room windows, which 'for a
wonder' were fastened. The third time she was awakened by the sound of cut-glass followed by a great
bang, whereupon, with a loaded pistol in her hand, she
descended bravely to the hall to find that it was a
policeman who was knocking. The parlour-windows
were both open! 'I could not help laughing [she wrote
to Mrs. Russell at Thornhill] at what the man's feelings
would have been had he known of the loaded pistol
within a few inches of him.' By the time of Carlyle's
return the alterations to the interior of the house had
been completed, but to escape from the odour of new
paint, they went to the Ashburtons where he, too,
found 'no right rest.' His journal is full of sick reproaches, of 'smothered rage and despair.' He com-
plains of growing old, of 'solitude of soul,' of his 'diseased liver.' Depression is perhaps the only mood that
is fed by everything that occurs. It was with distaste
that he saw the public funeral of the Duke of Wellington; Tennyson's verses upon the occasion were 'naught'
to him. At such times, the unfortunate man could be
conscious of nothing but his own biliousness.

This continued with little interruption during 1853,
when the writing of *Frederick* was actually started. In
these moods, even in solitude he could not always
work; in company he might be no happier. At the end
of this year his mother died, she who of all people was
nearest to him. The simplicity of her character and

the honesty of her life, an active life of eighty-four years, were the substance of his own idea of religion. The symbols of her faith and the terms of her creed he had abandoned, but his own life was the attempt to formulate a belief, credible to him, that should embody the principles upon which she and her like acted.

In spite of the sound-proof room with its double walls, constructed at the top of his house, he could not reduce the enormous literature of the eighteenth century relating to Frederick to order. He had horrible dreams, of desolate wastes, symbolical of his own condition.

V

A curious commentary on his blindness and his receptivity is seen when, in February, 1855, Mrs. Carlyle presented him, in writing, with the Budget of a *Femme Incomprise*. Prices had risen; her housekeeping allowance had remained unchanged; her exchequer was empty; and she had, she says, spoken to him of her situation in vain. She needed a supplement of £29 a year to set her right. When she had mentioned the matter, he had impatiently complained, she says, of being pestered, so she resorted to a literary appeal. The result was a carefully drawn document of some three thousand words. Carlyle, the most bookish of men, would always read when he would not always listen, and we are reminded of their love-letters when we meet this forensic argument again. Half-amused and half-convicted, Carlyle immediately surrendered. It was characteristic of him to be more open to writing than to speech. He called the budget the work of the 'thriftiest, wittiest, cleverest of women.'

Her journal for the autumn of 1855 is starred with phrases pregnant of her frame of mind: 'That eternal Bath House... setting up always another milestone and another betwixt himself and me'; 'fine weather outside, but indoors blowing the devil of a gale'; 'my most constant and pressing desire is to keep out of Bedlam.' By this time he had now settled down to the composition of *Frederick*, and was more or less in his stride by the end of the year. Downstairs, as we have seen, Mrs. Carlyle was also writing, having begun the private journal that he was not to discover until after her death.

The following summer was the occasion of the unfortunate journey to Scotland when the Carlyles accepted Lady Ashburton's hospitality in transit. They travelled in a compartment attached to that lady's royal saloon, a compartment which they shared with the Ashburtons' doctor and the lady's maid. Mrs. Carlyle resented the arrangement, and it is not clear why either Carlyle or Lady Ashburton herself permitted it. Though the journey was undertaken in a state of tension, Carlyle did not hesitate to pass on the proposal that they should return in the same manner, and he was hurt that his wife should decline sharply to do anything of the kind. Mrs. Carlyle was in no mood for this suggestion for she had not been too much pleased that he should rejoin the Ashburtons during his Scottish holiday. These lamentable misunderstandings seemed to arise out of trifles, but trifles are the occasions which bring latent states of stress to light. On this holiday, which the pair spent among their several friends or relatives, Carlyle was happiest, as usual, in the quiet and fresh air of Scotsbrig, surrounded by his devoted family, and when he left them for the Ashburtons he did not much enjoy himself. His hostess also had her prickly moods, and, unless his dubious letters from her different houses are read with some qualification, the wonder is that he should have accepted invitations which were often productive of little pleasure. Lady Ashburton was not a person who liked to be crossed; her invited guests were expected to accept her invitations, and she is the one person by whom Carlyle appeared to be dominated. So brilliant a hostess must have known how to flatter her guests, and how to remind them, when occasion arose, of the obligations that she assumed to be due to her. When she died, unexpectedly at Paris, in the following spring (1857), Carlyle suffered 'a great and irreparable sorrow.' The epitaph that he found for her is characteristic: 'Her work — call it grand and noble endurance of want of work — is all done.' Carlyle believed that if Lady Ashburton had not acquiesced in a fashionable existence, her capacities would have been more conspicuous.

It was in 1857 that the plan of separate dinners was tried in Cheyne Row, and this probably explains a sentence in one of Mrs. Carlyle's letters to her husband during the summer. She was staying at Haddington, and wrote: 'I cannot write, I am so wearied ... if you could fancy me in some part of the house out of sight my absence would make little difference to you, considering how little I see of you and how preoccupied you are when I do see you.' Whenever she left him, she was as anxious as a mother for a young child at the mercy of servants, and yet, when she was with him, something was wanting still. On the other hand, there was never any rift in her sympathy for his work, never any diminution in her admiration for his writings. Before she returned from this very visit, the instalment of *Frederick* that was submitted to her evoked tactful praise: 'What a magnificent book this is going to be, the best of all your books.'

The winter was chequered by Mrs. Carlyle's ill-health, and troubles with servants complicated existence. For these latter troubles Carlyle found a perfect phrase; they were 'dirtier for the mind [he said] than even brushing of boots oneself would be for the body.' In the summer of 1858 he was again in Scotland, and

wrote letters to his wife bewailing her condition: 'My
soul was black with misery about you. Past, present,
and future yielded no light point anywhere.' In another letter, he wrote: 'It is as if the scales were falling
from my eyes, and I were beginning to see in this, my
solitude, things that touch me to the quick. Oh, my
little woman, what a suffering thou hast had, and how
nobly borne! with a simplicity, a silence, a courage,
and patient heroism which are only now too evident
to me.' Again, he begged his wife to be of good heart.
They had had, he wrote, a sore pilgrimage together,
and he pleaded for forgiveness for 'the much that I
have thoughtlessly done and omitted to do, far far at
all times from the purpose of my mind.'

Such words as these are important, for they fore-
shadow the tone of self-reproach which, in his later
Reminiscences, has sometimes been attributed wholly
to the exaggeration of grief. Both Carlyles professed
to be martyrs to sleeplessness, and, though both indulged in exaggerations which only unimaginative
beings will misunderstand, from this time onward
Mrs. Carlyle's signs of distress became so pronounced
that no one living with her could be otherwise than
sorry and alarmed, least of all a husband who had
begun to realize that her physical condition was beyond his power to remedy. Carlyle was coming to regard her as an invalid, and, as he knew himself to have
no aptitude for nursing, he could only sympathize,
especially in letters, the one form of activity of which
he was capable. Such specialism of faculty is not very
uncommon, but he seems a glaring instance because
the evidence is so complete.

His peculiar helplessness in trifling emergencies is
shown by a little incident of this summer, and it is
pleasant to find that it occurred away from home. He
was about to pay a second visit to Germany, and the
fresh trappings that he needed before his journey in-

cluded a leather belt that he had been advised to wear on horseback. While he was staying with his sister this belt became a problem of the first magnitude, till at last even he became self-disgusted at the contrast between the 'industrious helpfulness' of his sister and his own 'unhelpable nature.' In the late summer he was inspecting the battlefields of Germany, and his letters on the discomforts of travel might have been written by a querulous child. At the end of this year, 1858, the first two volumes of *Frederick* were published. The welcome with which they were received did not seem to cheer him. The atmosphere of Cheyne Row remained bilious, and to Froude, now a regular visitor, Mrs. Carlyle looked 'drawn' and 'suffering.' Carlyle was now becoming conscious of her plight. His *letters* show increasing sympathy and anxiety.

At the end of this year Lord Ashburton married again, and his second wife, who had been a Miss Stuart Mackenzie, became a very good friend to Mrs. Carlyle, and to Carlyle himself before and after his wife's death.

In the summer of 1859 the pair went to Humbie, near Aberdour, a place of discomfort which made Mrs. Carlyle declare that she felt more like 'a keeper in a madhouse' than being in the country for 'rest and change.' According to her, Carlyle's walks, rides, and bathes had brought him to 'a bilious crisis.' To read these letters in bulk certainly leaves a feeling of depression, but because they are the most available evidence we must not suppose that the whole story is there. If Carlyle had been as gloomy as he averred, if his wife had been as sleepless as she stated, his suicide and her insanity would have been inevitable. All imaginative people have an exaggerative tendency because the vivid expression of their feelings gives to them an artistic pleasure, and this is particularly true of their troubles, since the exaggerated expression of these becomes not only a pleasure but a relief. To write a tragedy, if you have the faculty, is the surest way to recover serenity of mind.

In what they called the 'literature of desperation' both the Carlyles found an avenue to ease. The mistake was to indulge themselves so much in their correspondence with each other, for nothing is more depressing than to receive a Jeremiad at breakfast every morning.

VI

Allusions more cheerful, though we have to hunt for them, exist, and Carlyle was sometimes aware that his lamentations were monotonous. In 1858 we find him writing: 'A little *live* note to Goody will be a comfort to myself, and no displeasure to Nero and her over the tea to-morrow morn.' Again, 'the one thing that I objected to in your note was that of my being discontented with you, or having ever for an instant been. Depend upon it that is a mistake, once for all. I was indeed discontented with myself ... but not discontented with you ever at all. Nay, to tell you the truth, your anger at me (grounded on that false basis) was itself a kind of comfort to me. I thought, "Well, she has strength enough to be cross and ill-natured at me; she is not all softness and affection and weakness."' Is it possible, then, that Mrs. Carlyle was too obsequious to his moods? for her devotion was very great and his thoughtlessness, however unintentionally, was apt to become tyrannical. From some one whom Carlyle loved and respected, the Duke of Wellington's formula 'Sir, don't be a damned fool' might have turned an explosion into laughter, for laughter with Carlyle was never very far away.

There were tokens of practical kindness also, now that he was prospering. The first two volumes of *Frederick*, published in the autumn of 1858, rapidly sold five thousand copies, and Carlyle received 'some

£2,500' from this source. An immediate effect was
that Mrs. Carlyle now enjoyed an easy flow of money
and, since she had to give up walking, was ordered by
him to hire a brougham twice a week. A little later he
presented her with a carriage of her own. The gift of
this carriage was a keen pleasure to her, for Carlyle
overcame his repugnance to shopping and eventually
ordered it himself. This sign of his thoughtfulness was
precious to her, for attentiveness was not conspicuous
among his virtues.

Substantially, however, the atmosphere of Cheyne
Row remained unchanged, and work upon the subsequent volumes of his book reproduced his old moodi-
ness and her solitude. Work throughout the day, followed by a ride toward evening, a nap, dinner, and a
stroll in the dark, did not allow of much companionship. 'If any of us [says Froude] were to spend the
evening there, we generally found her alone; then he
would come in, take possession of the conversation and
deliver himself in a stream of splendid monologue...
the fiercest denunciations ending in a burst of laughter
at his own exaggerations.'

The year 1860 was a painful one for her in many
ways. At its beginning, she had lost Nero who did not
recover from an accident, and she wrote to the doctor
who had ended his sufferings: 'Nobody but myself can
have any idea what that little creature has been in my
life. My inseparable companion during eleven years;
ever doing his little best to keep me from feeling sad
and lonely.' In March she heard from Mrs. Rennie
that George, the faithless lover of long ago, was dying
at his house in London. His wife thought that Mrs.
Carlyle, his oldest friend, should know it, and it was
Mrs. Carlyle who was at his side when he died. 'By a
strange fatality [she wrote to Mrs. Dinning, the Grace
Rennie of her girlish days, whom she had not met for
forty years] it was I who watched by him thro' his last

night on earth. I, his first love, who received his last breath and closed his eyes. Was it not a strange, sad thing; after so many separations — so many tossings up and down this weary earth! His wife wrote to me on Tuesday... God bless her for that thought — death abolishes all forms and ceremonies; so I went to her at once, and begged to be let stay.'

To the naturally affectionate reply that this letter, one of Mrs. Carlyle's most tender, evoked, another followed in which she hoped to visit Mrs. Dinning in Scotland during the summer. She explains the situation at home: 'I should just have to provision my husband for two or three weeks, give my servant as minute instructions about him as if he were a three-years-old baby — Baby just old enough to get into the fire.'

In April Carlyle was the guest of Lord Sandwich at Hichinbrook, and his letters from there begged her to be patient with his moods, for he was 'the unhappy animal, but did not mean ill.' In August he was in Scotland. The workmen had been again in Cheyne Row, and Mrs. Carlyle's nerves were badly out of order. In reply to one of his letters she indulged in a characteristic thrust, saying that it would read charmingly in his biography and might be quoted in a Murray's guide, but that it had not charmed a solitary individual like herself. He replied as follows:

My dear little Goody, — I could have been somewhat fretted yesterday morning. First at your long delay in writing, and your perverse notion of my neglect in that particular, also of your scornful condemnation of my descriptive performance (which I assure you was not done for the sake of future biographers, nor done at all except with considerable pain and inconvenience and at the very first moment possible in my gloom and sickliness, if you had known of it). But all feelings were swallowed up in one — grief and alarm at the sleepless, excited, and altogether painful state poor little Jeannie had got into.

The sincerity and good temper of this are irresistible. Once his attention had been secured to another's feelings, Carlyle could write like the lover that he was. This attention, however, was not spontaneous. He was naturally too much preoccupied to enter into the feelings of some one else except by a direct stimulus or by an effort of the will. He gives us, in a letter to his brother John from Thurso, a glimpse of himself in the midst of a family party: 'I dimly intend to hold on for about a month... [my host] will perhaps be at bottom not so averse to the shorter term, there being such a cackle of grandchildren here, with governesses, etc., whom he sees to be a mere bore to me, though to him such a joy.' What would have been the effect on Carlyle of a numerous and obstreperous family? Did he really need it as much as, I think, his wife, and suffer without knowing from concentration on himself through being childless: the lack, of which she was still conscious, though her hopes had vanished long ago?

VII

A tiresome mischance now threw Mrs. Carlyle into renewed exasperation. She had fancied that his stay at Thurso would be indefinite and prolonged, and, as he wished her to refresh herself too in Scotland, from which she usually benefited, she had begun a round of visits. To the later of these she was particularly looking forward, when an indeterminate phrase in one of his letters and a delay in the post led her to believe that he had changed his plans, was suddenly returning home, and would be requiring her presence at Chelsea. Embittered by his fancied indifference to her convenience, she hurriedly concluded her visits and returned with angry impetuosity to town. She then learned that she was not to expect him, that he was going on to Annandale, and that her homecoming had been a mistake. He proposed, it was all that he could do, that she should 'rectify her huge error' by returning to Scotland, but her holiday mood had fled, and she reproached him for not having been more explicit. The disappointment had been acute; she was too tired to stir again; and Carlyle returned humble, full of regrets, sympathy, and good resolutions: 'I will be quiet as a dream [he said]. Surely I ought to be rather a protection to your poor sick fancy than a new disturbance. Be still; be quiet. I swear to do thee no mischief at all.'

Unselfishness causes a good deal of trouble in this world, and the present is a typical instance. If Mrs. Carlyle had consulted her own convenience, had refused to interrupt her holiday, and to suppose that she was indispensable in Cheyne Row, she would have been wiser even had Carlyle's plans been as she thought. People should not be more unselfish than is natural to them without excessive strain, for, when they overstretch themselves, they break down afterward by showing anger, even if their sacrifice has been successful. What was the good of Mrs. Carlyle returning heroically to town, if she was not heroic enough to feel no resentment when this return proved to have been unnecessary? That is the ethics of the case, but Mrs. Carlyle was now too nervous not to feel acutely any flurry or mischance. When two people live together the remedy for selfishness in one is not a similar degree of extra unselfishness in the other. We often find that a pair of selfish independent beings rub along much more comfortably than when most of the sacrifice is on one side and most of the thoughtlessness upon the other. Common as the Carlyles were in their affection, most of the sensitive love was on her side, and she suffered accordingly. On the whole, she had needed him more than he had needed her, and for this reason, among others, she found him more exacting.

In the hope of lightening matters for her, Carlyle now insisted that their maid of all work should be replaced by a good cook and a young maid. Mrs. Carlyle was not sure that the plan was an improvement, but then her trouble was more complex than mere servants could solve. Deep in the confusion of *Frederick*, so that the printers had to set his notes in order that he might disentangle them, Carlyle was in the throes once more, and his wife's health became so uncertain that, according to Froude, their friends began to see that the pair were best apart at regular intervals. When she went off to the South coast in the summer of 1862, he wrote: 'I am dreadfully low-spirited, and feel like a child wishing his Mammy back again.' When she had returned, she wrote to Mrs. Russell on August 30: 'I had set my heart on streaming off by myself to Holm Hill. Ah! my dear, your kindness goes to my heart and makes me like to cry because I cannot do as you bid me.... I tried him alone for a few days, when I was afraid of falling seriously ill, unless I had a change of air.... But the letter that came from him every morning was like the letter of a Babe in the Wood, who would be found buried with dead leaves by the robins if I did not look to it.'

VIII

In the autumn of 1860 Froude had settled in town, and for twenty years 'except when either or both of us were out of town,' Froude never ceased to see Carlyle 'two or three times a week, and to have two or three hours of conversation' with him. From this time forward Froude became the eye-witness of the story that he narrates, and is therefore entitled to peculiar attention. On their walks together Froude noticed how kind Carlyle was to beggars, to street arabs, to animals, and how the scorn for philanthropy and benevolence expressed in *Latter-Day Pamphlets* was directed against petty reliefs for enormous evils with the certainty that organized or institutional charity, when opposed to private generosity, sadly hardened human hearts. A subscriber, no less than a charity organization official, may easily become a person with a pigeon-hole instead of a heart. It is also interesting to learn that Carlyle was not impatient of contradiction in private talk, but the reverse of what he seemed to be in his writings and when holding forth in company even in his own house. One tends inevitably to think of him in the mood so monotonously characteristic of his letters, and for this reason to think that Mrs. Carlyle experienced little sunshine with him. His petulance and various humours, pronounced and trying as they were, happen to be the moods chiefly illustrated by his correspondence, but of the charm, the gentleness that his wife also enjoyed in their nightly dialogues, when he came to be amused by her accounts of the doings of the day, there is very little evidence in his letters. Yet Froude's experience, which came as a pleasant surprise, cannot have been unique, and it deserves to be remembered to-day when almost the only evidence we have is the bilious prose of Carlyle's letters. With the kindly converse that has perished has gone much that would explain why it was not impossible to be happy in his companionship. He was also fond of 'rehearsing' to Froude the scenes that he was describing in his history, thus showing, if we needed to be shown, that he had the mind of the novelist rather than the conception of the historian. It is true that Carlyle was talking to a friend, to a disciple, but the man comes before us in the anecdote of Mrs. Carlyle, on hearing from Froude that age was softening her husband, remarking to the latter: 'I wish that Froude had seen you an hour or two after you had seemed to him so lamblike!' A man's friends and his family will often give an account as contradictory as this, but one side of his nature must not be allowed to obliterate the other.

In the summer of 1863 the third volume of *Frederick* was published, and the remaining two were either being printed or nearly ready to be so. Mrs. Carlyle's time at home was largely spent upon her sofa, and her brief distractions were drives in London and periodic visits to her various friends. Her left arm was now giving her trouble, and the pain aggravated her chronic sleeplessness. Rheumatism was suspected, but when Dr. Quain saw her while she was staying with the Ashburtons he said the cause was neuralgia, once more making us think of the condition of her nerves.

Toward the end of October (1863) Carlyle returned in dreary mood from his ride, for his enormous book continued to expand and its end to recede while he worked upon it, when he learned that his wife was still out. He found that she had gone to see her cousin in the City. This cousin was a Mrs. Godby, widow of one of the officials in the Post Office, who had married her in Edinburgh. When he died she was matron of the Post Office Establishment with some forty maids to manage. Mrs. Carlyle was far from well, and her arm was too painful to allow her to brush her hair herself. Carlyle was disappointed to find her out, but he did not miss the bright fire and the talk that usually greeted him when he was told that, in spite of her weakness, she had gone for exercise. There would be more tales to hear when she came back, but dinner-time passed, and he waited on the sofa wondering what he would hear when she returned. She was making the journey by omnibus since she had as yet no carriage, though the brougham had been the subject of many talks. Naturally she wanted her husband to choose his promised gift, but *Frederick* reduced his time to zero, he said, so that the purchase was postponed and postponed. It was not one of her driving days in the hired carriage, and during 'the last seven years of the nightmare of *Frederick*,' he tells us, he 'did not write the smallest message to friends or undertake the least business' except when plainly compelled. Plainly compelled! What is plain to an author oppressed with a nightmarish task except to heed nothing that interferes with finishing it?

The evening was drawing out. The sound of wheels reached Carlyle. A knock followed. He was surprised that she did not appear. The servants, whom he called, gave evasive replies, so he ran downstairs to find his wife in the hands of Mr. Larkin, a friend, who was next-door neighbour, standing at her side. She was unable to move herself, and the two men had to carry her to bed. The doctor was hurriedly sent for, and, while he explained that no bones were broken, Carlyle learned how his wife, stepping off the kerb, to catch an omnibus at a point where the road was up, suddenly saw a cab bearing down upon her. In her attempt to regain the pavement, she made a spring and fell upon the flag-stones, falling, in spite of a wrench to save herself, upon her neuralgic arm. Some people who saw the accident placed her in a cab, and after a proper examination it was found that the sinews of the thigh had been badly twisted, though oddly enough the arm seemed little the worse. There followed three days of excruciating pain, sleepless nights, but by the end of the week she appeared to Carlyle to be over the worst, and was proudly displaying to him her contrivances of ropes, pulleys, and a patent champagne-tap which she had invented or discovered to help her to shift her position and to be less dependent on the bell. At the time, he says, he 'merely thought how lucky beyond all my calculations!' Apparently the doctor and she did not tell Carlyle the whole truth, and the result was the painful incident, which she described to Froude. Her whole side was affected even to the face. When her jaw dropped she could not shut it, and he, in ignorance of this, and hating the sight of a mouth open, said to her more than once, 'ye'll find yourself in a more compact and pious frame of mind, if ye shut your mouth.' The comment was a cold one, and he did not make it better when he added that she might be thankful that the accident had not been worse. At that she turned on him, and he retreated with regrets for her rebelliousness.

That is Froude's anecdote; and, if it arose from doctor and patient agreeing to keep Carlyle in partial ignorance, the explanation for such tactics is provided by Mr. Larkin.[1] In *A Ten Years' Reminiscence* he wrote:

I recollect the evening perfectly... and Carlyle little thought it was his own presence which had suddenly produced the collapse which struck him so painfully. To make the picture which thus fixed itself on his memory intelligible... few men have been constitutionally less able to cope with unexpected difficulties than he was. In any case of confusion or embarrassment, it was sheer misery to have him even standing by and looking on; his own irritable impatience was at once so contagious and so depressing. It was a constant struggle on Mrs. Carlyle's part either to keep him out of the way, or to take the opportunity of his being away from home, to effect any changes which might have become necessary; and this as much for his own sake as for hers. On the evening in question... I went instantly and found her on a chair in the back room of the ground floor, evidently in great pain. As soon as she saw me she said, Oh, Mr. Larkin, do get me up into my own room before Mr. Carlyle knows anything about it. He'll drive me mad if he comes in now!

For a month she was laid up. It was a great day when, leaning on a stick, she suddenly appeared from her bedroom in the drawing-room, and, when nearly two months had passed, Carlyle was persuaded that she was doing well. Once again she made an effort to

[1] *British Quarterly*, quoted by Mrs. Ireland.

disguise her state, and the effort, which was followed by a relapse, was apparently undertaken because Carlyle had found that still a further volume of *Frederick* was necessary, and she feared that he would be incapacitated by agitation if she did not seem to be on the mend. None the less, according to his Reminiscences, he began to perceive, without a hint from her, that this book 'was crushing down her existence, as it was crushing down my own,' and the thought that she 'must suffer so for it was occasionally bitter' to him. How far he really perceived this, how far it occurred to him at the time when his Reminiscences were being written to relieve his grief, it is not easy to decide. Some perceptions of this kind we have found already in his letters, but all he did, or could do at the moment, was to try to get this 'unutterable book' out of the way. He gave himself wholly to 'the dismal task.' He was 'day and night wrestling with it, as with the ugliest dragon, which blotted out the daylight and the rest of the world to me till I should get it slain.' Was not the moral of all this that a book which, in its latest edition, consists of eight volumes on the life of one man, which took thirteen years to write, was too long from the first?

IX

He has drawn his own portrait of himself at this time: 'Sitting smoking upstairs, on nights when sleep was impossible, I had thoughts enough; not permitted to rustle amid my rugs and wrappages lest I awoke *her*, and startled all *chance* of sleep away from her.' The winter waxed toward Christmas. Mrs. Carlyle, who could walk very little, was able, however, to take a few drives, during one of which she caught a cold, which proved obstinate. It produced a recurrence of her neuralgia, 'under which, it seemed, as if no force of human vitality would be able long to stand.' The doctors said that her nerves were diseased, attempted many remedies, but accomplished nothing. Indeed Carlyle formed the opinion that their opiates, and their medicines, and their appliances, only made matters worse. At times she suffered from 'a hideous pain,' and this was so acute and so exhausting that, while her intelligence, her husband says, was never clouded, she dreaded that it might snap under the strain. He recalled her twice saying to him: 'Dear, promise me that you will not put me into a mad-house, however this go. Do you promise me, now?' Of course, he did. 'Not if I do quite lose my wits?' Never, he answered, and besought her to compose her terrified heart. Another time, the fruit of her wakeful nights, she gave to Carlyle punctual directions about her burial, and told him precisely how he was to distribute her belongings, for she was anxious that these should go to needy friends in Haddington, survivors of past times.

By day the lower part of the house was almost crowded with visitors, doctors, nurses, while overhead the author sat alone, steeped or trying to steep himself in work. A double solitude seems the acme of all solitude, and it is not broken by such fixed visits as were all that she could then receive or he pay. Early in the morning, he would look in to see her, and again at midday. Sometimes he was able to enter again at three o'clock, but sometimes only, for he might hear that she was dozing at this hour, the time for his ride. When he looked back on this time, he wondered how he could have gone on working. We need not. There is no mystery, and no charge. But, even with *Frederick* on his brain, occasionally in the mornings he shuddered 'As of conviction, that here did lie death; that my world must go to shivers, down to the abyss; and that "victory" never so complete, up in my garret, would not save *her*, nor indeed be possible without her. I remember my morning walks, three of them or so, crushed under that ghastly spell... generally, before the day was done, I had decided to hope again, to keep hoping and working.'

Most of the nursing, at first, fell to the servants and to Maggie Welsh, for whom Carlyle had sent, and in whose 'almost obstinate placidity' he trusted. But, as the weeks went on, a nun was summoned, because a Protestant friend of Mrs. Carlyle had great faith in the nursing virtues of the sisterhood to which this nun belonged. A young Irish nun appeared, and for a few nights answered well. Then, without warning she was replaced by another of the sisterhood, a French nun of middle age, rigid air, and fixed despondency of expression. About three in the morning Carlyle was awakened by the violent ringing of his wife's bell. He called Maggie, rushed downstairs, and was met by the words 'put away that woman,' so the nun was bundled out of the room, and relegated, with rugs and pillows, to the sofa in the drawing-room, on which Mrs. Carlyle would sometimes try to sleep herself. When Carlyle asked his wife what the nun had been doing to her, Jane said that the nun had begun with prayers, had gone on to ghostly consolations, had then advanced to admonishment, whereupon Mrs. Carlyle had cried out: 'Hold your tongue or I will ring the bell.' At this the nun had tried to prevent her patient, but she rang the bell just in time. Carlyle somehow felt sorry for this misguided religious, and believed that she had been prompted by some priest. However that may be, his wife would have none of the consolations, which the sage compared to poisoned ginger-bread!

The doctors were so many, as time passed, that Carlyle did not even see all of them. Aid was needed so desperately that they brought their scepticism to try even animal magnetism. A male magnetizer and then a female offered their ministrations, in vain. The last straw, as it generally is, though not without reason, was to try a change at the sea.

Early in March 1864 therefore, she was carried downstairs into an expensive 'invalid carriage,' low, black and base-looking (Carlyle thought), a carriage which you entered hearse-wise by a window, to St. Leonard's, to the house of Dr. Blakiston who had kindly offered his hospitality. The skies were grey, the very wind was rainy, the sea hoarse when they arrived, but two rooms, with one near by for Maggie Welsh, and with a servant within call, were more cheering. Carlyle naturally was oppressed, he had to return by the last train to *Frederick* in London. Twice or thrice perhaps Carlyle visited her at the sea, but, though she seemed somewhat better, there was no hope in her face. Maggie wrote every day, and the fourth volume of *Frederick* was published.

In April 1865, not caring to trespass on the friendly Blakistons any longer, the Carlyles took a furnished house at St. Leonard's whither Carlyle joined his wife in May, as did also, for a time, John his brother. To continue at *Frederick*, Carlyle ensconced himself at the new house in 'a poor closet on the ground-floor,' in which 'there was hardly room to turn,' and he 'felt as if crushed, all my apparatus and I, into a stocking, and there bidden work. But I really did it withal, to a respectable degree, printer never pausing for me, work daily going on; and this doubtless was my real anchorage in that sea of trouble, sadness and confusion, for the two months that it endured.' On one of her daily drives Carlyle would accompany her, and despite her wretchedness, she would try to talk. They were dismal drives, however. Not only did he recollect her to have been visibly sad and ill, but they had to keep to the streets to avoid the dust, for beyond the town they met the 'haggard, parched lanes, and their vile whirlwinds.' Carlyle kept odious memories of the place. Yet he would ride for at least two hours each day, and bathe too, and the old rustic lanes, the breeze on

Beachy Head, were blissful, but they all ended in his return to the new, developing Resort, where was 'nothing but dust, noise, squalor, and the universal tearing and digging as if of gigantic human swine, *not* finding any worms or roots that would be useful to them.' The houses, the house that they rented, were bandboxes, as if intended for 'nomad apes' rather than men. Every local person seemed to be bent upon Development; sites and values were the talk, with wise whispers of judicious investment or appreciation of capital, while railway-shares went up almost as fast as the new houses. He returned late from his rides, usually not till half-past eight in the evening, when he took tea with Jane, who tried to talk for a short while before retiring to the solitary silence which was all she seemed fit for at that time. By the middle of June the sound of the sea begun to keep her awake, and she changed rooms with her husband, but for once he too found the sea no longer a lullaby but a disturbance. Even at the back, dogs and fowls banished repose, so at the end of the month they decided to return to Chelsea.

It was not an easy decision, for Jane had a natural horror of returning to the rooms in which she had been so wretched, but all they could do was to have these repapered and re-arranged. While this was being considered, she went to Mrs. Forster's, Palace-Gate House, Kensington. John Carlyle escorted her to town, but almost at once she determined to travel to Annandale, and pay a visit to Mary Carlyle at The Gill. On the night of her arrival she slept for nine hours, a blessed change after the restless nights which had preceded her departure from St. Leonard's. These good nights, however, were not continued, and in a week or so she moved to Nithsdale, where Dr. and Mrs. Russell entertained her. The quiet, the drives, the air, brought improvement at last, and enabled Carlyle, now back in

London, to grind away at *Frederick* with a heart less heavy than before. The end of this summer was, he says, the end of their most tragic days.

X

Though Mrs. Carlyle slept no better and was frequently in pain, it was noticed that her spirits improved during this, her last, autumn. He remembered 'mornings when he found her quite wonderfully cheerful as he looked in upon her bedroom in passing down.' Hope re-awakened; and 'it was an inestimable mercy to me (as I often remark) that I did at last throw aside everything for a few days and actually get her that poor brougham.' As Carlyle recalls, 'it was indeed useful, and necessary, as a means of health; but still more precious, I doubt not, as a mark of *my* regard for her.' He regretted, when he looked back, that he could not 'show her in my heavy-laden miserable life how *much* I had, at all times, regarded, loved and admired her.'

The condition of affairs during the eighteen months that followed Mrs. Carlyle's accident has been sketched in the light of Carlyle's recollections. After all we cannot dismiss his own version of his own case, and, though he was writing in the freshness of his grief, the indications that insinuated themselves into his letters show that, to some extent, or at certain moments, his self-criticisms began while his wife was still alive. To dismiss them as hysterical, or to concentrate upon them alone, would be equally ill-judged; but (read with the qualifications which his previous letters about himself to her, and hers to him, suggest to every impartial reader) they make an intelligible picture of the pair at the end of the greatest strain in all their experience. The originals are darker than this sketch since here we have to be upon our guard against Carlyle's exaggeration, but it is also true that the letters written by him to his wife during the summer of 1864 contain poignant sentences. One will suffice: 'Oh, you have had a hard life! I, too, not a soft one: but yours beside me!'

When she was away, he definitely missed her, partly because he could not manage when he was alone, could rely on no one else to find his missing scissors, and partly from a sense of loss, distinct, but not easily to be disentangled, from a dependence half-selfish and half-affectionate. The smallest improvement in her condition would disperse his fears, and, like most unpractical people, anxious to be relieved of a problem that they cannot handle, he instinctively took an optimistic view. Perhaps it was the same incapacity that made him welcome any signs of piety and submission which he detected, for these, too, are often forms of acquiescence whereby a situation to which we are unequal can be shelved by 'casting it upon the Lord.' Mrs. Carlyle, active and capable by nature, with that fighting quality that looks like rebellion, and with a quick tongue, the voice of an alert mind, had few of these crumbs for him. She never became resigned to the disappointments in her life, and clung to him not because she was weak, but because she was possessive. Her husband was a treasure which she was fully conscious that she 'owned.' Very gradually, age was reversing their relation to each other. She was outgrowing dependence on him, and he had really become more dependent on her since experience had taught him that his work, once naturally his first concern, gave him no final satisfaction. This illness had brought out his tenderness, and her apparent recovery gave sunshine to their days. Besides, the huge book on *Frederick* had been finished at last, and Carlyle's feelings when the final word had been written may be compared with Gibbon's famous note:

'On Sunday evening in the end of January 1865 I

walked out, with the multiplex feeling — joy not very prominent in it, but a kind of solemn thankfulness traceable that I had written the last sentence of that unutterable book, and, contrary to many forbodings in bad hours, had actually got done with it forever.'

PART THREE
A WIDOWER AND A SAGE

But, in any case, what hope have we in turning over those old interminable Chronicles, with their garrulities and insipidities; or still worse, in patiently examining those modern Narrations... — what hope have we, except the for most part fallacious one of gaining some acquaintance with our fellow-creatures, though dead and vanished, yet dear to us; how they got along in those old days, suffering and doing; to what extent, and under what circumstances, they resisted the Devil and triumphed over him, or struck their colours to him, and were trodden under foot by him; how, in short, the perennial Battle went, which men name Life, which we also in these new days, with indifferent fortune, have to fight, and must bequeath to our sons and grandsons...

THOMAS CARLYLE: *Essay on Biography.*

CHAPTER TEN

'THE UNUTTERABLE BOOK'

I

THE last volume of Carlyle's works, before the enormous length of which we quail instinctively, needs to be considered, first of all, in relation to the writings which preceded it. His reputation, made by the *French Revolution* and confirmed by *Past and Present*, had received an enormous fillip when the long volumes upon Cromwell appeared. These came at a time when success would be enhanced if the new book looked more important and more imposing than its predecessors. As we have seen, the collection of Cromwell's speeches had this appearance; the time was fully ripe for the reversal of the extreme anti-Cromwellian legend; the documentation was impressive; and length suggested that a masterpiece had come from one expected to create a masterpiece. Yet the *Cromwell* was not more than, at most, a piece of original editing. Considered as a book, it shows a decline, a decline disguised by the applause of the public. At last Carlyle had achieved the literary success which had been the earliest of his ambitions. His denunciations of fame, a little later, had been the reaction of a still disappointed young man; but he was extremely ambitious to the end, a man whose religion forbade him to admit it, and ordered him to express contempt for this desire of his heart. There seems to be little doubt that his delight at this public recognition encouraged him to fulminate more loudly than before, and partly explains the abuse contained in *Latter-Day Pamphlets*. By the publication of these Carlyle's popularity received a check, and his sense of this, combined with the gentler sympathies of his nature, led him to recapture his admirers by the almost innocuous and otherwise charming *Life of Sterling*. The new subject that he found, at last, in *Frederick the Great* occupied him for many years, but his latest hero should be seen as the youngest of the heroic pedigree: Burns, well understood; Goethe, the master-model of Carlyle which he fairly soon abandoned; Knox, the scourge of Scotland; Luther, the scourge of Europe and the Pope; Cromwell, the rich man who ruled England and only just declined the Crown; lastly Frederick, a king's son, who extended his dominions, was successful on the battlefield and in diplomacy, and has been named the Great: a sort of emperor of acquisitive mankind.

With the exception of Goethe, whom Carlyle never fully understood and whose finer teaching he soon abandoned, all these heroes show an ascent in power, social influence, and birth. No man could set so much store by worldly success who had not been humbly born and who would not be likely to yield to some of its corrupting influences. In the height of his popularity Carlyle was the guest, almost the inhabitant, of a few great houses. He rarely stayed elsewhere, though he entertained eminent commoners at home. There is no doubt that his susceptibility laid him open to these surroundings, that the arrogance of the proud and obscure peasant who meant to rise and was aware of latent and overlaid abilities, gradually merged into the arrogance of an autocratic temper. Not having been humble in obscurity, he was not humble in success. Whether the world was above him or below him, his imperious instinct was to rate it soundly. His circumstances, not his character, had altered, and so his heroes, being projections of himself, were similarly transformed. Thus he passed insensibly from the splendid Burns to the splendidly successful Frederick; from the poet, the superior of the world which spoilt his life, to the king who played his cards triumphantly. Force had always at-

tracted Carlyle's weakness. Triumphant force was what
he came to worship at last.

This decay in his finer sensibilities, which was the
price that he paid for his vast popular success, lends an
interest to *Frederick* which it needs, for both as a book
and as a history it is open to damaging criticism. That
it proved to be exactly what Prussia and the Hohenzollerns wanted is scarcely to suggest the masterpiece of an
impartial historian. The Frederician tradition in national politics was preparing the attack on Austria in
1866; and the same year which saw the victory of Sa-
dowa was the one in which Prussia conferred the Order
of Merit on Carlyle. After the defeat of Prussia in the
late War, one does not want to press the point offen-
sively. Enough to say that the creator of modern Prussia was idealized in an historical epic by Carlyle, and
that the descendants of that king fully appreciated its
value. While reading Carlyle's version, we need to remember who his heroes had been, their order in his
regard, and their change of type, success, and social
status. Then, the assertions which may exasperate,
and the length which must fatigue, regain an interest,
as we note the light that they throw upon the encomi-
astic author.

II

Certain other causes of confusion have to be removed before this curious history can be read with
pleasure or profit. As a study of Frederick's character
and policy, it is one-sided to an extreme; its estimates
are false, its morality is bad, its reasonings in defence
are intellectually trifling. In other words, it is the consecration of a legend, but, as the epic of that legend, it
deserves the abundant praise which has been bestowed
upon it. Faithfulness to a conception is not fidelity to
truth, though Carlyle's name is still quoted as an example of accuracy. That particular quality it is for pro-

fessional historians to assess. Mr. Belloc has lately
written: 'We have in Carlyle not only in his *Frederick*,
where every one concedes it ... an admirable example
of care and correction.' This sentence, from Mr. Belloc's introduction to the *French Revolution* (Dent, 1929),
occurs in a passage where details are under discussion,
and presumably applies to the details, and especially
the military details, of Carlyle's later history. For a
recent, though severe, examination of the substantial
value of *Frederick the Great* the reader can refer to the
chapter on the subject by Mr. Norwood Young, who
followed up his own life of that monarch with a very
interesting book entitled *Carlyle: his Rise and Fall* (Duckworth, 1927). The main point for us is that Carlyle
started by swallowing the legend, ended by glorifying
Frederick in all his acts, though half-way through his
work he seemed to have doubts — doubts which, since
two volumes had already been published, remained
interior because he did not wish to contradict the impression that he had already begun to create. His wife
told him that he could not make a silk purse out of a
sow's ear, but Carlyle was in a dangerous mood, the
mood in which a man, wishing to enforce a certain
view, does not greatly care whether he has chosen the
best illustration for it.

Some of the hero's acts were less noble on a near view
than they seemed when merged in the general record
of his greatness, and it is curious to observe how, in his
fine Edinburgh address, Carlyle had come to worship
authority, to exalt the figure of the obedient soldier, to
recommend regimentation in civil life, and to affirm
that the aristocracy 'by title' were among the salt of
the earth because they still, then, had the power of
wisely ruling their estates and of rooting out injustice
and baseness. He thought more kindly of his former
butts when he had become their intimate, and, regarding himself from the first as a natural aristocrat, he had

come to identify himself with the circle to which he had penetrated.

This was human and natural. It is his original defect in its latest guise. Originally all wealth was corrupting, and, when Carlyle himself was poor, poverty was a grand virtue. When he became eminent and successful a similar praise was showered on rank, authority, and success. What we miss, first and last, is the intelligent recognition of a principle: the veneration of a hero, apart from the accidents of birth or rank, of poverty or triumph. Carlyle's teaching is marred throughout by his personal egoism, which leads him to exalt whatever may be his own station in life. It also cannot be denied that the strenuous endeavour which he began by preaching degenerated into the justification of any policy that strength could by force or skill impose successfully on the mass of men, who were at last, in Carlyle's eyes, the natural slaves of their superior neighbours. If half the people who have praised Carlyle as a popular champion had studied his longer and later books they would have kept more silent. He was the first recent writer of repute mentally to divide people into rulers and ruled, and to visualize the servile state before that name had been invented. The exceptions that he made by his frequent private generosity, engaging as these were, did not modify his cult of success and predominance. A despot is allowed to indulge himself with favourites, and Carlyle had the despot's trick of being kind to individuals who crossed his path while remaining blind to, and contemptuous of, classes and men beyond his personal acquaintance.

The excuses that he made for Frederick's invasion of Silesia, for his partition of Poland, for his want of good faith when his obligations proved inconvenient, take two suspicious forms. He abuses the reader who questions his hero's honesty, and then asserts, without much evidence, that Frederick, from the first, was surrounded by corrupt sovereigns and is to be admired for proving himself the most astute dissimulator of them all. In fact, they copied Frederick's own example. The book is a quaint example of the scaling-down of a man of genius, who, in proportion to his own success, shows the corrosion of his own standards; but the weakness of these standards was apparent from the first, though at first excuses offered themselves readily.

III

Carlyle, it will be remembered, on the famous walk when he received his moment of illumination, had flung 'defiance' at the skies. In an early chapter we noted that he experienced defiance, not acceptance or humility. The sequel proves that this 'conversion' was impure. The defiance which began by being directed at the world, through a young man's rage at its ignorance of his merits, ended by becoming the defiance of the successful for his neighbours and his dupes. In other words, Carlyle did not overcome the world but was corroded by it; and his early sublimities were mixed with the inordinate self-interest of the egoist, and the arrogance of a poor man ambitious for public recognition and success. This was probably why the *French Revolution* had not its obvious sequel in a life of Napoleon Bonaparte. Once, Carlyle had been attracted by Napoleon, but, in the end, he could not bear the thought of a success turned to a failure; could not see that it is to Saint Helena that Napoleon owes his dignity in the eyes of history. Saint Helena is the Golgotha of Cæsar, and, by a profound instinct, to Failure alone do men look for a sublime symbol of nobility. That which was common in the clay of Thomas Carlyle, which rejected humility and trusted in defiance, had its inevitable issue.

The hero-worship to which he called mankind blended into the worship of Success and Selfishness. The sublime egoist ended on his knees before the Ego, the Scottish peasant, once he had been acclaimed by the world, set up boldly his idol of the self. No wonder that the world rejoiced over its seduction of Carlyle's genius. It had made its apparent critic admit its own standards in the end. But, before Carlyle had half-accepted, there had been a quality in his criticisms that did not wound. They were tainted with superiority, blunted by pride, innocuous by their vagueness. The absence of constructiveness of which all his readers complain was, at bottom, a sign of practical incapacity. Thus his ideal came to be the successful Man of Action. The man, too, who attacks the world because his real quarrel with it is not all disinterested cannot look evil in the face. If one of his desires is for its recognition, unless he is a Frederick he dare not say this, but must cast about for something else. Carlyle was captivated by Frederick's candour. But, once this desire is gratified, he can be bolder. He can then praise his likeness in the conqueror, and turn contemptuously upon inferiors. The instinct which led Carlyle from the French mob to Cromwell, from Cromwell to Luther, and from Luther to Frederick, was ingrained. He made his choice freely and must abide by it. He has passed judgment upon himself. No apparently objective writer has, through the medium of history, told us more of himself than Carlyle, whose own personal or fictional confessions do not come half so close to the whole truth. As usual, the egoist is most revealing when he is not consciously writing of himself. Luckily, his last and longest book is not that which is best known. The nobler element in him being absent, from much of it, led to a discursiveness which has induced most people to take the merits of the *Frederick* for granted. Thus the change has been concealed, and his better, shorter, and earlier works maintain his reputation, and are even preferred, because they provide a convenient excuse for passing over the monster-history of his declension.

This is not altogether fair to the book, for, if we read it and waive its premisses, the excisions suggest themselves, and, with even one-third eliminated, the merits begin to become clear. We find an author happily engaged on the epic consecration of a legend, and, once this bias, which is sometimes overweening, has been recognized, we can consider his fine artistry and gain a glimpse of him in the act of confessing unawares a good deal about himself.

IV

The book does not really begin until the Great Elector has been reached, for not even Carlyle can find anything to say of the barbarous origins of Brandenburg, and of the clashes of the shadowy robber-barons who in the Germanies lagged so far behind the rest of civilization. Because they did so lag, Carlyle of course idealizes them, but the scraps that he can gather are even duller than our own Wars of the Roses. With the Great Elector a comparatively civilized ruler appears, and as soon as Frederick William, the father of Frederick, has been reached, the book becomes very readable and interesting. Frederick William was a man after Carlyle's own heart, and Carlyle's portrait of him is plainly an ideal projection of his father. Strong, industrious, thrifty, practical, a stern ruler and father, almost inarticulate except in action, violently anti-French in tastes, with a hobby, unscrupulously pursued, for gigantic soldiers, and, in moments of relaxation, inclined to horseplay and the infliction of humiliating practical jokes upon his butts, without favouritism, but inclined to bully, and devoted, apart from the army, to military amusements and the regimentation of his people, mildly contemptuous of science, philosophy, and art, a heavy drinker, an inveterate huntsman, capable, for all his shrewdness, of being led by companions subtle enough to make their flatteries seem the counsel of loyal and honest men, Frederick William was the embodiment of heroic kingship to Carlyle.

His private weaknesses are glossed, and no distinction is drawn between the capacity of the ruler and his domestic limitations. We are invited to admire the rattan that Frederick William always carried, and with which he would belabour some subject dawdling in the street, in moments of fury his ministers or his daughter, frequently and for several years the Crown Prince himself. The bully in Frederick William was not uncongenial to Carlyle, who, years before, when sketching the country life that he would most enjoy, had described how he would rise early and 'go forth like a destroying angel among my lazy hinds,' with, no doubt, the big stick appropriate to a ferocious gaffer. This is not to imply that Carlyle was personally violent; only that his imagination was susceptible to violence in others, as well-meaning but partly inhibited men are apt to be. An odd instance of his partiality occurs in the first pages which deal with Frederick's accession. One of the young king's first acts was to abolish legal torture. On the universal applause that greeted this — and the young man had once been threatened with it — Carlyle observes: 'Applause, in which surely all of us still join; though the per-contra also is becoming visible to some of us and our enthusiasm grows less complete than formerly.' Carlyle, too, loved to belabour his readers, to write with the big stick, and had some envy for his opposite, for the man of action who could wallop people's bodies. Had he ever had the power to torture anyone, how revolted he would have been!

The character-drawing of Frederick William is very curious. Carlyle's way was to form a conception, an estimate, of his sitter, and his portraits are only vivid within the limit of this frame. The conception is wonderfully alive, but we are always conscious of the artist, since no complexity, no contradiction, is allowed to modify the chosen design. Thus, the qualities of Frederick William the ruler being, on the balance, praiseworthy and remarkable, are equally praised in private life where the benefits were none. To insist that the old women who sold flowers in the streets of Berlin must occupy themselves with knitting, lest in the intervals of trade they should be idle, is a relatively harmless insistence on the value of industry, but to insist also that one's eldest son should have exactly the same tastes and occupations as oneself, to bully and beat him to such a length that he tried to run away, and then to convict him, and an officer who abetted his attempt, of desertion from the army, and to execute the officer for treason, was the act of a tyrant, of a father so stupid that he could conceive no form of persuasion but force. There is no real light and shade in this portrait, because no shadows are allowed which the reader is not ordered to venerate. Carlyle's picture of father and son needs to be supplemented by facts he glosses over, and here Miss Margaret Goldsmith's book is of value.[1]

All this shows the weakness of the gospel of hero-worship: a man-made religion in which, as in those it was designed to replace, criticism is treason, and heroic right is invoked as wildly as divine right had been. Throughout the book, which, by the way, is called a history and not a biography, the interest is centred on families and different courts, so that Carlyle, who never had a profound sense of historical perspective, is mainly a dynastic historian. The dull places in this history, once the central figures have been overtaken, are made to live, but, as we read, we become increasingly conscious of the author's handling, and this consciousness expands as we observe that he confers all the importance, so that his work loses its authority almost in proportion to the vividness of his effects. We notice with

[1] *Frederick the Great*, by Margaret Goldsmith (Gollancz, 1929).

some amusement the increasing fascination that royalty has for him. It is hardly too much to say that the original conception of a man worthy to rule becomes slowly changed into a panegyric of royal pursuits, so that anyone who fails to be promoted is dismissed as unworthy. Carlyle began by drawing a sharp distinction between the man of sterling and his social superiors. He went on to exalt the superior being in a position of authority. He came near to end by excluding all in unrecognized positions. Ability rather than supremacy eventually was fading from his mind. He had come a long way from Burns and Abbot Samson.

V

Frederick, being a more complex character than his sturdy father, became less congenial to Carlyle. He was never fully content with the idea of a philosopher-king. More and more we see Carlyle drawn from intellectual concerns into admiration for active and military exertions, and falling under the spell of success. By a curious, but not unnatural, transition the earnest struggling man of Carlyle's original conception changed into the worship of ability, and into ever-increased respect for able men in the position of worldly power.

Within the frame of Carlyle's arbitrary premisses, the character of Frederick is clearly drawn. We are shown a man of extraordinary ability, who makes his first stroke toward aggrandizement out of ambition, and is praised for proving capable of carrying it to success. The seizure of Silesia, on these immoral grounds, involved Frederick in all his future wars, but we are asked to sympathize with him over the machinations of his enemies without being reminded that Frederick was the original aggressor. Military history is not to everybody's taste, but the best part of the immense book is the impression left by the detailed story of the three Silesian wars; for in the stress of these campaigns it is impossible not to admire the tenacity, the ability, the unquenchable resolution and resource of the King of Prussia. Frederick is shown to have been very like an extraordinarily superior millionaire who, once his ambition has been gratified, is prepared to put his talents to public service. Pressed by his enemies, he will stick at nothing, but let alone with his gains he will rule uncommonly well. Necessity is his sole principle, and the Partition of Poland is justified on the ground that Frederick had no other means of keeping his enemies quiet. Poland, we are expressly told, did not concern him, and Carlyle's want of perspective made him assume that the nation was dead, and would never survive this skinning. It is no merit of ours, to-day, to recognize that this was a gross mistake, but it reminds us that 'necessity' is only an expedient, that successful expedients are never final in grave matters, and that Frederick's original doctrine, being quickly copied by his enemies, gave him no rest, because, once moral foundations have been destroyed, there can be no virtue in any settlement. Frederick was the original cause of all his own troubles, and is interesting now as a person of extraordinary ability confronted with self-originated difficulties that would assuredly have overwhelmed every one else.

We are also invited to watch how much good an exceptionally capable ruler can accomplish, and this personal autocracy is that which Carlyle came to admire. The less agreeable side of Frederick's character is glossed over. We hear almost nothing of his treatment of his butts, but the story of his relations with Voltaire is very well told, and, if it seems too favourable to Frederick, we must remember that Carlyle was anxious to counter Voltaire's famous exaggerations. This is one of the masterly episodes of the immense book.

If it is still to be read, the history badly needs curtailment, for it comes near to being a history of all Europe in the eighteenth century, with Prussia for the central theme. The canvas is too gigantic, the excursions are too numerous, but it is impossible not to admire the zest with which the author cruises from corner to corner of his enormous field. The energy does not flag, the interest of each fraction of the huge mosaic is unfailing. Not unless the book has been read to a finish, can the feat be sufficiently admired. One of its valuable memories is the explanation of a later Prussia and of the latest Hohenzollerns. The growth of their house and the nature of their ideals, their military strategy and their social conceptions, become a possession from these volumes. It is easy for any but themselves to question the value with which Carlyle credits their great originators, but Carlyle's mysterious sympathy for a type the antithesis of his own is a valuable element in the picture. If he had been capable of realizing whither the worship of Fact and Self-reliance lead in the destiny of nations, he would not have painted them for us so vividly. We are offered a false religion by an imaginative but uncritical mind.

A peasant of genius was carried in a dream to the top of an exceeding high mountain, and there was tempted by the thought 'If I were King.' He wrote his dream in the form of an historic legend, in which he left his natural inhibitions behind him and glorified the counterpart, if not the opposite, of the noblest of his own gifts.

CHAPTER ELEVEN

CARLYLE AND HIS EXECUTOR

THE reception of *Frederick* was completely favourable, and this success set the seal of national approval upon Carlyle's literary work. The book was almost immediately translated into German, and became, there, the standard life of the hero and creator of modern Prussia. The English admired the portrait-painting in which the book abounded; the Germans, in addition to the pride that they took in this example of the Scotsman's hero-worship, marvelled at the accuracy and enormous detail, for these were German qualities. Having won his way to eminence, Carlyle was ripe for public recognition, for the public likes to applaud success in pursuits which it despises. To it success is the main thing, for this brings the great man down to the general level of comprehension. The first step was taken by Edinburgh University, which offered him the Lord Rectorship in 1866, the year after *Frederick* had appeared. The welcome of the students, the newspaper reports of his Address, the large sale that this had when reprinted as a pamphlet, emphasized the popular acclaim, and the familiar situation was repeated of an aged author being canonized in his lifetime. 'It was now admitted universally [Froude writes] that Carlyle was a "great man." Yet he saw no inclination, not the slightest, to attend to his teaching. He himself could not make it out, but the explanation is not far to seek. The Edinburgh address contained his doctrines with the fire which had provoked the animosity taken out of them. They were reduced to the level of church sermons.... Carlyle, people felt with a sense of relief, meant only what the preachers meant, and was a fine fellow after all.' Until his death in 1881, no one again ever murmured against him.

'A perfect triumph' ran the telegram which announced the happenings at Edinburgh to Mrs. Carlyle, who had feared the strain of being present. Her belief in his genius was, at last, shared by the country of his birth. If she looked back upon her early faith, it must have been a triumph for her also. His return was slightly delayed by a sprained ankle, and — before he had left Scotland — she was dead. She died suddenly, in her carriage.

The blow was doubly severe because it necessarily was unexpected by her husband who, moreover, had always assumed that he, as the elder, would be the first to die. He had never thought to lose her, and the stroke came, as we have seen, at a time when his independence had weakened and his dependence upon her had grown greatly. To retain that which could be retained, and to ease his heart by the means most natural to a writer, he began to collect her *Letters and Memorials*, and to write his *Reminiscences*, first of her, then of his father and of his early friends. This work itself was a refuge and a solace, and what was to be done with it, whether published or destroyed, was a matter too remote to be determined.

'Somewhere about the first week in May,' within a month of Mrs. Carlyle's death, Froude received a message from Carlyle asking him to come to Cheyne Row. 'He came down to me [Froude writes] into the library in his dressing-gown, haggard and as if turned to stone.' Then, or in the meetings that regularly followed, Froude heard how the old scenes recorded in her notebooks and journals had revived Carlyle's memories and self-reproaches; and the desire for atonement, for something that Johnson's public penance at Uttoxeter suggested, was mentioned 'many times' to Froude.[1] In the vivid memory of that desire Froude acted. The idea

[1] *Carlyle's Life in London*, II, 323. See also p. 241, *ante*.

won his respect. 'In his [Carlyle's] most heroic life there was nothing more heroic, more characteristic of him, more indicative at once of his humility and his intense truthfulness. He regarded it evidently as an expiation of his own conduct, all that he had now to offer, and something which removed the shadow between himself and her memory.'

Before discussing this attitude of Carlyle, we should recall the freedom which Carlyle conferred upon his chosen executor.

In a subsequent conversation, when Carlyle was anxious to know what Froude proposed to do with the documents entrusted to him, this passage occurred: Carlyle

was nervously anxious to know my resolution. I told him that, so far as I could then form an opinion, I thought the letters might be published, provided the prohibition was withdrawn against publishing his own Memoir of Mrs. Carlyle.... It would have been hard on both of them if the sharp censures of Mrs. Carlyle's pen had been left unrelieved. To this Carlyle instantly assented.... I required, and I received, a direct permission to print it.[1]

Again, apparently in 1878, Froude tells us (p. 466, *op. cit.*) that he asked Carlyle whether the *Reminiscences* 'of his father, of Irving' etc. should be incorporated in the biography or in a separate volume:

I consulted him about it. He had almost forgotten what he had written; but as soon as he had recalled it to his recollection he approved of the separate publication, and added that they had better be brought out immediately after his death. The world would then be talking about him, and would have something authentic to go upon.

This, to those who can look behind the consequences and can see the matter as Froude saw it, justifies the publication of the *Reminiscences* and even the strange

[1] *Carlyle's Life in London*, II, 411-12. J. A. Froude (Longmans).

promptitude with which they appeared. In my recollection of the anti-Froudian writings, neither passage, here quoted, is set against the written prohibition which Carlyle's MS. admittedly bears. Only the sincerity of Froude's recollection could have blinded him to the accusation he was risking when the prohibition was omitted from his edition of the *Reminiscences*, and the MS. passed once more out of his own hands. Froude's astonishment at the reception of his work as editor and biographer shows that, in the mass of confused instructions, he did not see that his judgment could be impugned with apparent warrant by any one able to quote a written word against numerous conversations. Froude was, in truth, more careful of Carlyle's reputation than of his own. His unwariness, to my mind, is excellent evidence of his honesty.

A touch on this wearisome controversy has been unavoidable, but our interest lies elsewhere. What are we to think of Carlyle's proposed expiation? What do the documents themselves suggest? We cannot doubt that, in the shock of his loss, Carlyle was haunted by the memory of Johnson at Uttoxeter, but I fancy that the idea did not long dominate his mind. As the *Reminiscences* were written, an old man's wish to recapture the past came exclusively to possess him, and like many a stricken widower, he saw his wife with the original vision of his lover's days. Sad and self-reproachful as his memories were, I do not feel, as I read, that self-reproachfulness entirely explains them. Throughout his life, all his memories were sad. All his reflections tended to be mournful. A picture rather forms of the Carlyle with whom we are familiar, sadly revolving, now, not about some work he could not find, not about some labour in which he was steeped despairingly, but about the loss that tormented him. The egoism that led him to complain of the universe, of his historical authorities, of his health, of society, of the discomforts

of travel, was at its familiar lamentation, only now the
object of his criticism was Himself. In the very exaggeration of his remorse, it is the personal pronoun, as
usual, which diminishes our assent to his propositions.
His eyes had certainly been opened to some sufferings
which he had not perceived himself to have caused; but
he had changed his part in the stormy panorama of his
inner life. From being the earnest struggling man he
had become the chief of sinners, for that, too, is one
form of an egoist's dream, and it is he, not only the wife
whom he was mourning, that still dominates the page.
The loved figure of Mrs. Carlyle was naturally the
centre of his sorrows, but it was not by any means all
remorse that placed her there. His egoism, a disorder
rather than a fault, always revolved around some external or semi-external grievance, and we have, I think,
to recognize the persistence of the egoism as much as,
indeed more than, its latest adopted cause. Only because the loss of a partner is a cruel experience that
seems to explain itself, have people been ready to accept Carlyle's self-reproaches literally, or to take refuge
in the plea that he could never have intended them to
be known.

Carlyle was a born writer. His activity was limited to
the written word. To write — he often said this of his
work — was his only consolation. Of necessity, a writer
by profession assumes that publication will probably
follow anything which he himself does not destroy. To
the questions When and Where he becomes, in time,
indifferent. The assumption, which is not the same as
an intention, lurks almost unconsciously in his mind: a
mere practical matter to be decided at some future time.
Carlyle scarcely went beyond the idea of preservation.
His thoughts varied with his moods, but he could never
bring himself to destroy these papers. Whenever the
question came up, he was painfully uncertain, and,
very naturally, only too glad to entrust the final deci-

sion to his executor and his trusted friend. All this is human and understandable. It is an author to the life.

Froude, I think, took Carlyle's first notion of penitence somewhat too literally. He accepted as a fixed intention what may have been the dramatization of grief. What we have now to consider is the reception of Froude's work, for that he deserved the trust imposed upon him no impartial person can doubt. Why, then, did he create this uproar?

In the first place he acted with unusual speed, and in the second he misjudged the mood in which the fruits of his executorship would be regarded. The *Reminiscences* of Carlyle appeared in 1881, the year of Carlyle's death. The first two of the four volumes of Froude's biography were published in 1882, the *Letters and Memorials of Jane Welsh Carlyle* in 1883, and the two concluding volumes of Carlyle's *Life*, a year later. There was neither delay nor pause. The story too punctually followed the funeral. Such speed looked very like inconsiderate haste to people at large, who did not know that the preparation of the *Reminiscences*, even if prepared, though not edited by, Carlyle, had been occupying Froude's attention for years, and could scarcely credit that the first half of Froude's biography had been written before Carlyle himself was in his grave. In the speed of publication there was, then, already something on which objectors, should there be any, could fasten. No time was allowed to soften a possible shock.

As we have seen, Carlyle died in the odour of popularity. He had been acclaimed on both sides of the Atlantic; in Germany as warmly as in England. Since the great ceremony at Edinburgh and the death of his wife, criticism had been still. In 1869 Queen Victoria received him. The Grand Cross of the Bath had been offered to Carlyle, with a pension, by Disraeli in 1875, that is after the Prussian Order of Merit had been bestowed on him through the German ambassador in London. These honours had followed his installation as Lord Rector at Edinburgh, and for fifteen quiet years before he died his figure, face, and hat were familiar to the omnibus-drivers in London. People would recognize him respectfully in the streets, and pilgrims make their way to Cheyne Row in order to inspect the outside of his house, or would linger in the hope that they might catch a glimpse of him going or returning. Remoter and less considerate admirers would approach the sage of Chelsea through the post, and every morning his table was littered with missives from correspondents. He was occasionally the subject of respectful caricatures, and had assumed in the public mind the image of a revered sage which they worshipped delightedly. Even his pamphlet on 'Shooting Niagara,' published in 1867, and his letter to *The Times* protesting against Disraeli's policy over the Russian-Turkish War, were allowed to pass without demur. His warnings were treated indulgently. Were they not, too, appropriate to the Sinai on which his public image had been pedestalled? The retiring man with his private idiosyncrasies was lost in the reverend public figure, and people naturally wished that anything further published about him should confirm the ideal image that they, its creators, had formed.

With Carlyle's own conception of biography before him, Froude, a writer of high distinction with several vivid historical pictures to his credit, could not, in any event, countenance a simulacrum of this kind. Carlyle himself was utterly opposed to these abstractions, and a man who had worked hard to clean off the tar from people like Luther, Cromwell, and Frederick of Prussia would thank no one for the trouble of making a snowman of himself. It happened, moreover, that Carlyle was a man of marked idiosyncrasy, with an inhibited man's respect for action and a weak man's worship of force; an author with all the crotchets that are popularly attributed to his tribe. It also happened that his wife was one of the most vivid of our English letter-writers, that she could be acid in her wit, and that Carlyle had chosen, in regard to his relations with her, to paint himself in sable and repentant colours. He had wished that she should have the Memorial of her own letters, and, if these were to be understood fully, he had agreed that his self-portrayal must stand beside them.

Thus, it was at the most unexpected of moments that Froude's volumes hastened to appear. At the centre of interest for so long himself, Froude was almost necessarily oblivious of the conception of Carlyle that ruled the outside world. The first to object was a feminine member of Carlyle's family, and, as Carlyle, in the end, had told Froude to return to her the original documents when he should have finished with them, she was provided with the necessary ammunition. Now experience shows that the family circle of a great man is much more self-conscious than himself; and the same is true of near disciples. The reflected light in which they glow is very sacred to themselves, and, since they are of different clay, they set more store than he by the figure on the pedestal, the public estimation, the accident of popularity. The family of Gladstone is another example of this.

Few words that Froude ever wrote fell upon indifferent ears. He had the power of enforcing an exasperated attention. The admirers of Carlyle, in proportion to their fervour, exclaimed loudly at the shock, the more perhaps because Carlyle's own self-portraiture appeared to accuse *them* of misconception and stupidity. His own words seemed to them like treachery, for he upset their idol himself! Since he was beyond their reach, they turned instinctively upon his editor. It is an instructive case of popular psychology. What idolized public figure had sanctioned such a trick upon his admirers before? Rousseau had hobnobbed and apologized. Carlyle appeared to blurt out. The storm burst. Disconcerted for the moment, Froude offered to retreat, but he withdrew his offer and is more to be admired for retracing a false step than to be blamed for a momentary weakness. He carried out his task to the end, and the long and dreary controversy began.

From the beginning, all the obvious arrows were in his enemies' locker. There had already been a long campaign, on the part of rival historians, to discredit his accuracy. Almost from Froude's cradle, the demon of personal controversy had been eager for Froude's scalp. The written prohibition in Carlyle's handwriting was explosive ammunition, and Froude, instead of Carlyle, had to endure the attacks that the inevitable reversal of a popular reputation involves. Inevitable? The reason is, not that great men do not deserve great reputations, but that great reputations which are also popular reputations necessarily mistake the accidents for the substance of renown.

This is what happened with Carlyle. It explains the agonized reception of his *Reminiscences* and of Froude's biography. Nevertheless, upon the facts the truth seems clear. Carlyle, an extreme example of the type of author, was by no means an exceptional example of a husband. The trouble is that, viewed under a microscope, every marriage looks like an extreme case, and the Carlyles, having provided the microscope themselves, are seen out of proportion. He had married, moreover, a woman who knew what to expect, who had kindred interests, and whose chief misfortune was that she had no children and no profession to compensate her for her husband's whims. The whole interest of their story is that it is not exceptional except in the extraordinary completeness of the record furnished by themselves. Blessed are they who have no memorials? No! Records of any marriage are as rare as they are

precious, and people who do not rise from reading
theirs with a deepened sympathy for man and woman,
and with an enlarged understanding of the complexity
of married life, are beyond teaching. We have here
the reality behind a hundred romances, a priceless picture of a common truth. The story of the Carlyles is
an authentic history substantially repeated in a thousand homes. It holds, interests, and at times exasperates
us, as living problems do. The love, and the difficulties,
the misunderstandings and the unity, the friction on the
surface and the devotion at the core, are the mirror of
the confusion of daily life. To reduce this record of experience to a miserable game of tying labels would be a
contemptible return for such a gift.

But, it may be asked, what of Froude's treatment of
his materials, apart from publishing Carlyle's own
words? As was mentioned in the preface, the present
writer did not open Froude until he had studied
Froude's critics. So far as he came to Froude with a
bias, it was with a bias of suspicion. When Froude's
volumes had been read, the impression left was utterly
different from that of the heedless husband and the suffering wife which had been anticipated. It is a wild dis-
tortion to assert that Froude gives any picture of so
crude a kind. Froude has written a very fine biography
on a most interesting human being: rich in contrast,
alive with light and shade, and far better balanced
than any to be met with in the same inquiry. Indeed,
the others, which ever side they take, suffer from want
of balance, and the 'inaccuracies' which they detect in
Froude are neither vital nor confusing. The same
scrutiny applied to any standard work would not return
with empty hands. The scrutiny itself would not have
been pressed with equal zeal, if it had not been the
stock charge to bring against him. Yet Froude, and
Froude alone, of these biographers, seems to have been
equally attached to *both* the Carlyles. One point — on

which I have ventured to question his judgment — was his acceptance of Carlyle's wish to pillory himself. This can only be conjecture, since Froude alone heard Carlyle's words. But it is also possible that Froude was tempted to embrace them literally, because he vaguely felt that a biography of Carlyle (written upon Carlyle's theory of biography) would be likely to annoy when the theory was applied to a popular contemporary, at a time too when, in consequence of the prevailing insincerity, biography in England had sunk to its lowest ebb. Froude's work has to be contrasted with the biographies of his own generation for us fully to appreciate what a fine piece of living portraiture it is.

The recoil from it has two further characteristics which are worth a moment's attention. It was led and has been maintained either by namesakes of Carlyle or by men who were grown when he died: who thus virtually belong to the surviving circle of his disciples. The voice of that past generation, not of posterity, is the voice which has troubled our ears. Carlyle was one of those writers who meant much to the young whom they influenced, and to the books and the authors to whom we are earliest indebted we can only be grateful, we can scarcely be fair. One must be tender to feelings which arise from generous springs, and such feelings are the portion of some in every generation of readers. Those who were boys when *Tess* and *Jude the Obscure* were published will be reminded of Thomas Hardy. These two books meant much to some of us, but the day came when Mr. George Moore subjected these novels to some damaging particular criticism. Were we, then, to renounce an admiration, or to turn furiously on the distinguished novelist who had exposed spots to which we had been blind? Surely the reasonable attitude was to be convinced by the convincing? and to retain that part of our experience which survived the disconcerting attack? This the Carlyle party would not do, because of the personal element in the controversy. They were loftily indifferent to criticisms of style and had never felt any vagueness in their master's writing; but they could not part with the cherished figure of their Sage, could not admit that an angular and somewhat disordered soul was more interesting, more valuable, and more impressive, than the popular conception of a prophet, the romantic conception of an ideal husband.

The generation of these admirers, like their hero, has proved long-lived, but the resentment will pass with the generation. Such an eye as can be kept on the men born since 1881 seems to indicate a change. Such references to Froude by men born after that date as I have happened to meet have praised his biography for its departure from the standard pattern of that day, for its attempt at truth, for its living contrasts. As to the position of Carlyle's own histories in current estimation, it is impossible to dogmatize. How far he is read is a doubtful question, more doubtful than the critical indifference to him. The critical neglect that ignored Trollope for years had no effect upon Trollope's influence; for the critics like the mass of readers have their fashions. It may prove so with Carlyle. The curious can look at the second-hand catalogues to see if collectors turn their eyes on these first editions, for collectors are sometimes signs. Whatever such researches indicate, it seems at least certain that the *French Revolution* is safe, and *Sartor Resartus*, but the *Cromwell* is too one-sided, and the *Frederick* far too long, to be steadily, or perhaps permanently, read.

The letters which both left behind them would remain unalloyed good reading were their enormous number not fatiguing, and had not the controversy which defaces them become a distraction and a bore. Apart from their letters, the book about the Carlyles which is most indispensable remains the long life by Froude. That has neither been dislodged from its place nor will it disappoint any open-minded reader. Once, indeed, we have passed unscathed through the clouds of controversy, we meet a very human and distinguished pair, and this wonderful record of experiences, to which so many unrecorded marriages bear witness, remains of exceptional interest. Of the present book I can have nothing to say, except that the relief and contrast offered to biography by the joint story of two lives has, once more, tempted the present writer. For the second time, he believes the condensation required by this method to have compensations enough to justify it, though it has added difficulties of its own.

The final impression left by the story is that Carlyle was most appealing in his person, and his wife through her pen. All *her* moods issued in her letters, whereas his glooms are over-emphasized in his; and his books are deficient in the humour and geniality that his intimates discovered in his company. There is plenty of evidence of this. His written volumes, therefore, do some injustice to the man. In some degree, he remained an inhibited author to the last, for his humour and his gaiety were scanted of expression. Yet these two beings, who charged each other's lives with so much electricity, were equally rich in friends; and, even at this distance of time, they tempt us, for all their angularities, to enrol ourselves in the charmed company which was drawn to the far cottage at Craigenputtock, or gladly invaded the cosy, curious household which, when all is said, managed to survive, there and in Cheyne Row, for forty chequered years.

THE END

SHORT BIBLIOGRAPHY

1. *The Life of Jane Welsh Carlyle.* By Mrs. Alexander Ireland. Chatto and Windus. 1891.
2. *Early Letters of Jane Welsh Carlyle.* Edited by D. G. Ritchie. Swan Sonnenschein. 1889.
3. *Letters and Memorials of Jane Welsh Carlyle.* Edited by J. A. Froude. 3 volumes. Longmans, Green & Co. 1883.
4. *New Letters and Memorials of Jane Welsh Carlyle.* Edited by Alexander Carlyle. 2 volumes. The Bodley Head. 1903.
5. *The Love Letters of Thomas Carlyle and Jane Welsh.* Edited by Alexander Carlyle. The Bodley Head. 1924.
6. *Jane Welsh Carlyle: Letters to her Family.* Edited by Leonard Huxley. Murray. 1924.
7. *Jane Welsh and Jane Carlyle.* By Elizabeth Drew. Cape. 1928.

8. *Reminiscences.* By Thomas Carlyle. Edited by J. A. Froude. Longmans, Green & Co. 1881.
9. *Reminiscences.* By Thomas Carlyle. Edited by C. E. Norton. Macmillan. 1887.
10. *Early Letters of Thomas Carlyle.* Edited by C. E. Norton. Macmillan. 1887.
11. *History of the First Forty Years of Carlyle's Life.* 2 volumes. By J. A. Froude. Longmans, Green & Co. 1882.
12. *Carlyle's Life in London.* 2 volumes. By J. A. Froude. Longmans, Green & Co. 1884.
13–17. *Life of Carlyle.* By David Alec Wilson. Six volumes, of which the following five have appeared:
    Carlyle Till Marriage (1795–1826). Kegan Paul, Trench, Trubner & Co. 1923.
    Carlyle to 'The French Revolution.' Kegan Paul, Trench, Trubner & Co. 1924.
    Carlyle on Cromwell and Others. Kegan Paul, Trench, Trubner & Co. 1925.
    Carlyle at his Zenith (1843–53). Kegan Paul, Trench, Trubner & Co. 1927.
    Carlyle to Threescore-and-Ten (1853–65). Kegan Paul, Trench, Trubner & Co. 1929.
18. *Carlyle: his Rise and Fall.* By Norwood Young. Duckworth. 1927.

All but two (Nos. 4 and 9), and these but prefatorially, of the volumes on the controversy have been omitted, except the following because, although the author makes his own attitude clear, it is mainly a history of the subject:

19. *Froude and Carlyle: A Study of the Froude-Carlyle Controversy.* By Waldo H. Dunn. Longmans, Green & Co. 1930.

INDEX

INDEX

Addison, Joseph, his prose, 203, 204

Age of Reason, The, Thomas Paine, 12

Aiken, Mrs., letter of Mrs. Carlyle to, 233

Aitken, Margaret, marries James Carlyle, 27. *See also* Carlyle, Mrs. James

Allingham, William, his *Diary*, 37

Andrewes, Lancelot, 203

Annan Academy, 12, 29, 35, 40

Anti-Romantic Movement, 143

Aquinas, St. Thomas, 143

Arabian Nights, The, 28, 35

Art, Carlyle on, 150

Artistic temperament, the, 165

Arts, the practice of the, 140

Ashburton, Lord, William Bingham Baring, 250

Ashburton, Lady, Harriet Montagu, Mrs. Baring, 225–27, 234, 236, 247; death, 248; Carlyle's epitaph for, 248

Ashburton, Lady, Stuart Mackenzie, 250

Ashburtons, the, 245, 247

Austin, Mrs. John, 187

Authors, 164, 166; English and German, their situations compared, 151, 153; the wives of, 191

Autobiographies, 167

Baillie, James, cousin of Jane Welsh, 71–74

'Ballet, the home of,' 40

Baring. *See* Ashburton

Barnet, Bessy, 186

Barrett, Elizabeth, 128

Belloc, Hilaire, quoted, 274

Bentham, Jeremy, 154, 178

Besant, Mrs. Anne, 22

Bismarck, Otto von, 136

Blake, William, 51, 153, 188; his

advice, 'to be humble to God but haughty to men,' 41; and Voltaire, 147, 149

Blakiston, Dr., 264

Books, 205, 220, 221, 222

Border, the, 28

Border families, 6

Boswell, James, 106, 107

Bridekirk, laird of, 25

Brontë, Charlotte, her love-letters, 100, 101

Brown, William, mason, 26, 27

Browne, Sir Thomas, 145, 203

Browning, Robert, 43, 106, 188, 189, 238

Brownknowe, 25

Buller, Mrs., 130, 187, 234

Buller boys (Charles and Arthur), 65, 132

Bullers, the, 65, 132

Bunyan, John, 50, 198, 199, 221; his prose, 204

Burke, Edmund, 200

Burns, Robert, 28, 30, 31, 39, 201, 203, 272, 281; Carlyle's admiration for, 35; Carlyle's portrait of, 220

Butler, Samuel, and Lady Ritchie, 72

Byron, Lord, 19, 20, 39, 176; Jane Welsh writes poem on, 63; a hero of Jane Welsh, 73, 74

Calculus Made Easy, The, 39

Campbell, Thomas, 35

Cant, 33, 155, 175, 242

'Captain of industry,' 228

Carlyle, Alexander, brother of Thomas, 76, 85; takes Craigenputtock, 133–35

Carlyle, James, father of Thomas, his character, 25–29; becomes apprentice to William Brown,